Guilloché

A History & Practical Manual

Calina C. Shevlin

4880 Lower Valley Road • Atglen, PA 19310

Copyright © 2017 by Calina C. Shevlin

Library of Congress Control Number: 2017931604

All rights reserved. No part of this work may be reproduced or used in any form or by any means—graphic, electronic, or mechanical, including photocopying or information storage and retrieval systems—without written permission from the publisher.

The scanning, uploading, and distribution of this book or any part thereof via the Internet or any other means without the permission of the publisher is illegal and punishable by law. Please purchase only authorized editions and do not participate in or encourage the electronic piracy of copyrighted materials.

"Schiffer," "Schiffer Publishing, Ltd.," and the pen and inkwell logo are registered trademarks of Schiffer Publishing, Ltd.

Designed by Justin Watkinson
Cover design by Matthew Goodman
Type set in Didot LT Std/Minion Pro/Futura Std

ISBN: 978-0-7643-5017-7
Printed in China

Published by Schiffer Publishing, Ltd.
4880 Lower Valley Road
Atglen, PA 19310
Phone: (610) 593-1777; Fax: (610) 593-2002
E-mail: Info@schifferbooks.com
Web: www.schifferbooks.com

For our complete selection of fine books on this and related subjects, please visit our website at www.schifferbooks.com. You may also write for a free catalog.

Schiffer Publishing's titles are available at special discounts for bulk purchases for sales promotions or premiums. Special editions, including personalized covers, corporate imprints, and excerpts, can be created in large quantities for special needs. For more information, contact the publisher.

We are always looking for people to write books on new and related subjects. If you have an idea for a book, please contact us at proposals@schifferbooks.com.

Contents

Foreword

Guilloché: a most rare and exotic form of engraving, one which exhibits an optical play of light like nothing else. The art and technique of guilloché is one very dear to my heart, having been fascinated with the machines, and the creations made on such machines, for most of my forty plus years as a silver and goldsmith. Very little is written on the topic of engine turning and guilloché: a few books, some centuries old, others more recent but not complete. Though there is little written on the subject, there are numerous examples of the finished work in most museums and collections. Most notable of the designers that utilized guilloché in their designs was Peter Carl Fabergé and Abraham-Louis Breguet. Fabergé used guilloché on many of his famed eggs, picture frames, boxes, opera glasses, and cigarette cases, just as Breguet used guilloché in his watch faces to great effect.

Calina Shevlin has brought together her first-hand experience with these engine turning machines and her research into the history of these machines. She also writes with personal knowledge gained from her experiences spent working at the most prestigious watch making factories in Switzerland. I am most proud to call her my protégé.

The history that is presented here is more than we have ever seen in print. It is hoped that with time others will research further and share what is learned. Knowing a bit of the history behind the technique and the machines gives the guillocher a sense of pride, along with a sense of legacy by being a part of that history.

One of the earliest books that touches on the subject of engine turning and guilloché is Bergeron's *Manual du Tourneur* (1816). In Bergeron, the information given was enough to expand the use of the decorative turning of wood and the engraving of metal known today as guilloché.

The technical information presented will assist the first time guillocher in creating beautifully engraved patterns on metal—precious or non—to be left as engraved or enameled, as did Fabergé. It will also greatly benefit the experienced craftsman by now having a go-to book with recipes and proven techniques.

No technical book is ever complete with all there is to know about a given subject. Instead, we evolve and slowly add to the general knowledge with books such as this volume. The philosophy of sharing knowledge originates in the Age of Enlightenment. Denis Diderot's *Encyclopedie* has been said to be the most influential publication of that age. With it knowledge that was typically held secret by the trade guilds was now freely given to all that were interested. The secrets of the machines of the age became known to any craftsman or lay person desiring such knowledge.

I clearly remember the day my first engine turning machine arrived. The rose engine was almost 100 years old at the time and required several days to take apart, clean, and reassemble before I could start engraving on metal. For mechanically inclined individuals, the rose engine represents a world with few limits. Whether it is simply cleaning and repairing an old machine, or building a new machine from the ground up, or inventing some new accessory to be used with these machines, working with these machines can certainly be a lifelong endeavor. It is said that with only one rosette a good craftsman can make hundreds of different patterns to engrave into metal; I'd state this is a very low estimate. Given the number of variables on an engine turning machine, the number of patterns that are possible by using only one rosette, or one pattern bar, might well be in excess of ten times that, and more than likely is only limited by one's imagination.

The art of guilloché is experiencing a new beginning. Many artists from around the world are now rediscovering its beauty and techniques. Many are also looking at guilloché in a new light, asking "How can I use this process in new and exciting ways?" By fully understanding the history and the techniques as presented in this volume, the question can now be answered with greater clarity. My hopes lie with the reader that they will now better understand and appreciate the artwork when seen, and for the craftsman in finding new ways to express their ideas using guilloché, both traditional and inventive.

G. Phil Poirier

Preface

This book is the product of my long-time affair with and research about guilloché. From the moment I saw my first Fabergé egg to my accidental discovery of a pattern created by Bonny Doon Taos on a roll pattern steel plate I was hooked. I have compiled what I know to be tried and true and what I have learned about guilloché into the first written history and how-to book on the subject to date. I began my research and my work officially in 2009, when I was searching for sources on guilloché. I found only brief passages and passing mentions of the art, and at a chance meeting at a Society of North American Goldsmiths (SNAG) conference, I met a gentleman who told me I should get in touch with Phil Poirier. I had a long conversation with Phil where I felt like he had told me everything about guilloché in one go. Phil invited me to his studio to see my first machine in person, and at the very moment when I first laid hands on one, I knew this was what I was meant to do. I spent every moment thinking about guilloché patterns and figuring how I could maybe work some into my own jewelry work in graduate school. I had visions of helping to bring about a guilloché revival, and I consistently wondered why it was not more popular. Some people who are fluent in another language often dream in that language; I dream in guilloché.

As I continued through graduate school I began really understanding the processes of creating guilloché and started thinking about how to do what I love and how to create a job when I graduated. A few years later, after earning my MFA in metals and jewelry at the University of North Texas, I ended up working for a prestigious, high-end watch manufacturer in Vallée de Joux, Switzerland. At the time it seemed my dream job had landed in my lap. The company I worked for has expressed their wishes to remain anonymous, but I must credit them with teaching me how to pump out pieces in serious production numbers almost like a machine with emphasis on absolute perfection. I may not have had the opportunity to learn this anywhere else at any other time in my life. It was here I realized I did not have any desire to work like a robot and be limited by choice of patterns; I wanted to have my own voice, and do work that I could say was 100% mine that I could be proud of. I yearned for patterns that were not authorized but innovative. After a seemingly long two years of production work, I broke away and began to slowly traverse into independent consulting, and later independent work for several companies, as well as independent horologers. As I had landed in the Swiss Romande region, which is exclusively French speaking, I learned French on my own and I have been able to communicate with and interview a few independent guillocheurs to see how they got their start and where they learned about guilloché. I have largely found that, while the system of apprenticeship has been somewhat in effect, the current practitioners were mainly taught from generation to generation, with information passed down through oral instruction—nothing written, but simply remembered.

My goals are to disseminate what I have discovered and give insight to what can be done, including what I call a recipe section, where you can follow along and create the same patterns from written instruction. I have also included information for finding, building, and preserving the rose engine and straight-line machines necessary to create guilloché.

This book would not be possible without the guidance, insight, and information of so many people. I have wandered into the lives and picked the brains of people who have much more experience than I that were more than gracious with their information and time. Without the free dissemination of this information this book would be theories and hypotheses. I would like to specifically thank my mentor and friend Phil Poirier: he has nudged me into exploration of more nooks and crannies than I knew existed and has always encouraged me to do better and to keep pushing on if only for personal development. A big thank you to David Wood-Heath, Phil Bedford, Fred Armbruster, Celia Kudro, David Lindow, Mike Stacey, Georges Brodbeck, Catherine Corthesy, and the plethora of other people who contributed to my knowledge and encouraged me on this journey. Without the information I was presented and an unending stream of encouragement and fact checking I would not have been able to assemble this book and disseminate it to a wider audience.

C. S. 2014

CHAPTER 1

The Leap from Ornamental Turning to Guilloché

Guilloché has a troubled history, with scant written accounts detailing its legacy. Much of the history of guilloché has been recounted to me orally, so to fact check, I have asked many guillocheurs to tell me their stories and how they personally began their journey with guilloché and what they learned and know about the history. Almost all of them had similar stories, with very slight differences depending on the region and language spoken. What I learned at an early point in my studies and later career was that although many dictionaries will attribute the word *guilloché* to one person, this is simply not true. The original word *guilloché* was used to describe an architectural detail either on the base or the top of columns rooted in Greek and Roman times. This was an intricately interlaced pattern consisting of interwoven cord forms all carved out of stone, and it was quite an accomplishment to create a pattern that gave the impression of woven cord. This is one of the earliest examples of a decoration that leads the eye to follow along and see all of the detail carved into columns. The pattern seen was often not the intended pattern, much like in what we now call guilloché. It is from this that the word guilloché was repurposed.

The decoration found in ancient times was very intricate for the time and led the eye to follow or see a pattern that did not intentionally exist. These patterns were nearly always depicted as interlinking circles or braids. It is commonly thought the word *guilloché* was so similar to what was happening when cutting the facets into metal, especially the unintentional patterning, that the name guilloché was given and later adopted to become what the current term embodies.

The Metropolitan Museum of Art (MET) Bridge and Double Spout Bottle with Guilloche, fourth to seventh century BC. Ceramic. *OASC*

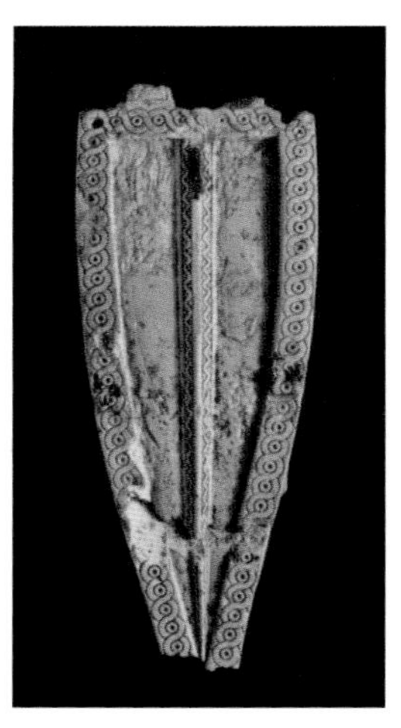

(MET) Horse Frontlet with an incised guilloche design, ca. eighth century BC. Ivory. *OASC*

(MET) *Portrait of a Man* (ca. 1778), French painter. Ivory with guilloche. Oval 36 × 28 mm. Gift of Mrs. Louis V. Bell, in memory of her husband, 1925. *OASC*

Guilloché is of French origin; although it is a decoration used in the United States, England, Germany, Switzerland, Canada, and many other places, the name stays the same. It is pronounced with a hard "g," as in "gee-oh-shay." There are variations on the word to describe it as an action, a job, and so forth. For the sake of clarity I will introduce these terms now. A *guillocheur* is a male who works in guilloché. A *guillocheuse* is a relatively new term, as the art was historically practiced almost exclusively by males, but is a term for a female who works in guilloché. *Guillochage* is the word that makes guilloché an action and is the act of creating guilloché. There is no past tense; to make it easy to say as a past action it is correct to add a verb. For example, "I applied guilloché," "I decorated with a guilloché pattern," "The guillocheur works in guilloché," and so on. Guilloché is the decoration, and is often referred to as engine turning, because an engine (rose or straight-line) is being turned by hand. This term conveniently allows for the use of past tense—*engine turned*—and is why I believe it is so often interchangeable with the word *guilloché*.

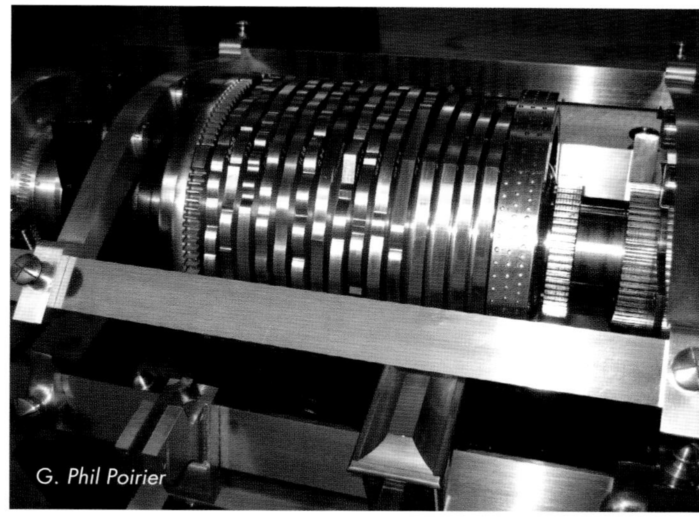
G. Phil Poirier

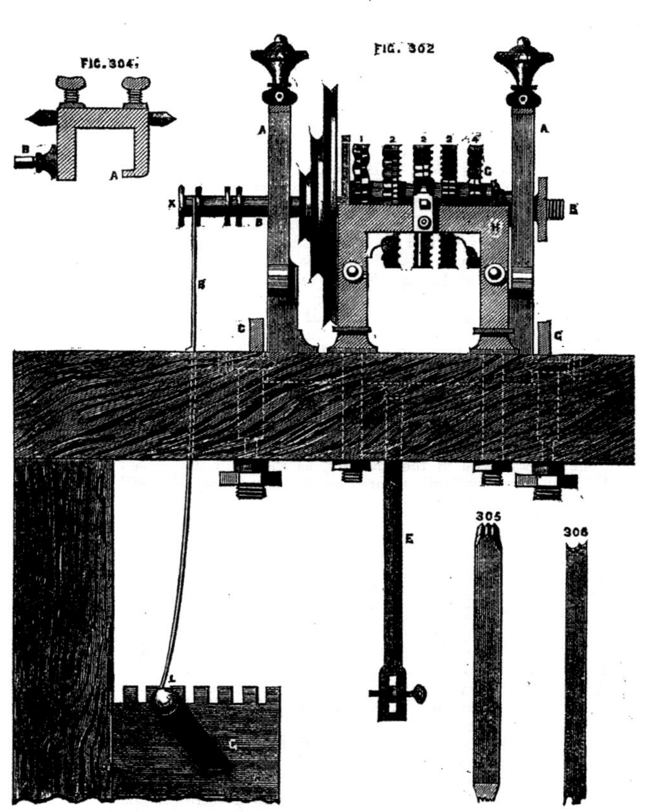

Diderot et D'Alembert

To really understand a complete definition of guilloché one must know the most basic account of a technique called *ornamental turning*. Ornamental turning is used in creating a three-dimensional pattern on a soft material such as wood, ivory, or plastic. This is created on a lathe that is similar to the rose engine with several small differences. In fact, the engine turning lathe was created *after* the ornamental turning lathe and is an adaptation for exclusive use with metals. One of the main differences in the lathes is the amplitude of the rosettes. For ornamental turning the amplitude is much higher and the lobes are much less multitudinous, meaning pointy but few. A rose engine has lower amplitude and more lobes with standards such as 96, 124, and so on. This is because for soft materials fine detailed work would not show up well due in part to wood grain and material behavior. With metal the work is much more detailed and requires patterns with lower amplitude and cuts in two dimensions. With lower amplitude the vibrations from the rotation are greatly reduced. Some other differences between engine turning and ornamental turning are the tools. For engine turning, the cutter is fixed and aided by the use of a guide (said with a hard g, "geed") and the decoration must be applied to a piece using hand turning, which cannot be too fast, or there will be vibrations in the facets known as *chatter*. With ornamental turning, the tool is rotating as is the work, and both are turned by a motor. There are two people whom I know that do not use the two together: Jean-Claude Charpignon and Jeremy Soulsby.The surface of ornamentally turned works is in heavy relief.

G. Phil Poirier

The easiest method of discerning if a piece has been created by way of ornamental turning or guilloché is to remember the following: ornamental turning changes the shape and overall dimensions of a piece and is a more three-dimensional change in form. Guilloché is the decoration of a surface on an already existing piece in a more two-dimensional fashion. Guilloché does not significantly change the dimensions, as the cuts are relatively small. Ornamental turning has traditionally been applied to wood, ivory, plastic, and now solid metal stock, such as brass. Guilloché has traditionally been practiced primarily on metal, with some examples in horn from the 1700s and mother of pearl in the watch industry. With the right tools almost any type of two-dimensional surface can be decorated.

Over many years and minute transformations the rose engine was born from this ornamental turning lathe. What we see now as a rose engine from the late 1800s to early 1900s is considered the modern rose engine. The straight-line machine has remained relatively the same since its conception with little improve-

G. Phil Poirier

Calina Shevlin

ments because the straight-line came to light from the rose engine and has needed almost no transformation. The first rose engine appeared between 1730 and 1740, in the far eastern French to far western Swiss regions. I believe the cradle and birthplace of guilloché was in the La Chaux-de-Fonds area of Switzerland, less than two kilometers (1¼ miles) from France. There are two types of machines associated with guilloché; the terms *engine turning* and *guilloché* assume one or both are used and are equally interchangeable. Guilloché does not refer to a machine, but rather a process of applying decoration to a surface. The first of these tools is the rose engine, named for the flower-like rosettes (cams) that are used to transfer the pattern to the material. The rose engine turns in the round and follows the rosettes. The second is the straight-line machine, which was born out of the rose engine. This machine uses pattern bars, runs in an up and down fashion, and can create radials (like sunburst patterns). The straight-line is perhaps most commonly used to make pens and other cylindrical objects with the aid of a special pen chuck.

The straight-line, like the rose engine, has a hand wheel to turn, but instead of turning on the x-y-z axis all the way around, its pattern bars rest fixed and the rubber travels exclusively on the x-y axis. The rose engine is used to create patterns that are round, and the straight-line creates patterns that are linear and radial.

Currently guilloché is seeing an exploration in experimental materials. I would really like to see guilloché applied *on top* of enamel, rather than just under it on the metal. I have not yet designed

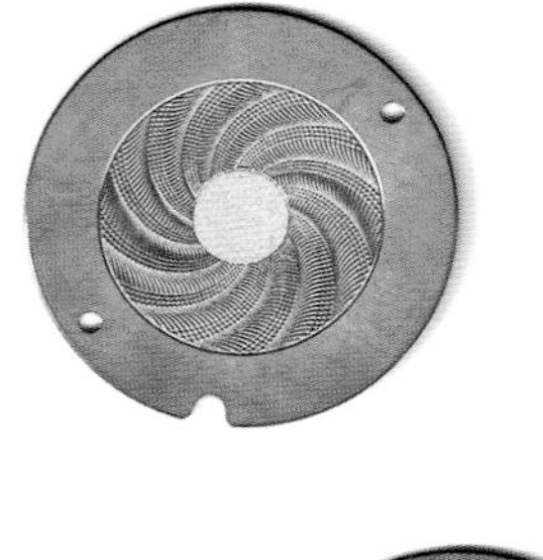

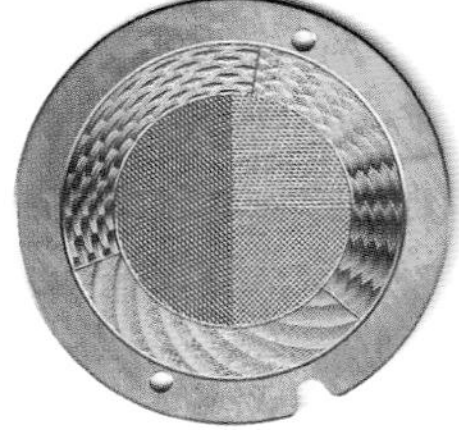

Calina Shevlin

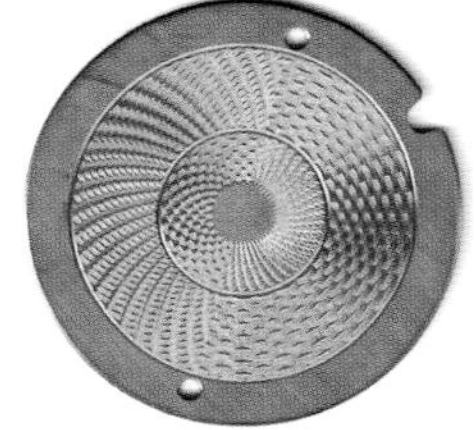

Calina Shevlin

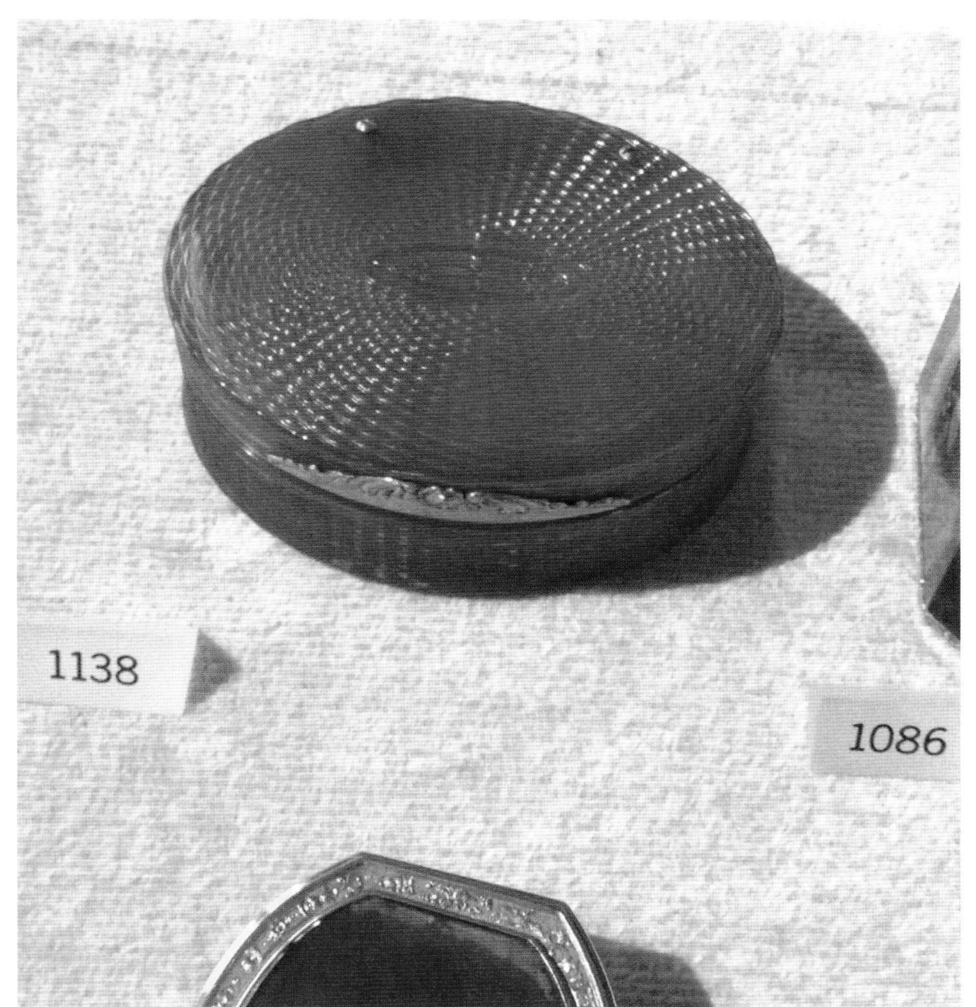

The Collection of the Alte Pinakothek, Munich, Germany

enameling (although there are a few examples that pre-date Fabergé), both enhancing the other and creating a perfect marriage of two highly sought-after art forms. Fabergé was also the first to have an actual workshop for guilloché, where machines were aligned for workers to create pieces in early production style.

Types of Machines Used in the Creation of Guilloché

There have been few changes in the overall mechanical design of the rose engine and the straight-line from their first manufacture, but rather small improvements. A rose engine is a machine that moves in a circular motion while pushing against a form—known as a rosette—and making a copy of that form on the work.

The piece to be worked is attached to the headstock and rotates with the machine while the cutter rests in place and is applied to the work, thus cutting the pattern into the rotating work. The straight-line machine moves in an up-and-down motion and follows pattern bars fixed at the side of the machine; it can also create radial patterns by turning the headstock. The straight-line is also capable of working with a pen chuck a cutter that would serve this function; although I did mention this curiosity to someone in 2012, it has not been realized to my knowledge. Unfortunately, the most innovative or creative things often take a back burner to production work.

While the history is largely forgotten, the two people who introduced guilloché to the world and brought its presence to the masses were Peter Carl Fabergé and Abraham-Louis Breguet. Neither of these men were the inventors of guilloché, but they both had a lasting impact in the field. Although neither Fabergé nor Breguet exist as family businesses, both enterprises are continuing to exploit the riches of guilloché and use the names of the original founders. Looking at Fabergé, we see a man who had a vision of preserving the facets that were gently carved by hand turning with a rose engine. Fabergé was one of the first to publicly combine the arts of guilloché and

Calina Shevlin

FIG.01-09A

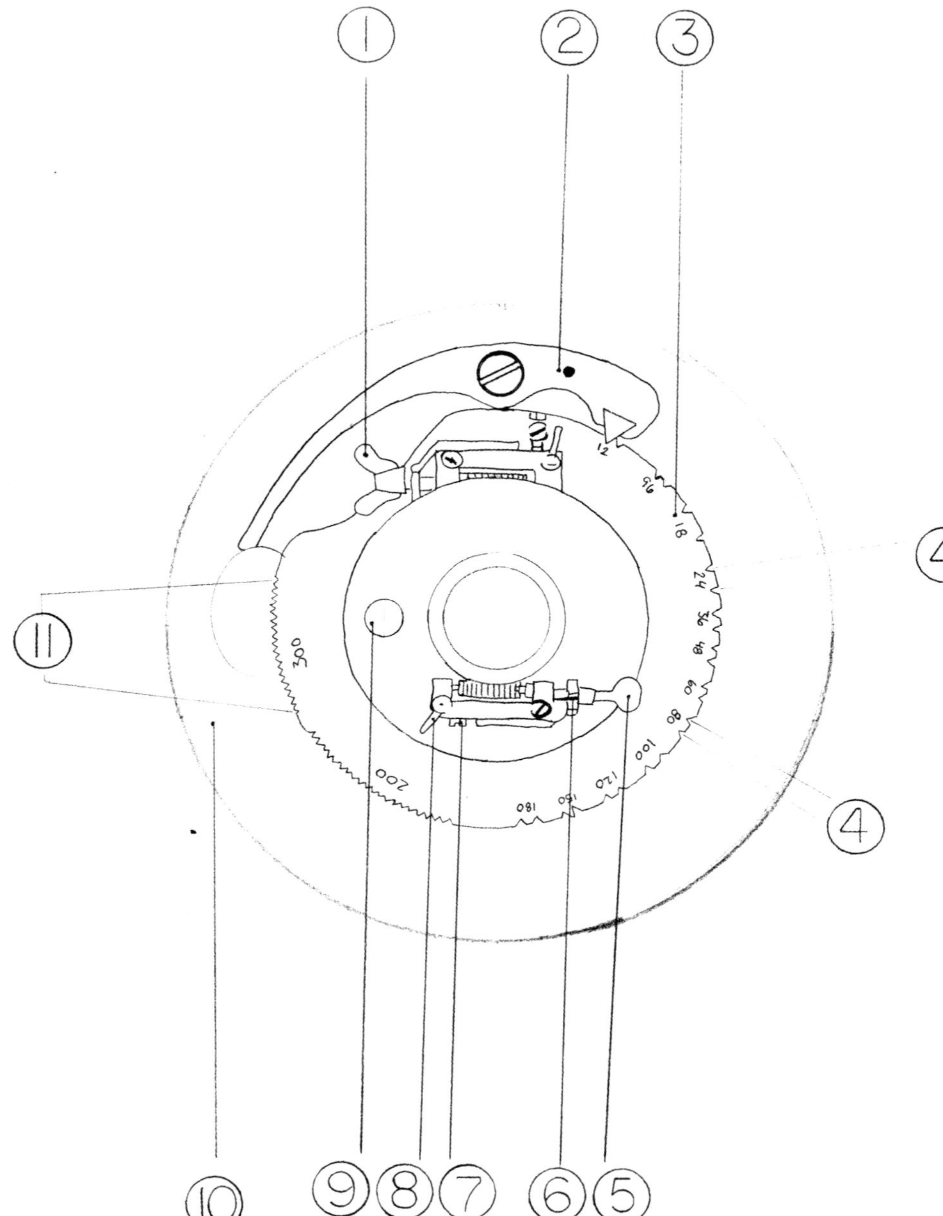

Illustration re-drawn from Lienhard Operators Manual 1895 by Calina Shevlin
A view of the Flywheel and Indexing or Division Plate from the point of the operator.

1. Worm: This is the worm for moving along the large headstock. The worm screws that exist now, and that are replacing the old ones, have notches cut into them in eight equal parts that allow counting the clicks and more precision than before.
2. Selector: This is for selecting the division plate, but is mounted on the flywheel. The oval just below the handle of the selector is a hole in which the operator can place fingers from the backside to get good leverage while turning the wheel for selection.
3. Division Plate/Indexing Plate: Where all of the divisions are located; from the old Lienhard machines you can see that there were fourteen different divisions.
4. Divisions: These are showing that the first line—or the top line of each leading to the number 4—would be considered 1, which I write with permanent marker on the left side, and 2 on the right side just under the notches.
5. Worm Screw: This is for displacing the small worm wheel on the small barrel.
6. Counter: This has notches in it and works the same as every other counter mentioned.
7. Screw: This is to block the worm in place, keeping it fixed.
8. Release Lever: Releases the worm to be freely moved larger distances.
9. Steel Pin: Used to block the barrels together.
10. Flywheel/Drive Wheel: This is what the cord is connected to the top of and allows the machine to rotate smoothly.
11. Fibonacci Sequence: The 200 and 300 teeth are a faster method with less counting using Fibonacci counting. I still like to make ticks under each notch, alternating colors so I can easily keep track of where the selector should go each time I move the division plate.

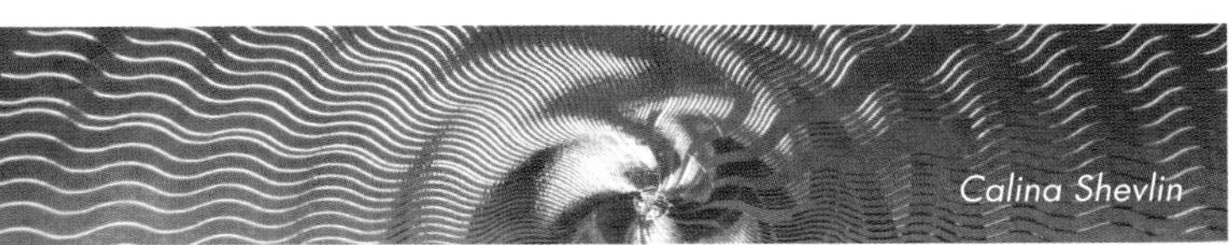

attachment, allowing up and down movement and turning a cylinder 360 degrees to apply the decoration that way as well.

The first rose engines had many different types of chucks, and the straight-line chuck was one of them. From this attachment the straight-line machine was born. The chuck was large and cumbersome, taking hours to attach and align before using. The independent straight-line machine took up a little more space than the large attachment; many workshops adopted the independent straight-line machine. Both the rose engine and straight-line machines are used to create guilloché. Although many people will argue the brocading machine is also a machine for creating guilloché, I say it is not. Even though the brocading machine uses small rosettes to create a background pattern when tracing a plate to create an image I do not consider it a machine for creating guilloché for several reasons. The main reason is it is a direct descendant of the pantograph, also called the reducing machine, which was also used for copying images and reducing them to make medals and other keepsakes. This brocading machine—called a *tapisserie* in French—uses guilloché as a background, and it does not have the facets that identify hand made guilloché; it is merely a tracing of guilloché. The brocading machine does use parts of guilloché machines such as the rosettes, but it is not hand operated; it is run by motor, so the work can be put on, a switch is turned, and the operator can go off and do something else—not requiring too much skill. I am not saying this machine is not interesting or useful, but it does not create what is defined as guilloché.

Straight-line chuck on a rose engine. *G. Phil Poirier*

While Louis-Abraham Breguet used guilloché exclusively on his watches, there are no records that exist to explain where he learned or if he was self-taught. The first watch created by L. A. Breguet that showcased guilloché was around 1775–1780. This is when Breguet marked his pieces as unique, as indeed they were, and people really started to see and pay attention to guilloché. From this guilloché gained a popularity not seen before. Collectors and buyers alike were pulled in by these handcrafted watches with their unique decorations.

Interestingly, some of the patterns that exist can be created with either the rose engine or the straight-line and look almost exactly the same. For example, the barley corn pattern is almost the same, and only close scrutiny can provide the answer as to rose engine or straight-line; a passing glance would not really register the difference. The basket weave can also be created on both machines.

I find that these two machines are complimentary, and it is really useful to employ one of each if you are thinking of making a living from guilloché. Different clients and pieces will require different patterns and applications, so if you can find them, it would be wise to invest in both machines. Multiple

Pen and pen chuck on the straight-line. *David Lindow*

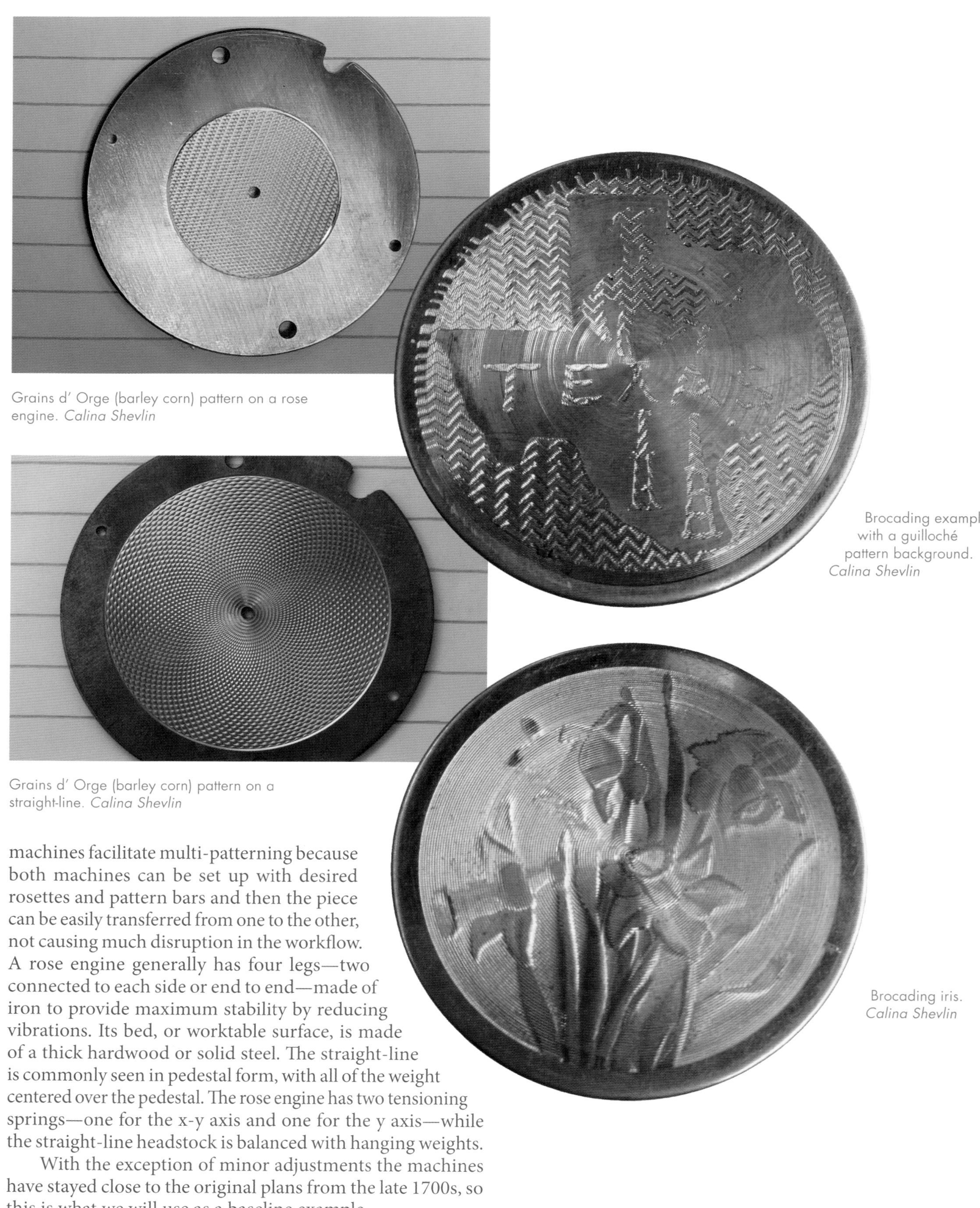

Grains d' Orge (barley corn) pattern on a rose engine. *Calina Shevlin*

Brocading example with a guilloché pattern background. *Calina Shevlin*

Grains d' Orge (barley corn) pattern on a straight-line. *Calina Shevlin*

Brocading iris. *Calina Shevlin*

machines facilitate multi-patterning because both machines can be set up with desired rosettes and pattern bars and then the piece can be easily transferred from one to the other, not causing much disruption in the workflow. A rose engine generally has four legs—two connected to each side or end to end—made of iron to provide maximum stability by reducing vibrations. Its bed, or worktable surface, is made of a thick hardwood or solid steel. The straight-line is commonly seen in pedestal form, with all of the weight centered over the pedestal. The rose engine has two tensioning springs—one for the x-y axis and one for the y axis—while the straight-line headstock is balanced with hanging weights.

With the exception of minor adjustments the machines have stayed close to the original plans from the late 1700s, so this is what we will use as a baseline example.

Brocading machine. *G. Phil Poirier*

Hall straight-line machine with pattern bar roller. *G. Phil Poirier*

Lienhard rose engine. *Calina Shevlin*

CHAPTER 2
Instruction and Learning

At one time there were official classes in guilloché in the School of Applied Industrial Arts in La Chaux-de-Fonds, Switzerland. This region is the birthplace of guilloché because two major machine manufacturers were situated there, as well as the physical classes. There are documented pieces that were 100% made in Switzerland in the mid- to late 1700s that have beautiful guilloché applications. Between 1896 and 1932, there were classes at the aforementioned school, and at the height of enrollment for guilloché there could be up to ten students at one time. The rest of the time there were one or two registered every year, then due to war the classes saw a drop in enrollment, stopped, and never resumed.

I have spent many years in the Chaux-de-Fonds region researching, digging, and photographing all things guilloché. The beautiful and technically challenging student works were innovative for their time and are proof of what could be done with a little instruction. The shapes created by students were incredible and followed the rules of form: finish then guilloché, and enamel if applicable. The rules of today are quite different, but from a production point of view they were more than adequate.

To my initial disappointment I arrived at the school—now called the École d'Art Appliques (EAA)—inquiring about classes and was told they never existed, but after a bit of digging and persuasion to see old records just for curiosity's sake I struck gold. I found all of the records pertaining to the creation and closure of the guilloché courses. I initially knew to go to this school because a gentleman—now retired—who did guilloché in La Chaux-de-Fonds told me his grandfather took courses in guilloché at the school.

There was the apprenticeship method of learning guilloché, the school method, and the self taught, which I will go into a bit later. The following is a detailed and accurate record of the goings on in La Chaux-de-Fonds, providing a clear view of the rise and swift fall of guilloché. I have translated the school records from their original French.

In 1886, in La Chaux-de-Fonds, Switzerland, there was a school called École Municipale D'Art Appliqués à l'Industrie (the School of Applied Industrial Arts). The school exists today as the École d'Art Appliqués (School of Applied Arts), which teaches watch, fashion, and jewelry design and hand arts like engraving. I first visited the school in spring 2013, to find answers to my questions about guilloché as a course. I was intrigued, as I had been in the region for a month visiting every museum and library searching for information about guilloché. I was told at every place there was no information on the subject and no one believed guilloché had been a subject of study in the region. I stayed at each place for a day or two, reading any book I thought might even mention guilloché, enameling, or engraving, only to be disappointed again and again. I was really skeptical to try to find information at this School of Applied arts, mostly because I thought it would encompass more industrial type arts, but I went anyway. Sadly, the librarian told me there was no information because there had never been a course in guilloché. Not to be put off, I asked if I could just have look at the school records because I was also interested in enameling. Finally I was handed the records and was told the records only went back to 1886, so this is from whence I begin my discussion on education.

In the school year 1886–1887, Mr. Eugène Gauthier was nominated to the post of teacher of guilloché in the school of engraving. This is not to say he was strictly teaching guilloché in a hands-on manner, but he was giving lectures periodically as more of a special topic a few times a year. Mr. Gauthier was taken from the working world of guilloché, where he had a private workshop and several prestigious clients. He was also asked to give demonstrations, but when he was not talking about or demonstrating guilloché, Mr. Gauthier was busy in his own workshop or was working as the part-time mechanic for the school. He was the one who kept the machines in working order and fixed things as needed, in addition to regular maintenance. This is where I would venture to say an introduction to guilloché began in this school. Throughout the following text, when talking about the school, I feel it is important to mention a few students not of guilloché, but who were enrolled in the school at this time. These students later became guillocheurs, or patrons to guillocheurs with their watch companies. James and Eugène Calame were brothers enrolled at the same time in engraving and had descendants who formed Calame et Cie., a company in Le Locle that makes watch cases and jewelry occasionally adorned by guilloché. Fernand Droz was an engraving student at the school and later became known as a founder of Jacquet-Droz, a watch company specializing in enamel dials with some use of guilloché.

In 1889–1890, the school curriculum stayed the same, with guilloché being taught as a special topic. Mr. Eugène Lenz was put in charge of giving the theory of guilloché, again in the engraving school. One of the notable students who attended school in engraving and other "professional arts" during this year was Henri Perregeaux of the Girard-Perregeaux watch manufacturing family.

I believe as the students knew one another from school, they later decided to branch out and start their own workshops, which ended up being passed down to their sons and their grandsons. These workshops are what are now disappearing, leaving nothing more than a legacy from the cradle of guilloché.

In 1891, the first straight-line machine was acquired by the school, but it lacked tools—I presume pattern bars and touches—rendering it initially unusable. This would have been no problem for Mr. Gauthier, now a mere part-time mechanic, as he would have known about guilloché if he were giving lectures and demonstrations on the subject. This straight-line was a gift, and was really a useful commodity used to initiate students who would later go into the field of guilloché. During this school year the professor of guilloché—still in lecture format—was again changed to Eugène Gauthier. Mr. Gauthier taught the principles of guilloché to the engraving class for two hours per week. In this year, the students and the board of directors visited various architectural marvels and it was decided that what was learned in the courses of design would be applied on more varied objects in future years. It is also in this year that painted enameling was added to the curriculum, a direct effect of those inspired visits. Enameling was slowly gaining popularity again in the late 1800s, and was a literal method to apply designs in miniature to pieces that could be portable.

Collection D'Arts Industriels De L'École D'Arts Appliqués, Ville de La Chaux-de-Fonds

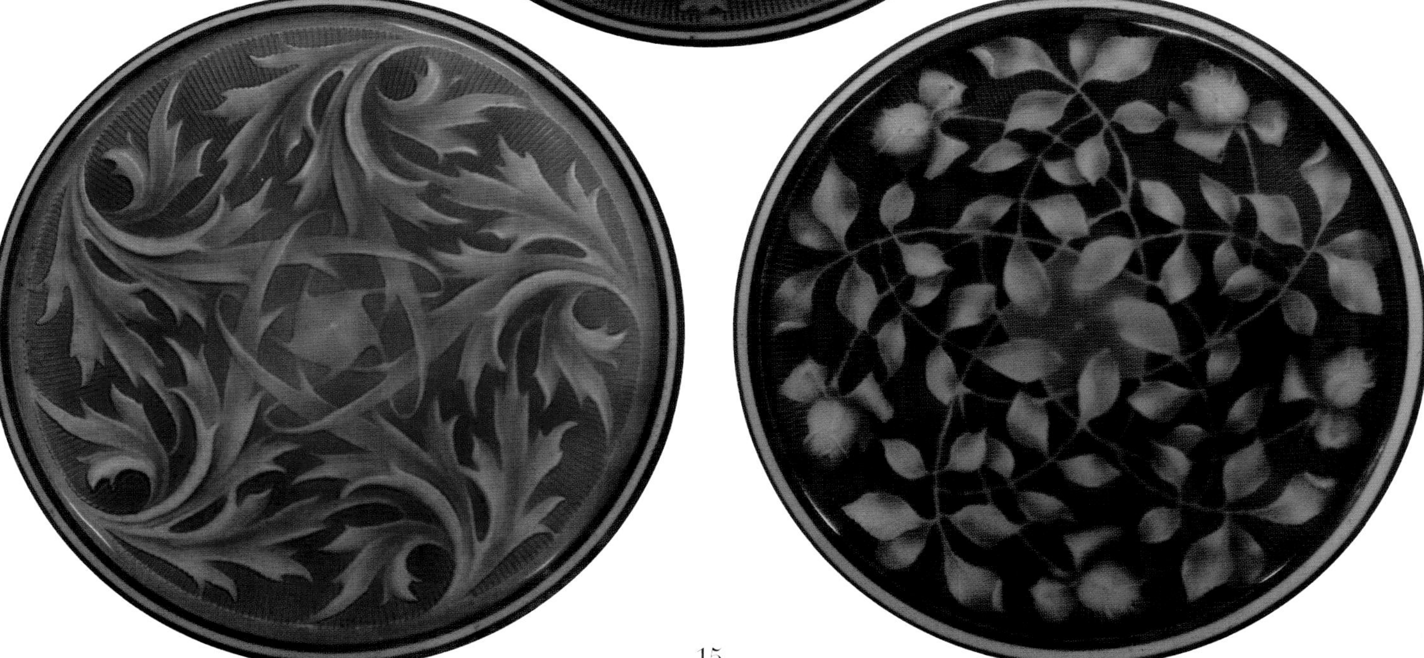

From 1891–1892, the students were so plentiful that they were only being enrolled on a case by case basis after several interviews with members of the school board and teaching staff. The engraving class was more than full and it was the technique to learn at the time. As the classes were so popular and the students needed work to enamel and engrave on, the board began looking for someone with guilloché experience to create guilloché plaques to give to the enameling and engraving students for something to experiment and hone their skills with. Most notably, the Syndicate of Workers in Engraving and Guilloché asked for authorization to use the tools at the school for professional guillocheur training and studies. This was for the training of apprentices in the workplace; they would now have additional time, resources, and a place to teach them in the evenings, with additional tools for their own workshops. This was the first apprentice training supplemented with school materials in a location different from the workshop. More time was spent with the apprentices than usual, as they were training many more hours than the norm of the time—fifty hours per week.

From 1892–1893, the school purchased a straight-line machine with all of the accessories necessary for a professional class to be held in the evenings, and for use in regular exams. This was a direct product of the boom in students from the previous school year. There were enough apprentices/students that the school now officially had two straight-line machines, and I suspect three or four rose engines, as well.

From 1894–1895, the engravers began using guilloché to practice different effects in their work; more shadows and light play were developed depending on the patterns used. The students could engrave their pieces, then send them to the guillocheurs to finish, or they could receive the pieces with guilloché and would painstakingly add engraving over top. The plaques made available to the enameling and engraving students originated in the enterprises around the city and were not cost effective for a level of learning. The effects of engraving over guilloché really made the pieces have a more three-dimensional look to them, and some students used the light play from the guilloché in a painterly manner.

Between 1895 and 1899, there was no mention of the curriculum including guilloché in any form. It is assumed the courses continued as normal with a lecture, but if the teacher was no longer at the school they very well may have stopped altogether. There is no mention of either probability and all I can do is speculate.

The year 1899–1900 proved that with the influx and high interest of incoming and continuing students it would be necessary to acquire more guilloché machines, a competent teacher, and a building—or at least a classroom—dedicated to this art form, rather than carrying on with a lecture and some meager demonstrations. The search was put into motion, applications were accepted, and machines were purchased or gifted from nearby enterprises and manufacturers. The birth of the first courses for students was well underway.

The study of guilloché was said to be vast and varied; since the introduction of the rose engine would open doors in terms of imagination and skill set, the guillocheurs were to be knowledgeable in drawing, have an idea of decoration, and understand mechanics for maintenance—their ability to repair of their own machines would be indispensible. The students were expected to carry their art into the world and make a career of it.

In Switzerland a student begins to study for what they will do for the rest of their lives at age fifteen or sixteen. It is rare one would spend years in an apprenticeship and then have a change of heart and try to find another job. This can be equated to trade schools in the United States. In Switzerland trades are also highly respected, as is the education to achieve one of the professions, and are equal to a university education.

The employers who would take students in after their schooling also had their own kind of apprenticeship program that was for another few years; then the apprentice would work their way up until they eventually became a master, which was after roughly twenty years—in their mid- to late forties. The students needed to be able to become masters of their tools (the rose engine and straight-line, plus all of the cutters, the sharpening, the rubbers, and maintenance and upkeep). It was in that year the school asked the commune (a commune in Switzerland is like a county in the United States) to authorize an official guilloché class, as well as a class specific to engraving letters, to start the first of the year in 1902.

In 1901–1902, the budget for organizing the two new classes was an astonishing 60,000 CHF ($65,000), with a contribution from the public of another 13,180 CHF ($16,000). That amount was enormous for the early 1900s, and even today would be an acceptable sum to acquire a machine and the tooling necessary to start a small class in guilloché. This amount, divided 70% for guilloché and 30% for letter engraving, would have been enough to buy eight new guilloché machines, all the necessary tooling, and rent a decent-sized space. That year there was a detrimental shortage of skilled guillocheurs in nearby cities, a direct consequence of the suppression of apprentices in a creed from 1899. Thus the interest in training guillocheurs was astronomical, as potential employers waited for the first students to graduate in three long years.

In the search for a qualified guilloché teacher, the school board prohibited the school from asking the bosses and heads of workshops to teach the guilloché class, as there was already a minute decline in the art that was never overly populated to begin with, as well as a high demand from existing workshops to produce. The school of art ultimately wanted to create an elite group of worker artists that would be able to fight against any foreign competition for guilloché jobs in Switzerland. It should be noted this is generally the same goal or mind-set that still exists today in Switzerland, so while a lot has changed, many things have also stayed the same. In creating the guilloché class, all efforts were to be put toward training the workers, so that when they finished, they were measuring up to current requirements in the art and decoration of watches, watchcases, jewelry, and small boxes.

> Votre commission se joint aux craintes qu'exprime la rapport du Conseil communal et aux réserves qu'il contient quant aux consequences possibles qui pourraient résulter de la création de nouvelles classes de guillochis et de gravure de lettres, si cette creation devait être mal comprise et faire dévier l'Ecole d'art du but principal qui lui fut assigné lors de sa fondation. (*École d'Art Appliqué a l'Industrie: Rapport de la Commission sur L'Exercice 1901–1902*. La Chaux-de-Fonds Imprimerie du National Suisse 1902, translated by Calina Shevlin)

The school commission expressed they had reservations about the creation of a guilloché class because there may have been repercussions from the community, meaning the patrons of the school and the professional guillocheurs. The commission was afraid the principles of the art school would perhaps be deflected in creating this new (first ever) guilloché class. At that time guilloché was only beginning to be considered artistic and not just some skilled trade.

Collection D'Arts Industriels De L'École D'Arts Appliqués, Ville de La Chaux-de-Fonds

Despite the concerns of the commission, the new classes were approved due to the insufficient number of new apprentices for guilloché in the working world. The letter engraving class was created simply to supplement, not to transform the engraving program. After all obstacles were cleared the first ever guilloché class commenced at the art school on January 6, 1902. The instruction included the operation and repairing of the straight-line machine, the rose engine, set-up and operation of the eccentric chuck, operation of the automatic rose engine (which I believe we now call the brocading machine), and use of the engraving machine. There was also some instruction to begin with on the reducing machine, which would have been what we call a pantograph today, or a brocading machine.

The class structure and overall hours were rigorous and demanding; just the instruction of guilloché was for five hours *per day*. In addition, there were six hours a week in geometric drawing and six to nine hours a week in decorative composition depending on the season (more for spring and summer, less for autumn and winter). There were also four hours a week of artistic drawing, four hours a week of practical mechanics, four hours a week of mechanical theory, and two hours a week of general instruction, including art history and other areas of interest. Thus there were fifty-one to fifty-four hours a week spent on instruction alone, and the students were encouraged to work on projects and ideas in their spare time. The students began their instruction using nonferrous metals such as brass, but quickly advanced to using precious materials such as gold and silver. Students were motivated to move on to precious metals because gold and silver were primarily used in the industry. The class highly encouraged new and innovative applications of guilloché, as opposed to working on watch dials and watchcases, as was the habit in the past for guillocheurs.

In the school year 1902–1903, the inspector general stated that students of guilloché deserved a huge congratulations, but also that they should feel privileged to have the opportunity to learn the professional secrets of their instructors.

> I have visited many workshops in the United States, France, Germany, and Switzerland. I have found that European workshops are very closed about sharing their "secrets" about how they work, set up a machine, sharpen cutters, etc. All of the "secrets" I have seen are nothing more than what I like to call simultaneous innovations or inventions. I have seen almost the same thing in most workshops.

The first years in the guilloché class were good, with the students making satisfactory progress (*satisfactory* in Switzerland means "on schedule"), and held real promise for the future. Thanks to the zeal of the teachers, the students easily completed thirty hours of guilloché, plus twenty-six hours of other classes, each week for the entire school year. This included many evenings and frequent Saturday lessons.

During the 1903–1904 school year the school had seven new guilloché students enrolled. It was during this year the students began working on specific forms and sizes. The directions for the class were very specific and gave students the number of pieces needed per year, per project, and so forth, like syllabi do for students today. The students were also given various patterns to make and told what distances were required between cuts—a sort of formula to see if they could understand and follow written directions as well as pay attention to each little detail. This is the practice in many production facilities today. Each student made twelve plaques, with eighteen lines of grains d'orge (barley corn), six oval plaques of a free design using the elliptical chuck, three plaques flinqué for enamel, and so on through the various patterns. In this era, it seems to follow a program would have been fairly simple, as long as one was willing to come in and work hard and could follow directions.

From 1904–1905, there were six students enrolled in the program, and the third-year students (the first students of the course) began working with soft gold. There were many pieces to create on the engraving machine, as well as work on the rose engine and also some straight-line work. The third-year students finally began to explore working on three-dimensional objects such as goblets, table clock structures, and boxes.

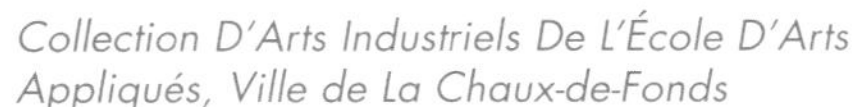

Collection D'Arts Industriels De L'École D'Arts Appliqués, Ville de La Chaux-de-Fonds

The second-year students were designing entire watches that could be executed on the machines and were really starting to explore and experiment with the straight-line in general, a machine essential to guilloché and popularized in the decoration of cigarette cases and picture frames.

In the 1905–1906 school year the first guilloché class graduated and moved into practical working life in workshops around the city. The owners and bosses of the workshops welcomed the students enthusiastically. The seven men who were still in class were all following along well and the professor, Mr. Rossel, was content with their progress and excited to be teaching. He was encouraged to continue the line of courses and method of teaching, as it was working well for everyone and producing desired results. The products created by the students were of good quality and the students could continue to dials, silver boxes, and gold coins (the coins were made more like medals using the brocading machine).

The year 1906–1907 proved the new graduating class was also in a position to be respected by their new bosses. It was in this year that the guillocheurs were finally striving to make their decorations regular, more precise, and machine like; they were going for perfection and not just operating, beginning to really know the machines and their mechanics, as well as the depths and pressure required to make a good cut and be able to reproduce the effects accurately every time. The students executed their art on special steel blocks and small metalwork objects. This is the first time the creation of stamps is mentioned, and it continued to be a focal point hereafter. It was stated that the room for guilloché was not sufficient for student working conditions, and I completely agree based on the following description: "…le local affecté à cet usage a été un peu rafraichi pendant les vacances d'avril, mais il est insuffisamment éclairé, deux fenêtres pour 10 outils" (There were only two windows and ten machines, and the inspector as well as the board stated light was insufficient for this kind of work). (*Rapport de la Commission sur L'Exercice 1901–1902*)

The 1907–1908 school year saw another eight students enrolled—keep in mind this was a four-year apprentice program. The students were found to be taking advantage of their education by being persistent, giving a good impression, and excelling at their chosen craft. The board wanted to change some projects to really highlight the guilloché, but they were told this was not possible, as this was not the school of guilloché; it was merely a concentration under the school of engraving in the school of art. One of the Fehr brothers was a first-year student in this school year and would later be one of the Fehr and Cie. founders, a company still active in La Chaux-de-Fonds that creates stamps for guilloché.

A quick word about stamps: They are steel bars to which guilloché is applied and then used as a model for dials and other items that will become stamped with it. It is making an impression on a material much harder than the material to be imprinted. The guilloché stamps were what led to the downfall of guilloché in the first place. It is clear the brothers decided guilloché would not be the most efficient method of disseminating their craft, but rather made stamps to emboss as many objects as possible with the pattern of guilloché. Fehr and Cie. still use this method of stamping for several large watch manufactures; it gives aesthetic pleasure with little cost involved and not much skill or craftsmanship.

The year 1908–1909 was the first the school started to realize the importance of practical work and not only the rote creation of samples. The students began making watch dials and cases, as well as starting on clock bodies for the tabletop clocks that were becoming more popular. The guilloché class had always given good results for the practical; aside from the evening class for the apprentices in town, the students and teacher had started developing relationships with many of the workshops in the area, where the students would hopefully be working after graduation. The students were well versed and profited immensely from the teaching of Mr. Rossel, but the board of directors wanted students to pay more attention to the technical teachings and to apply themselves more seriously to geometric drawing courses. The board was also keen to see more interest and effort put into the research aspect of the students' compositions. The directors found the progress to distraction ratio for the younger students was difficult to control. (Note the board of directors was like the school staff in the United States; they were usually charged with noting progress in all school aspects, much like the modern principal and their staff.) They felt that sports and other varied events were detracting from the drawing course and so forth. The students of this year were Camille Jeanneret, brother of Le Corbusier; and Armand Fehr, later a founder of Fehr et Cie.

In the school year 1909–1910, many of the students had attendance problems and difficulty arriving in a timely manner. This caused Mr. Rossel to become very strict with many aspects of the students' training. The program remained the same, with equal amounts of work on old and new rose engines.

I would be curious to know what exactly is meant by "new" and "old" rose engines, as during this time frame they were a fairly standard make and had not changed much since the early 1800s. There is also an automatic rose engine mentioned, which again, without photographic evidence, is difficult to imagine. The only machine that is like a rose engine and could be automatic is the ornamental turning lathe.

The fourth-year students did not attain the required or desired results in skill level, and this was almost certainly a direct result of the fact that more than half of the students' time was occupied with various practical work from the trade industry. From previous years it was decided that only making samples was not a good use of time, but now making actual pieces was not a good way to learn. The school needed to find a balance between these two aspects to ensure quality guillocheurs were produced. While this was a good introduction to the students' future workshops and working conditions, they missed out on a lot of information that would have further progressed them in the field. Because the guillocheurs were not abundant in this school year, work began to pile up from outside businesses. In my opinion, guillocheurs were never abundant like other artists—there have never been several thousands of guillocheurs. Outside the school and in the program, twenty-six decoration businesses used the school and students for their work throughout the school year. Several employers and workers also arrived at the school seek-

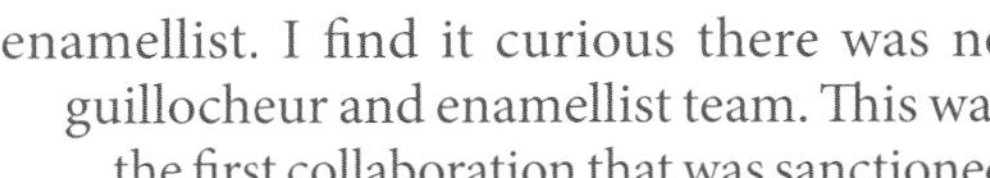

ing advice on the craft of guilloché. This is a prime example of the problem of not giving written information; when one master retired, if he did not have an apprentice with whom he shared his information, or only had apprentices that were short-lived, the information went away with the master. The board mentioned the method of teaching had remained the same for the last eight years because it had established a class that had the proven knowledge needed to have a good base for going into workshops and starting successful careers as guillocheurs. The fourth-year students again needed to do better work, and we can see they were working almost full time for these companies. Only one student started an apprenticeship in the 1909–1910 school year.

Collection D'Arts Industriels De L'École D'Arts Appliqués, Ville de La Chaux-de-Fonds

A professional course was started in the evenings in the 1910–1911 school year, directly stemming from the heavy use of the students in guilloché in the previous two years. Before 1910, professionals were simply using the school and tools, but there was no actual professional course other than the exams and occasional training in 1891. The classes were started on a trial basis, but there was no doubt professionals needed this course to supplement and hone their skills. The third- and fourth-year students in guilloché, engraving, and jewelry started to have an obligatory enameling class for two hours per week. This class was taught by a Mr. Kocher, and was important because during the early 1900s, enameling was becoming more and more popular and the school thought it necessary to give more in-depth information on enameling, and also because there had not been an evolution in the courses for such a long time, so this would perhaps entice new students to join the school. This was the first year that cross-pollination among different arts became extremely important and integrated into the curriculum. Students of guilloché were given a project with absolutely no parameters, no advice, and no corrections; projects were envisioned and executed by the student team, consisting of two people. This came about because a gentleman from Zürich who was a celebrated professor and curator introduced a sort of contest in the school so he could choose a few of the projects to be in an international show he was curating. The board of directors, as well as this gentleman, judged the students' work and one to two of the best projects were selected. The teams of collaborators needed to be in one of the following categories: a guillocheur and an engraver, a jeweler and a guillocheur, a jeweler and an engraver, or an engraver and an enamellist. I find it curious there was no guillocheur and enamellist team. This was the first collaboration that was sanctioned by the school, whereas before, the students would have to create pieces based on very strict guidelines and a plethora of feedback, as well as create "production" pieces for the students in the other arts to use. These pieces for other students' use were not counted in the final requirements, but were nonetheless expected and even heavily relied upon. The curator brought this idea to the school because he had found huge success in making his own students, who were studying textiles, work like this for the previous two or three years. The board of directors mentioned it would be ideal to acquire the special machines to permit guilloché work to be applied to small metalwork. Again my curiosity abounds, as all rose engines were capable of accommodating small three-dimensional metalwork. With the other six students in the entire four-year program, only two new ones started in 1910, a huge decline in popularity as seen in 1898–1902, where there were many students interested, and once the first official diploma in guilloché was introduced, students had to pass exams to get into the program.

During the next school year (1911–1912) enrollment for engraving was down by more than 40%, and not just at the school; general interest in engraving was being exchanged for other methods of decoration on watchcases and bracelets,

Collection D'Arts Industriels De L'École D'Arts Appliqués, Ville de La Chaux-de-Fonds

such as guilloché, stone setting, and enameling. In La Chaux-de-Fonds, the inhabitants were extremely pleased that students of the decorative arts and compositions were all at one school and collaborating, ensuring the students were exposed to more than one art. This would allow the city to have many different types of workshops should students stay in La Chaux-de-Fonds, thereby drawing more tourism to the area. The art deco period was really starting to take off, especially at the school, and nature was the basis for the new style. There was only one style purely of Swiss invention in the art deco period called "Style Sapin," meaning "pine tree style." (This style bucked the system of art deco with the whiplash curve, being a very geometric pattern. This was a direct result of the school of art when Charles-Edouard Jeanneret was studying in engraving, later to become known as Le Corbusier.)

The board of directors stated the class of essentially mechanical guilloché continued to bring satisfactory results every year. Of the eight students of guilloché six were very well advanced, but the second-year students needed encouragement; they were not on a track to be desired by the board. The practical work was well executed, as decoration companies who made watchcases could come to the school and its students with confidence. While there was not much work or teaching for the straight-line machine this year, the board strongly advised not to neglect those kinds of decoration, especially the application in the workshops in the city.

The drawings were limited and followed previous years' studies; the decorative compositions were followed eagerly, but unfortunately at the expense of the dial drawings. The drawings should not have been neglected due to their practical value. This year saw five new apprentices in guilloché, a feat compared to the two previous years, when numbers declined almost detrimentally.

In the 1912–1913 course for professionals there were seven people enrolled and out working in professional workshops. These seven were earning their diploma in an entirely practical setting. In the school there were ten students, the highest enrollment to date.

The 1913–1914 school year only saw the addition of two new students. Because of WWI, from 1914–1915 the school suffered terrible repercussions and very low enrollment in *every* course offered. There was an exhibition for the country, but due

Collection D'Arts Industriels De L'École D'Arts Appliqués, Ville de La Chaux-de-Fonds

Collection D'Arts Industriels De L'École D'Arts Appliqués, Ville de La Chaux-de-Fonds

to the poor and limited lighting the pocket-sized pieces of jewelry, engraving, painted enamels, and guilloché were all lost in the semi-darkness; their beauty was not appreciated as it should have been. This was not an acceptable representation of the work of the students at the school and shows a general lack of interest in promoting these arts during a time of war.

The guilloché and jewelry classes were improved with the addition of another rose engine, as well as a melting furnace. The masters of the practical classes in jewelry were fervently hoping to have their own bench press and rose engine with which to experiment and felt these were indispensable tools if they were to be able to meet the new requirements of modern industry with a complete and rounded education for their students. Guilloché was finally applied to small metalwork and jewelry this year and new information was taught in relation to three-dimensional works. There were only seven guilloché students this year due to WWI; people were being paid well to make bullet casings at a factory near the school. There were three students in the professional class, but the enrollment for guilloché had no new students; only third- and fourth-year students remained.

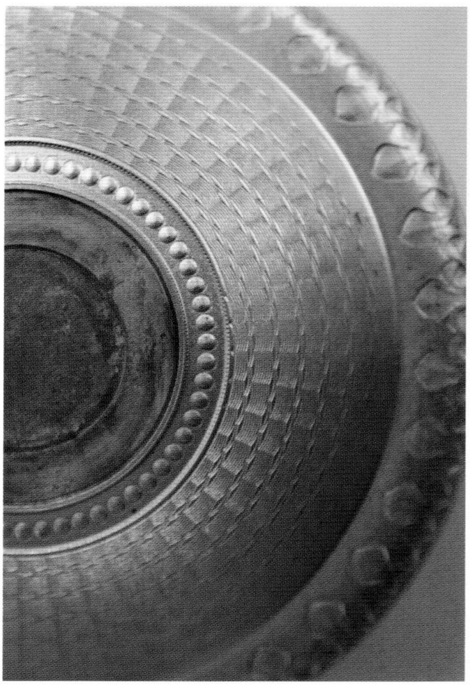

Collection D'Arts Industriels De L'École D'Arts Appliqués, Ville de La Chaux-de-Fonds

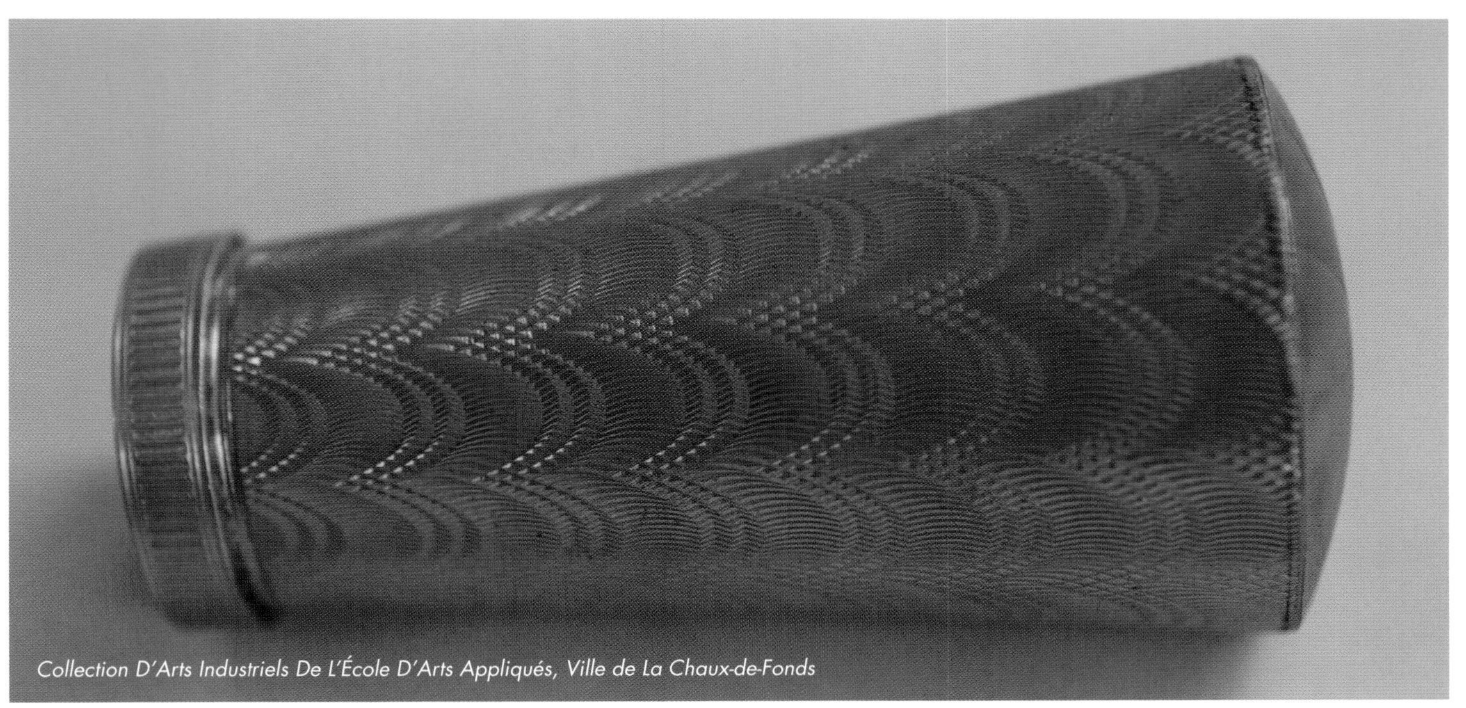

Collection D'Arts Industriels De L'École D'Arts Appliqués, Ville de La Chaux-de-Fonds

I found the board of directors to be very interesting during the 1915–1916 school year. Of the fourteen board members, three men were later to establish empires of guilloché that still exist in present day, even though they are trickling out of existence due to retirement and no new interested apprentices or operators: Gustave Calame, in Le Locle, Switzerland, would later establish Calame et Cie., which would much later turn into a watch parts business; Gervais Donzé, in La Chaux-de-Fonds, Switzerland, would later create Donzé Cadrans, specializing in guilloché and enameled watch dials exclusively (which was recently sold to Ulysses Nardin); and Fritz Flückiger would establish Flückiger Cadran in St.-Imier, Switzerland, also specializing in guilloché and enameling of watch dials. This school year saw the suppression of the guilloché class because there were no students to enroll. Although enrollment was non existent, the school did keep Mr. Rossel on to service the machines at the school and to teach essential guilloché to students, as well as the brocading machine. In addition to the lack of new students, two of the professional apprentices quit due to WWI. On the bright side, two students were added to the professional course to perfect their skills, so I feel this was a pretty good trade for the two that quit. The legacy of the two that went on to establish their own guilloché workshops continues in 2014; perhaps these workshops will remain in their families and continue on.

There was a student that attended the school for a four-month internship to learn the basics of the rose engine machine, as well as building it and taking it apart, and another apprentice that moved over from the engraving program. To finish out the end of the school year, the departing students applied guilloché to some small metalwork and donated it to the school. I was

Collection D'Arts Industriels De L'École D'Arts Appliqués, Ville de La Chaux-de-Fonds

Collection D'Arts Industriels De L'École D'Arts Appliqués, Ville de La Chaux-de-Fonds

lucky enough to see the entire collection and to photograph the many pieces.

The board stated that should the course return to normal one day, it would be necessary to attune the apprentices to this method of working with jewelry and small metals, and not primarily watch dials and cases that were flat or fairly flat. Again, in this school term, the companies that had been bringing practical work to the students stopped because almost all of the companies specializing in decoration had disappeared from the city around this time due to lack of work. This was a blow to the education of the students, and the board wrote that the discipline of guilloché was good but the spirit was not what it should and could have been. As a measure of self-preservation the school decided to re-combine the two engraving courses into one; the guilloché workshop would see a "modified activity," which I believe meant a paring down to just the bare minimum of lectures and little practical training.

Guilloché no longer existed as a complete course in the 1916–1917 school term, but was simply available for students in the other classes to learn various things about guilloché dependent on their year in the school. For example, first-year students would only hear a lecture on guilloché, while the second-year students would learn to operate and take care of machines and so on, progressing to hands-on activity only with the fourth-year students. This was in part a ploy to try to get students from other disciplines enticed enough to change their apprenticeship to guilloché. The school, without restriction to discipline, found increasing recruitment problems for all areas due to the concurrence of fabrication of munitions. Mr. Rossel was only giving demonstrations at this point and had to ask the board for more duties to stay on at the school. His initial contract was terminated, and he was given the task of maintaining the machines and operation of the brocading and engraving machines for thirty hours per week. With these two machines Mr. Rossel was making medals in then popular styles. The course description in 1917 was a lot more detailed and really encouraging in a last ditch attempt to attract any students to a program that officially no longer existed. The fourth-year guilloché students were concentrating on applying

Collection D'Arts Industriels De L'École D'Arts Appliqués, Ville de La Chaux-de-Fonds

Collection D'Arts Industriels De L'École D'Arts Appliqués, Ville de La Chaux-de-Fonds

guilloché to steel stock—what Fehr and Cie. used generations later for making stamps to press guilloché onto watch dials at a more affordable price. This also enabled more work to be produced in a day.

The year 1917–1918 was when the effects of WWI were at their worst and recruitment of students was nonexistent. Only one guilloché student remained and Mr. Rossel was only teaching two hours per week. He was giving lectures to the apprentices of other arts and he welcomed them to come and see the machines but none came—no one was interested in guilloché. Only the third- and fourth-year students followed these lessons with interest, but younger students were left indifferent. In the grand scheme of things, guilloché has always been an art with fleeting interest and minimal practitioners—more of a specialty niche. In this school year there were two external professional students and an engraver who were learning the machines. There was not any new work, but the people playing on the machines were testing out patterns on small metalwork and medallions. Engraving and guilloché classes were diminished. By almost obliterating these two programs the school was enabled to develop other areas that corresponded with the demand of new products and industrial art. The school did try to doubly employ the machines since they already had them. Most moved to making medallions with modern themes and interests. Poor student enrollment was attributed to the decline of watchcases and bracelets being decorated with engraving and guilloché in favor of other methods of decoration.

The year 1918–1919 is the last there was information for. The board of directors said that at least there was still one guillocheur. The school director stated he hoped the limited number of apprentices who became guillocheurs in recent years would contribute to raising the business of guilloché, and as can be attributed they did. Unfortunately, guilloché in its heyday was not a booming art form and was practiced only by the few who found their passion in intricate, time consuming, precise decorations.

From the brief rise and downfall of guilloché in a mere sixteen years, we see that pattern would continue in perpetuity. Guilloché has never been a popular subject to learn, even though many people find it interesting to look at. The tides come in with tens of people interested and wanting to learn more, but in the end of every cycle, only about 1% will continue on, and out of a very small group of people per decade, there is not much hope of reviving guilloché to what it once was with Fabergé.

How We Learn This Art

I have interviewed several people for the creation of this book who did not wish to tell me at first *how* they learned to create guilloché, but they eventually relented. Most people learned by trial and error; few learned through apprentice/master training. Trial and error lessons occurred via several factors—for some, a found machine led to curiosity, which in turn led to experimentation. Another factor is that it was a necessity for a watchmaker who wanted to make everything themselves from start to finish. This second method did not produce master guillocheurs, but rather very good practitioners who used guilloché in a purely practical manner. I know that for a time the US mint used a machine that was similar to a rose engine with a geometric chuck to create patterns of guilloché in the background of paper money. Sweden also had a similar machine, all of which have been sold to private collectors or machine enthusiasts. I understand someone who works in this position not wanting to disclose information because it is actually a secret, but watch dial making does not seem to be a reasonable art to keep secrets from others. It is not terribly hard once you get the hang of it, and in most cases it is not terribly interesting to do using classic patterns, either. A person who worked for a mint had a reason to keep secrets. This person was never allowed to write down the recipes of the patterns he created, but kept it all neatly tucked away in his mind, preventing anyone from successfully making counterfeit money. This is in part why the mint stopped using guilloché and has moved into computer programs that create new elaborate patterns. I could not keep all of the recipes I use in my head; I *have* to write them down so that if I wish to recreate them I can do so easily. I find this example to be an acceptable form of secrecy, but guilloché is no longer used in creating monetary notes; it is an art form and surface decoration. There will never come a time where there is too much guilloché. There simply isn't the demand, and should the demand arise for guilloché in everything from light switch plates to dinner platters, there aren't vast numbers of guillocheurs in the world to undertake all of the future varied projects. If the information on guilloché is simply passed down verbally, as it has been since the beginning, it will be lost. There are people that have a surface interest, wanting to know more about the craft, but guilloché is not their deep-rooted passion and they do not need nor want to know every detail about it, just basic information. As I write this, there remain somewhere around twenty-three people who actively practice the art of guilloché in the world for a living, and of these twenty-three, there are around nineteen who work professionally with guilloché. So pass on the information, write it down, give courses, learn all you can, and keep good notes.

I find that I learn best by writing something down—sometimes repeatedly—and seeing it. I have a photographic memory, which helps when I am using recipes and their corresponding charts. Different people learn in different manners. There are those who can read a pattern recipe and visualize the pattern straight away. There are others who simply need to hear the steps and can visualize the patterns. With all of the different types of learners in the world, it is important to have classes and disseminate the information as much and as widely as possible.

People who want to learn guilloché will often succeed if they have a steady hand, very good concentration, and a lot of patience. Hobbyists will be able to quickly pick up the technique and create pieces after only a few weeks of study, but it is the professionals that have the ability to have even patterns with no faults. This is why practice is key to a career as a guillocheur.

Collection D'Arts Industriels De L'École D'Arts Appliqués, Ville de La Chaux-de-Fonds

CHAPTER 3
The Manufacturers and Makers

Throughout the main period of manufacture (1760–1920) it is estimated there were less than eight thousand guilloché machines made. This encompasses all of the manufacturers (American, British, and Swiss) and all of the guilloché machines (rose engines and straight-lines). This does not seem like an impressive number by today's standards, but then, the makers did not have the same technology or means to make production pieces. These were planned and made almost entirely by hand, with hand-operated tools and the aid of simple lathes. Now we find it difficult to imagine the creation of parts and objects without the aid of motorized machinery practically capable of thinking for itself with little human input. Every piece or part created for these machines were so precise and custom that they were a great example of

Cast Duguet rosettes. *Calina Shevlin*

the "measure twice and cut once" principal. Sometimes entire rosettes were cast all at once on one solid block of varying diameters made from a wooden mold and cast in a bronze alloy, but there were also individually made rosettes to puzzle together a custom headstock variety.

On most of the machines I have had the pleasure of inspecting the screws were all individually made, as were the tap and die, per hole. This means on a 100% original machine, each screw only fits in the hole it was made for. This is a bit tricky to navigate if you wish to take apart and refurbish the machine, but is great to know so one can clearly label everything. The rosettes were made by creating a pattern in the smallest piece possible—a quarter, eighth, and so on—then repeating it by moving the pattern piece to create a perfectly even and flawless rosette.

As far as manufacturers go, there were major players and minor players, but all were working from similar plans and all were working toward the same goal: create a machine that would produce guilloché. Several components were a must, such as a stable base, a table to absorb any vibrations, a certain number of rosettes, a fixed cutter system, a tool slide that could turn 180°, and leaf springs or a weight system to stabilize the headstock, depending on the use. These are similar to the needs of a straight-line machine, with the exception of the tool slide and leaf springs. On a straight-line, the weight system allows the work to move up and down and the tool slide does not rotate 180°. I have seen a "farmer machine" that was made using a few stock parts, such as the flywheel, entirely by a presumed farmer. This machine came from a person who did not know too much about guilloché, as was common in the late 1700s, but made a machine for it and learned how to use it. This machine is almost an exact replica of a Lienhard machine—Swiss made—without any plans to work from. Even today there are watch-makers and workers in Poland that create machines out of necessity in their own home workshops to make the most basic guilloché.

The most prolific machine producer was a Swiss company called R. A. Lienhard. They were based in La Chaux-de-Fonds, not far from where the School of Arts was located. This is not to imply they were a result of the school, as La Chaux-de-Fonds was and is an industrially oriented city with a major emphasis on watches. R. A. Lienhard was started between 1800 and 1805.

There was a plethora of makers around the early 1800s to early 1900s. This was the most popular time for guilloché, so it makes sense the "rise" would be during this period. There were many manufacturers in England, as the rose engine evolved from the ornamental turning lathe and John Jacob Holtzapffel, in Charring Cross, made the first ornamental lathes in London. Holtzapffel was the most popular manufacturer and one of very few. From his work came the manufacturers of rose engines and later straight-line machines. While I say "manufacturers," each company could only produce so many machines, as most were made entirely by hand. An example of this handicraft is how the tool slides on most machines were scraped by hand to a uniform horizontal plane.

Geometric chuck detail. *G. Phil Poirier*

There are no written records, as with most dealings with guilloché, but based on research I have rough estimates of how many machines were manufactured by each company. There are some companies I may not have listed because I am not aware of them, along with individuals that made their own machines. There are also many unmarked machines. In the United States several companies manufactured machines, but as with many things from the war era more than a few were lost to smelting for parts and ammunition. I know of a machine that looks just like a basic rose engine that was used for guilloché that sits in a collection but was made at a farm with parts either found or ordered from a generic parts catalog, as they once could be. The table was hand made from wood and it still stands today, but more as a display piece than a working machine, although I know it is still used for demonstrations. This piece is a little rustic but functions as a rose engine should, and was made somewhere around 1780.

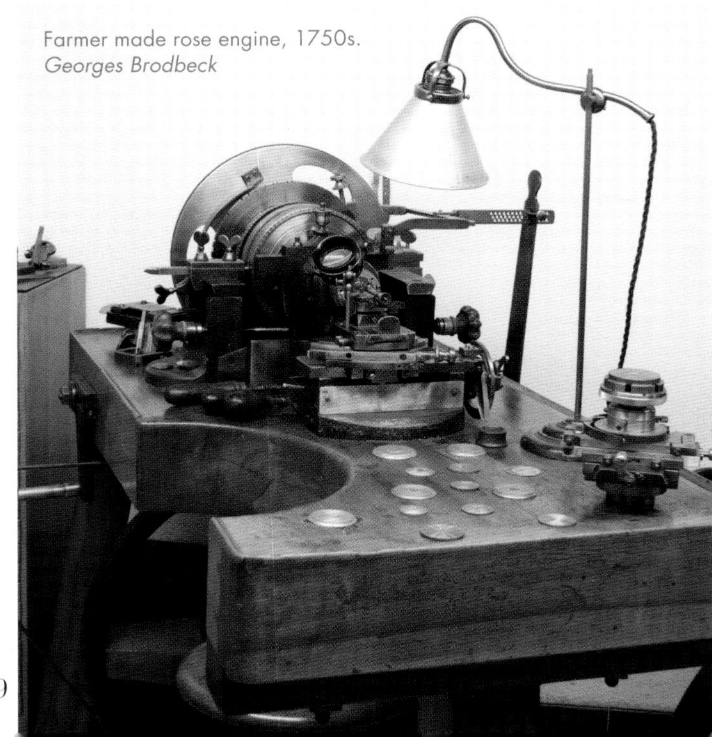

Farmer made rose engine, 1750s.
Georges Brodbeck

There is a known hoarding or storing situation among some collectors throughout the world, where either individuals or large companies buy the machines and put them away, or only use them for display in museums. While I find it a good idea to publicly display machines so people wonder and start to ask questions, I also think it is a travesty not to use them to perpetuate guilloché, and not just the idea of it. The original machines are fantastic. They have all mechanical parts, making them fairly simple to repair, and are rarely out of order for longer than a few days. The machines that can be found are not only magnificent works of ingenuity and art but mechanical beasts that never die.

Pertaining to the manufacture of new machines, I know of at least three watch companies that are fabricating their own machines, rose engines and straight-lines. The small number of antique machines that are available, or can be found, really limits the options for a business to have many operators or guillocheurs. There are several companies that are buying already scarce machines and storing them in garages just so they cannot be used by anyone else, thereby creating a monopoly. A representative from one such company told me they wanted to keep all of the machines and would find and buy them for exorbitant prices just so they could be the "guilloché Mecca of the world," where people would have to go through them to obtain any item with guilloché. These old machines are being used as a start-off point in the new manufacture of rose engines and straight-lines. In my opinion, this can bring mixed results, good and bad, along with increased creativity. This is excellent for getting machines back out to people and a lot easier to use, because many of these new machines rely on the use of dials and measuring tools that allow not only a skilled guillocheur to use the machine, but also simply operators, meaning they cannot sharpen or care for their own tools, nor can they diagnose a problem or repair a machine. It is becoming increasingly easy to turn the hand wheel and have everything already set and ready to work. Some of the operators I have met do not even know how to center the machine or sharpen their cutters; they have people that do that for them. These people are not true guillocheurs yet, but they have the potential so as long as the companies that employ them allow them to learn.

Many watchmaking companies are experimenting with different materials for the machines, trying to incorporate different woods, metals, and plastics, and even change the design of their guilloché machines. I have seen some machines with tool slides that actually cause more vibration to be distributed to the dials due to the material, feet that do not distribute the weight of the machine equally, and other such

Plant rose engine set up for three-dimensional guilloché. *G. Phil Poirier*

oddities. There does not need to be a big departure from the original machines; they worked and they still work. You do not need to change things that still work well and have already stood the test of time and are still around as a testament.

Some of the most well known manufacturers who produced many machines and made their business based on rose engines at one point in time are still identified with their mark. I will start with these manufacturers and then work my way down from there. I may not list all of the manufacturers or very much information about some of them, but what follows is a list of what I do know and have information about.

G. Plant and Sons was an English manufacturer of rose engines and straight-line machines in London, England. The machines I have personally worked with had the Plant mark and were painted a green or red color; I have not seen any other original colors, although now they are being repainted to a black or grey. The rose engines were made in two sizes. The first, a standard, was a rose engine with 17.78 cm rosettes (7 in.). This machine was made to be small for the times and was made specifically with the manufacture of jewelry in mind.

Plant tried to make small machines to be included in every jewelry shop to give jewelers access to a different technique that did not take up such a large space as the older machines. These machines had a shorter headstock for more stability, but this meant fewer rosettes at a time. The second rose engine Plant made was a monster of a machine; I only know of two examples, though there may be more. The large machine was fitted with rosettes that were 35.56 cm in diameter (14 in.) and was used to produce works up to one meter (39⅜ in.) in diameter.

These machines were primarily used to create silver coffee and tea service platters, as well as other large or unwieldy objects. I know David Pledge, formerly of Pledge & Aldworth in London (1975–2006), used one of these large Plant machines to decorate items such as platters, trumpets, and all large and bulky items that their customers demanded. This particular machine has been refitted with smaller rosettes and headstock and is currently being used in a jewelry type workshop. Plant probably made the most rose engine machines in the United Kingdom, estimated around 2,300 machines.

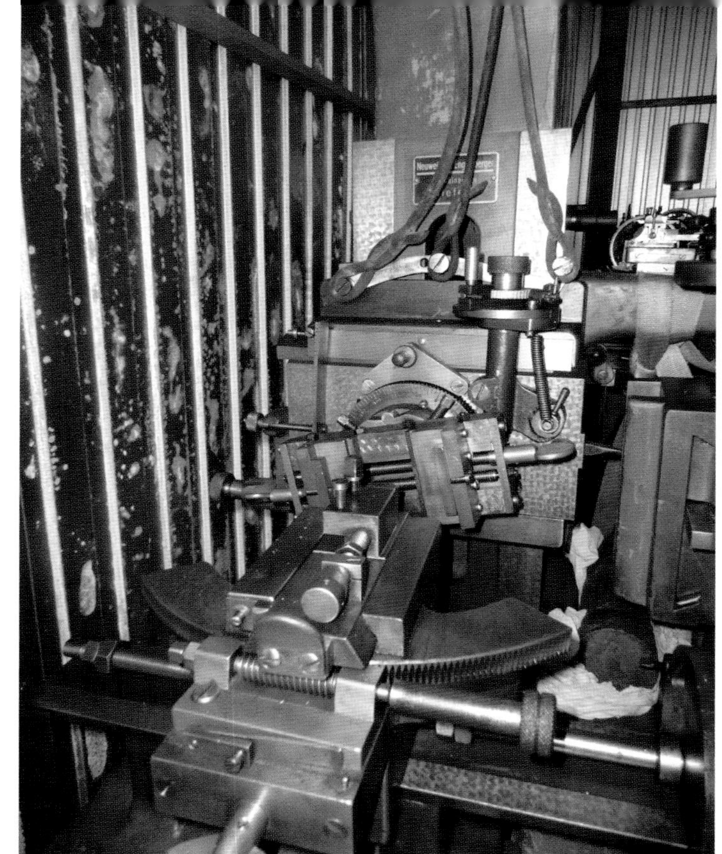

Neuweiler & Engleberger straight-line machine. *Calina Shevlin*

Neuweiler and Engelsberger was a German maker in Niefern, Germany. Niefern is a mere eight kilometers (five miles) from Pforzheim, Germany, a well known hot spot of guilloché in the past and up and coming now, with creative uses appearing regularly. This company only manufactured the straight-line machine, but their accuracy is like all of the other manufacturers and remains true today with little work needing to be done. In fact, any work or updates that have been done on these machines is purely optional and for the preference of the guillocheur, along the lines of adding calipers and other built on measuring devices. I can only guess at how many were made based on the people I know who are using them—somewhere in the realm of 200–250 machines.

Large Plant rose engine set up for work up to 1 m. *Calina Shevlin*

Lienhard S. A. was a Swiss manufacturer in the Le Locle/La Chaux-de-Fonds region, the birthplace of guilloché. The rose engines made by Lienhard were and are still of great quality, not unlike the other manufacturers. Lienhard S. A. still exists today, providing quality, solid machinery to many different

Lienhard with gears and tension holding chuck. *Calina Shevlin*

Lienhard started out as an industrial machinery manufacture initially and in later years began to manufacture rose engines, and even later a few straight-line machines, then brocading machines. In the years following the popularity of these machines Lienhard and Güdel combined to form LANG to prevent having to close their doors due to economic hardship. Under the LANG mark five to ten machines were made, and although I did some sleuthing, I could find nothing else written about it. After a few years the companies separated and went back to being two separate entities. Both companies continued to manufacture machines, but not rose engines or straight-line machines. Lienhard went on to manufacture all sorts of machines useful to the watchmaking world.

Güdel was a Swiss manufacturer in the Le Locle/La Chaux-de-Fonds area. Güdel was a top manufacturer of straight-line machines, but did make some parts for rose engines in conjunction with Lienhard. Güdel straight-lines were quite large for their time, but were also sturdy. After the LANG union and separation Güdel manufactured machines used for making six to seven pens at a time with 6.35 cm (2.5 in.) diameter rosettes. Güdel also made machinery specific to the watchmaking world and continues to do so today.

M. J. Brohen was an American maker in North Attleboro, Massachusetts. I have seen but one example in Kent, United Kingdom. I absolutely fell in love with this machine, and if I could find one, I would snatch it up in a second. This machine has the capability to create patterns similar to what the geometric chuck can do. The rose engine has a slightly complicated set of gears behind the rosettes that allow for the crossing over of patterns (think about what a Spirograph can do). This works similarly to the geometric chuck.

LANG Geneva rose engine. *G. Phil Poirier*

Brocading machine. *David Wood-Heath*

industries, notably watchmaking. They manufactured not only rose engines and straight-line machines, but also machines to create six pens at a time using a small set of rosettes, tool grinding machines, small presses, and a variety of other interesting machinery.

John Bower was an English maker from Clerkenwell, United Kingdom. Bower rose engines came about after Bower Ornamental Lathes. These were some of the finest production rose engines made in the United Kingdom at this time. Bower lathes can be found dated from the 1820s until the late 1840s.

Bower rose engine with a geometric apparatus behind the headstock. *David Wood-Heath*

Plant straight-line brocading machine detail. *David Wood-Heath*

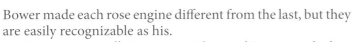

Detail of the Bower gears and rosettes. *David Wood-Heath*

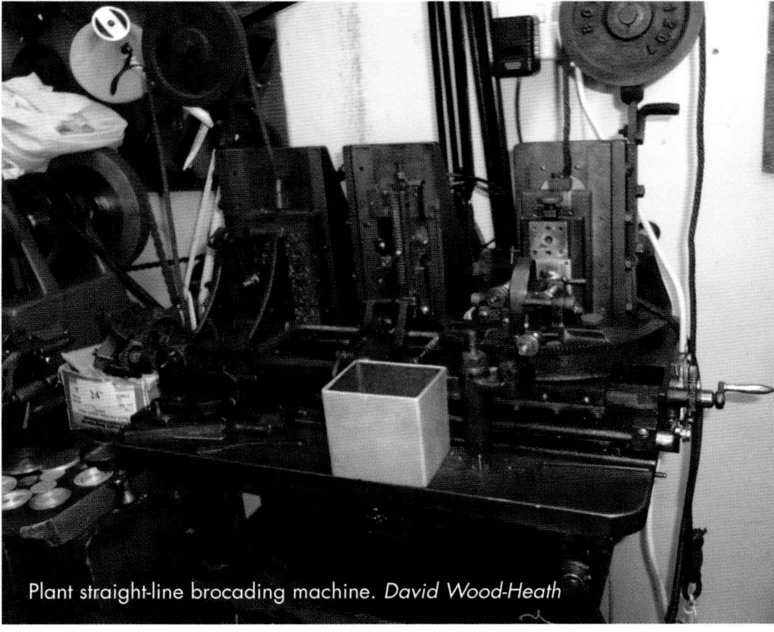
Plant straight-line brocading machine. *David Wood-Heath*

Bower made each rose engine different from the last, but they are easily recognizable as his.

I once saw a really interesting Plant and Sons straight-line brocading machine, but I have never encountered it since, nor have I ever heard of this. Perhaps it is an English specialty.

F. A. Hall was an American maker producing interesting looking rose engines; I have seen some with upward of sixteen rosettes on an extremely long headstock. They have also made some straight-line machines. The F. A. Hall straight-line and the Kenloc straight-line are almost identical to the nuts and bolts, but I am unclear as to the exact history, although Hall was known to use very similar styles and parts from Kenloc machines, as well as Charles Fields, and some even resemble an M. J. Brohen machine.

Charles Fields was an American maker of straight-line machines, with a few rose engines for good measure. His works were most notably compared to and used in conjunction with F. A. Hall and Kenloc.

Pear was an Italian maker; although I do not have a photo, it is worth working on one of these at least once. They are built to last and have a beautiful smooth finish.

Lienhard made many machines, both straight-line and rose engines. They were a Swiss manufacturer in the area of La Chaus-de-Fonds. At one point Lienhard merged with Güdel to preserve the company (estimated two years together), and they collaborated on at least three rose engines. Lienhard machines are some of the most prevalently found today; since

Hall straight-line with roller pattern bars. *G. Phil Poirier*

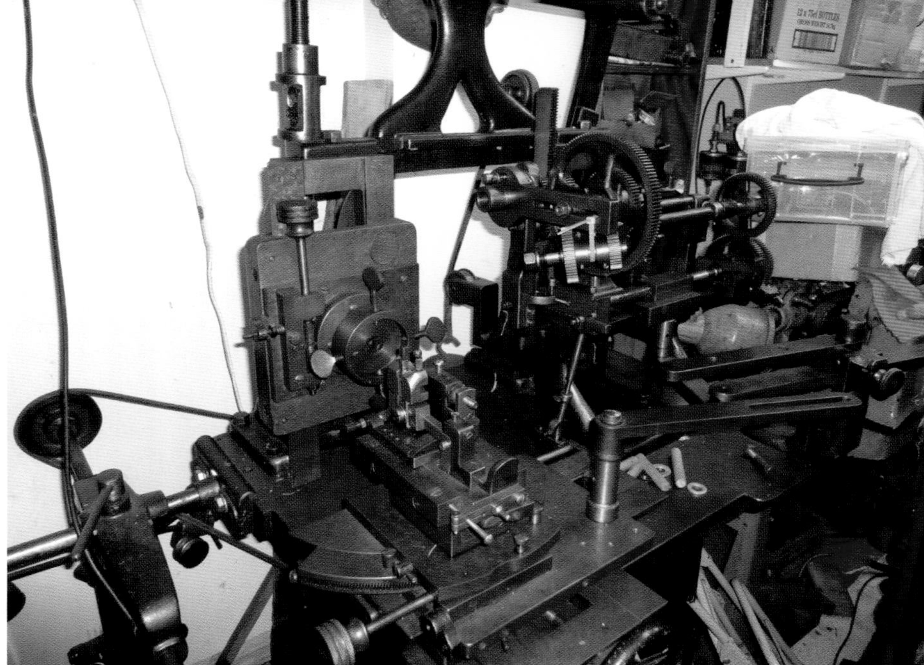

Plant straight-line brocading machine. *David Wood-Heath*

Switzerland has not had a war since 1291, the machines were never repurposed for other uses as American and UK machines have been.Duguet was a French maker who only made about ten machines. He was French but lived on the border with Switzerland around the Besançon/Pontarlier region. These machines followed traditional methods with a heavy wooden table, but the rosettes appear to be cast in several pieces in lieu of making all individual rosettes. This machine is from around 1840.

A. Droz was a maker in Besançon, France, which is close to the border with Switzerland, where a lot of cross pollination has occurred. He followed the lines of the Lienhard machines and, like Duguet, only produced a small number of machines.

French made Duguet rose engine, early 1800s. *Calina Shevlin*

Detail of the Hall headstock. *G. Phil Poirier*

A. Droz rose engine, Besançon, France, early 1800s. *G. Phil Poirier*

Unmarked straight-line machine with rosettes and pattern bars. *Teri Jo Kinnison*

William Mills rose engine. *G. Phil Poirier*

Lastly, I include this unmarked machine of which I have seen two and now heard of one. The first one lives in Arizona with a couple who use it in their jewelry work and care very well for it; the second one lives down the road from me in Switzerland, and the third is in a museum in Paris. This is a straight-line machine with pattern bars and rosettes, with the rosettes behind the headstock like on a rose engine. This machine is exclusively a straight-line, which makes having the rosettes so unusual.

The machines that are used in the creation of guilloché have never been plentiful if we compare them with other tools for decorative arts. There have been a good handful of manufacturers between 1740 and 1930. In this time there were an estimated 6,500 to 8,000 machines built, including rose engines and straight-lines. This number only accounts for the machines made by manufacturers and not those independently fabricated, such as the farm rose engine (see p 33). The manufacturers were from many different countries, including the United Kingdom, the United States, Switzerland, and Italy. The ornamental turning lathe originated in the United Kingdom, but the build of the rose engines and straight-lines were originally thought up and made in Switzerland.

It is becoming increasingly difficult to find any of the old machines, so anyone wanting or needing a machine, either rose engine or straight-line, would be obligated to manufacture a new machine. The people who have been making their own machines seem to be following the lines of the old but add one or all of the innovations I have mentioned.

Lindow is an American watchmaker in Pennsylvania that also makes ornamental turning lathes under the name MADE with his three other partners. The rose engine machines are made sturdy enough that careful engine turning with great results can be achieved. I have heard several people say they are more than pleased with their new, compact, easy-to-use machines. The rosettes are an acrylic, and they are aesthetically appealing, much like the old machines were and still are. Patek Philippe, in Geneva, Switzerland, manufactures its own straight-line machines and most likely rose engines. The straight-line headstock has become skeletonized and reminds me of a Knew Concepts saw frame.

Mercklein. French made rose engine/ornamental turning lathe by looking at the rosettes. *OASC*

Mercklein is a machine that is in a museum in Paris. I had never seen one before or since, so perhaps the name was simply added after the manufacture, or it may be like the random farmer-made machines in the late 1700s.

I have not added information about every machine here because I do not know an accurate or precise history or origin. I do know there are guillocheurs with all of this information, but for the sake of this book I provide just the images and encourage readers to search for more information on their own. There are many machines around, but they must be hunted down. I have found that individuals who own certain makes and models of machines know quite a bit about their own machine. It would be beneficial to meet and speak about the machines that particularly interest you at some length.

Innovations and Inventions

Simultaneous inventions were exactly that: people came up with great solutions to little annoyances—not exactly problems—all at the same time. Even now machines are being reinvented and remanufactured by several private companies, but they are using what they call proprietary secrets on their machines. I have seen quite a few of these machines and can tell you without a doubt that these improvements and solutions that companies manufacturing the machines wish to keep secret have all been tried and discarded before now.

There are a number of innovations that are really interesting, such as a vacuum method for attaching work to a headstock—albeit a bit complicated to install on an old machine—and I would assume many different shapes of tools would need to be made to fit with a sort of key-like system to this vacuum. This is not extremely practical, but definitely deserves to be explored a bit, as it is an ecological option to attach work to the headstock that would allow for easy mounting and dismounting. I do not know how this innovation would work with three-dimensional pieces, but I would have to assume that two-dimensional pieces would be held flat to the headstock, making adjusting to the cutter much easier, assuming the metal was perfectly flat. As you can see there are a lot of "ifs" in guilloché, which is a large reason why the materials have stayed the same over the years.

Something I would like to see or would like to experiment with is a pawl that not only allows a piece to move from left to right like the traditional pawl, but one that has a reversible gear, or rather two sets of teeth facing in opposite directions. This would allow the guillocheur to move the pin, thereby reversing the action of the pawl, allowing it to move from right to left in measured distances without having to use a micrometer. This would be advantageous with an extremely complicated pattern with many worm turns; once you reached the center you could click the pawl over and just retrace your steps using your recipe, rather than counting and turning the worm back hundreds of clicks. Another innovation I have seen in several different countries and various workshops is a worm that clicks. This simply adds notches to the worm and a peg above the worm so every eighth or quarter turn is one click, permitting the spacing to be quite large or very small, depending on the number of notches. I find this type of worm is much easier to use and gets an accurate turn every time. It should be quite easy to add tabs at the half and sixteenth turn points, and perhaps stamp them with numbers or dots to keep track of the position of the worm. All of which could easily be incorporated into the recipe.

More recently, I have encountered David Lindow's portable rose engine. It is fabricated using alternate materials, such as patterns for medium density fiberboard (MDF) legs; optional cast iron legs are also available. The rosettes are made of a thick Plexiglas or acrylic and with the rubber—which I would assume is wood, but could also be a mild steel that could glide really well and shows little wear on either one. This is a great example of an innovation that is helping more people gain access to the world of guilloché. The old machines are expensive *if* they can be found in the first place. There are even people building machines from scratch based on necessity. I have recently met several people who have made a rose engine and they function quite well. An enamellist and jeweler in Poland has just fabricated his own very simple rose engine out of eighth-inch steel, with a very minimal number of rosettes. The resulting pieces are well executed. These new machines are incredibly accurate and functional. There seems to be a revival in progress as I write this, and it is wonderful. Every twenty years or so there is a renewed interest in guilloché and rose engines and straight-line machines, but this time around it is more than a passing interest. We now have people lecturing and demonstrating guilloché, there are classes happening, and people are making more affordable machines for hobbyists and non-professionals who are interested in guilloché. All of these advances will help the field become more understood, as well as give access to simple patterning to use in non-watchmaking applications.

One of the most common additions to a rose engine and straight-line machine is an air hose attached to a compressor to blow burr off of the work piece; the operator does not need to touch the piece or cut their finger and the work can be more easily seen with less stopping to remove burrs. This also makes the work a bit cleaner, as you no longer need to blow air (and inevitably spittle) on the guilloché. This revelation came about around the same time for several guillocheurs, most likely in the 1970s.

With the advent of compressed air there arose a need to neatly collect as much of the gold burrs as possible in a container, rather than in your hair, on your sweater, or littering the floor.

Often the gold was not enough to be recuperated until someone decided to put a box under the work piece. It began with some cardstock; then ended up being an old cardboard box. I have seen people using the cardboard box method (which I personally use), but I have also seen plastic boxes affixed with double-sided tape and wooden boxes attached with cotter pins. There is no right or wrong way to catch burrs, but the recuperation of the precious metal is key. There are people who use more than one box, depending on the metal. They have a box for brass sample burrs, which are great to collect if you decide you wish to do some hand bluing of small steel parts. They have a box for silver, gold, platinum, and even steel. I think this system is best because it is quick to change out the box and all of the scrap bits are kept with their like metals; when full (or when full enough) they can be sent off to a metal refining operation.

For such a long time the tool slide has had a knob near the thumb rest to help control the depth of the cut. The inefficiency of this is that the depth was only known by guessing by sight, and the knob was not marked, so more guessing was involved. Then guillocheurs started making marks on their knobs to know how many marks to turn the knob for a fairly even depth. This also had some problems, as one could easily push through the knob. Every machine has some give, and if you push hard enough, then what was marked "one" on the knob could easily be a cut at the same depth as "two" or "three." Eventually a micrometer knob would be replace the unmarked knob. The micrometer knob had all of the markings and a solid steel bar stock to keep the cutter a set distance from the piece and a certain depth. It was quite accurate in comparison, but again, brute force wins here, so please remember to cut with a light (and even) hand. This little knob enables a measured stop to be incorporated, allowing for the depth to be selected and taken down one micron at a time.

After one shop used this micrometer the idea caught on like wildfire. This is now a staple in machine building and refurbishing. I also currently use this, mostly because I am a bit obsessive with the "perfect cut" to test my skill.

I have seen other substitutions of materials, but nothing beats the best combination: the original solid wood or steel base, bronze rosettes, and steel moving parts. They continue to be the best materials, and are still used by many people who restore, remake, and build machines from scratch.

Flexible neck lamps have been attached to the machine just near the work for increased visibility, in addition to microscopes and large loupes attached with wire and screws. Lamps illuminate the work and show the facets of the cut, helpful in spotting chatter, broken cutter tips, and line placement. A microscope can also provide a light source that is moveable, with the microscope attached to the tool slide. This is a vast improvement over using glasses mounted with powerful loupes. This also helps with better posture for the guillocheur: no more hunched backs or craned necks from straining to see the work they are creating. I use and highly recommend the stereomicroscopes of Leica Microsystem Corporation. They have parallel optics, making it simple to see your work as you go. They have a few different systems, but I prefer the M-60. It is easy to mount to the machine, or even better, to a rolling stand so you can move between machines, or from machine to table to check out a piece. They are versatile and can withstand a lot of wear and handling, and can be set up so the viewing angle is head on, while the eye pieces are vertical and quite comfortable.

With these few innovations and innovative uses of existing products the work that is created in this generation is less flawed, and at watch manufactures almost perfect. The nearly perfect watch dials are so perfect it seems as if a machine made them most of the time, but automated machines are not able to produce guilloché yet. There are many places that have been trying to get CNC machines to make perfect looking guilloché for years, but they have not succeeded and will not, because the cutter cannot mimic the angle or shape of a traditional cutter, much less remain in a fixed position while the work rotates. While perfection displays a mastery of skill, this begs the question, why *not* use a machine? Personally, I like to see a small variation in the pattern—not necessarily a mistake, but a human touch. This goes with the art versus craft discussion and the ideas of craftsmanship.

From photos of guilloché it might seem like it is easy to see when cutting, but these lines are around three to five microns deep. In the 1700s, conditions in workshops were much worse than they are today. A guillocheur would work only when there was daylight available because most ateliers were lit with candles in the evening, so a lot of the old farmer watchmakers/guillocheurs had their ateliers in the attic with a long row of north-facing windows, where the light was best and they could work longer. Most of the buildings that originally held guillocheurs even part time in Switzerland are like this. They are still used and many ateliers are still on the top floor, but not for guilloché or watchmaking: they are for crafts or a children's playroom. Even with advancements in modern lighting there are still quite a few guilloché ateliers that are northern facing.

The quality of the cut in the late 1700s and 1800s was hugely flawed by today's standards. The guillocheurs of yesterday were hard workers, and often used glasses in conjunction with large loupes mounted to a flexible stand near the work. Add this to the lighting conditions and the work that was created in guilloché was pretty impressive. Now guillocheurs often use a variety of visual aids to create their work, such as a standby jewelry loupe attached to a headband that is really a magnifying lens that can be adjusted up or down.

This has its loyal fans and many advantages. I find a disadvantage is the viewpoint of the piece being decorated changes with the slightest movement of the guillocheur's head. I do not find the magnification enough for my eyes, and I really like to feel like I am looking at a piece that has facets the depth of a piece of yarn. Next there are Orascoptic glasses. These come with a private consultation and include a pair of glasses with your prescription if you need one, plus two small loupes mounted to the lenses. These are good, but you must continually raise and lower them to look around when not working. They are a great alternative to a binocular and cost between $200 and $500.

GRS tools (Glendo Corporation) has some great models made for engraving work, so guillocheurs also need the GRS dual angle sharpening holder. This pairs nicely with the horizontal lapping machine to sharpen your cutters.

These binoculars have really allowed guilloché, enameling, and engraving to advance. The binocular has allowed me to make work with cuts so fine, shallow, and close together that when viewing with the naked eye, they look almost mirror-like; you can see slight reflections in them but they are patterned.

Georges Brodbeck is the man to whom guillocheurs who use Diametal cutters owe their thanks. The cutters came from his prototype, and he developed them with Diametal; now these are some of the most popular cutters on the market. All of the blades (cutters) fit into all of the holders in the DIADEC series. The cutters are made from various carbide grades and high-speed steels. The cutters come in 5 mm and 8 mm sizes and are long lasting.

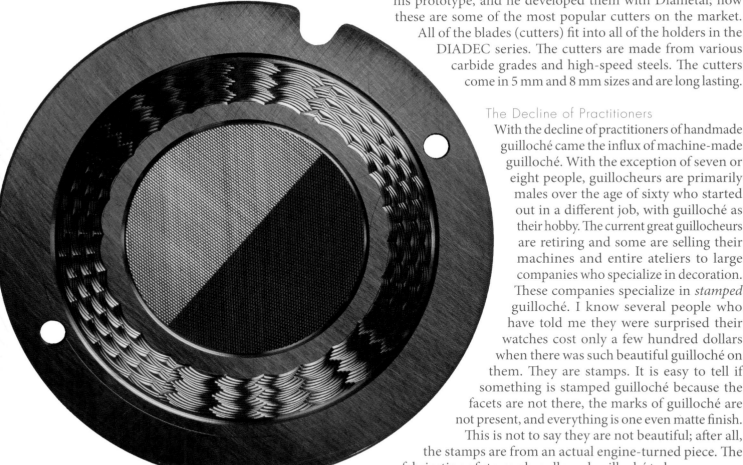

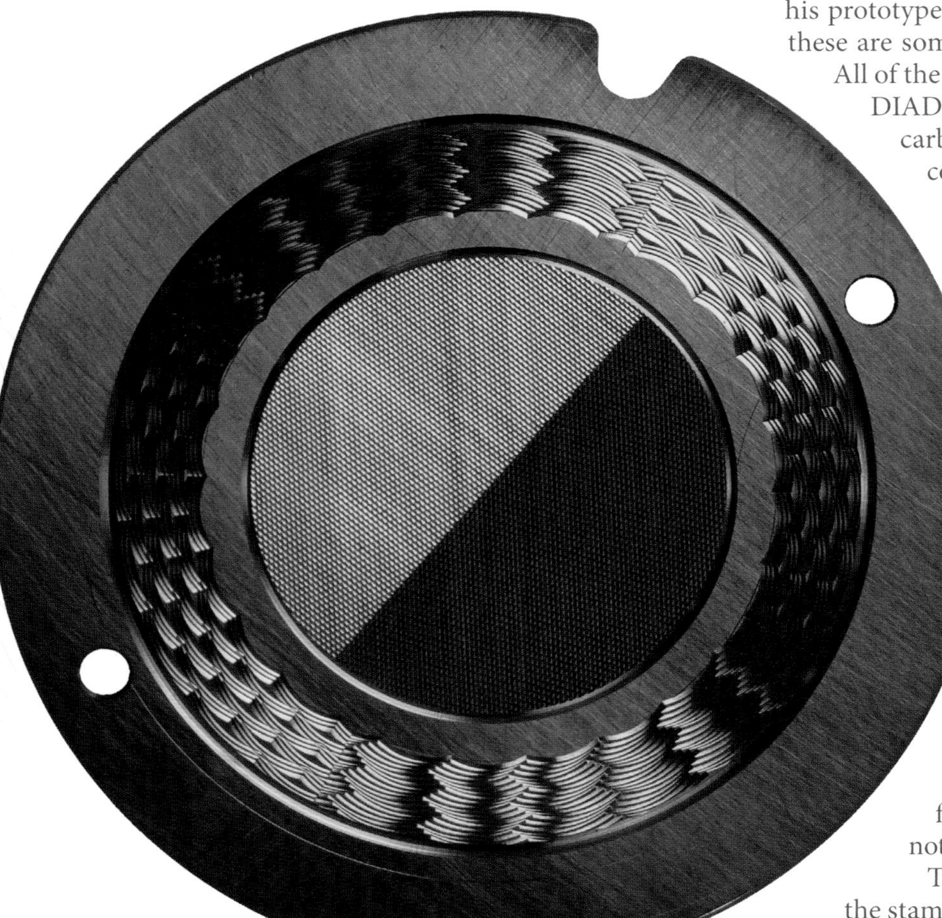

Super fine cut clous de Paris with 0.10 mm spacing. *Calina Shevlin*

The Decline of Practitioners

With the decline of practitioners of handmade guilloché came the influx of machine-made guilloché. With the exception of seven or eight people, guillocheurs are primarily males over the age of sixty who started out in a different job, with guilloché as their hobby. The current great guillocheurs are retiring and some are selling their machines and entire ateliers to large companies who specialize in decoration. These companies specialize in *stamped* guilloché. I know several people who have told me they were surprised their watches cost only a few hundred dollars when there was such beautiful guilloché on them. They are stamps. It is easy to tell if something is stamped guilloché because the facets are not there, the marks of guilloché are not present, and everything is one even matte finish. This is not to say they are not beautiful; after all, the stamps are from an actual engine-turned piece. The fabrication of stamps has allowed guilloché to become more widespread, but at the same time misunderstood. This is not a new process or invention. In the School of Applied Industrial Arts in La Chaux-de-Fonds, at the end of the life of the guilloché course stamp making was taught. This is partially why there are one or two large companies in La Chaux-de-Fonds who have been making stamps since the early 1900s, or faux guilloché if you will. It is these companies who are interested in buying the small independent guillocheurs' ateliers when they are ready to retire.

Diametal cutter with the holder ready to cut. *Celia Kudro*

CHAPTER 4
The Effects of War Lead to the Decline of Guilloché

During WWI a lot of things declined in the world and guilloché works were no exception. The students in the classes of guilloché that only began in 1902 were starting to drop out and find jobs that paid well at the ammunition factories. The enterprises that had provided watchmaking firms, independent watchmakers, and jewelers the dials and jewelry that were in such high demand were no longer keeping up with the work demand. In turn, companies began to close because people were not spending money on ornamented ornaments or watches. After a few years the people making guilloché just here and there wanted to move on to more profitable businesses, so they left their machines in warehouses and garages and on farms to rust and become almost unrecognizable. Switzerland was one of the leading manufacturers of ammunition at the time of WWI, and many people chose to move into the profession. The largest ammunition factory was in the La Chaux-de-Fonds area.

In other regions materials were scarce, and to fight a good fight one must have the proper materials, in addition to giving people incentive to change to a wartime job. Machines that existed in Italy, the United States, France, and England were unceremoniously scrapped for their materials. Many machines were disassembled and used to make ammunition warfare stores. The machines were not deemed a priority to maintain. Many of the Swiss and German machines survived for several reasons. Germany had a plan of attack and already had stocks for what was needed to fight the war; they were not searching for materials out of desperation. Switzerland was a neutral country and therefore did not need to assemble extra materials, as they already had what they needed to make ammunition and left the rest alone.

Along with WWI came the decline in need or want for guilloché. Many people who could still afford it did not order it because it would make them look as though they did not care about money, and that was not a good thing in wartime. As time moved on, with a lack of practitioners, a lack of clients, and a lack of time, guilloché started silently slipping away. People began to forget the existence of engine turning, and by the time WWII ended it was almost forgotten.

From the heyday of guilloché when it was a sought-after decoration, usually applied to ornamental objects, to its quiet disappearance, at a certain point people pushed it into the past and wanted to move on. More machinery was becoming automated; fewer workers were needed so people were moving into new fields of employment. There were a few diehards who held out and worked quietly. They kept giving the world guilloché in small doses and made a decent living at it. In 1910, there were around 150 guillocheurs in the world. By 1940, there were only twenty-five. By 1970, there were an estimated thirty-five, and currently there are around forty. In the grand scheme of things forty people creating guilloché for a job/living is not a lot, but it is with this forty that the knowledge remains and is being actively passed down.

A Flame Still Exists

There are currently a few independent guillocheurs in Switzerland in the La Chaux-de-Fonds region, the Val-de-Travers region, the Vallée de Joux region, and the Jura Franches-Montagnes region. There are a handful of guillocheurs in Pforzheim, Germany. In the United States there are around ten to twelve; most seem to be centralized around Colorado, with a few in the Pennsylvania and Ohio area. In France there are one or two guillocheurs, but as I have not met them, I can only assume they are in the regions close to the Swiss border. There are also one or two in the eastern region of Canada.

These are independent guillocheurs with small ateliers and perhaps a few employees, but usually not. They are all making a living creating guilloché pieces for watches, jewelry, ornamentation, and so on. There are also large watch companies who regularly use guilloché in their dials. Some of these companies say they have guillocheurs, which is partially true. They use the independents—almost all of them do work for the same companies—but they also have people in-house. I do not consider the in-house people—with the exception of one or two—guillocheurs. Most of the in-house people are simply operators. Several of the large watch manufactures have people who can turn a hand wheel but need to wait for someone, or a group of people, to carry out the rest of the tasks associated with a true guillocheur. A group effort does not effectively make a guillocheur.

Companies Who Revived the Art

Vacheron Constantin has helped revive guilloché in a big way. They have been using guilloché in their timepieces since 1755. While not every watch has guilloché, the pieces that do are very tastefully done. What I find most admirable is that Vacheron Constantin has not fallen to the classic eight patterns that have been floating around watch dials since the 1750s; they use creative patterns that have not saturated the market, and they are constantly thinking about how to change the game.

Audemars Piguet, in Le Brassus, Switzerland, has also contributed to the revival of guilloché on a small scale. In the 1970s, Roland Tille created the Royal Oak pattern while working at Audemars Piguet. This was created on a brocading machine, and for the past forty years has been demonstrated as guilloché. I have seen videos in watchmaking museums demonstrating the brocading machine and have always wondered why this was called guilloché. Years ago I interviewed for a position in guilloché at Audemars Piguet, and after I answered all the questions posed to me about guilloché—my knowledge of it and so forth—I was told they did not feel I would be happy in the position because it was automated guilloché. By this, they meant pushing a button to commence brocading, waiting for it to finish, then taking the piece off, cleaning it, and starting all over. I was shocked because I had seen some beautiful creations, though few pieces of actual guilloché that came from Audemars Piguet. I can only assume they must have one guillocheur and buy or commission the rest of the pieces from a small independent atelier nearby.

Fabergé has been revived in a way, but it is not the same family Fabergé. Nonetheless, this Fabergé is bringing back small egg-shaped charms for pendants and bracelets. Among these are some that have guilloché and then enamel. As I have only seen those that had guilloché before they were sent to the Fabergé factory, I can neither confirm nor deny if the enamel is kiln fired or cold application. The fact that they are contributing to reigniting an interest in what was once considered fit for the royal Tsar and Tsarina is a testament to the beauty and allure of guilloché and enamel.

From Independently Owned to Industry Owned

From the 1940s until about the late 1960s, almost all guilloché ateliers were privately owned and operated. Most were kept as a family business being passed down to each generation. Then the heirs to these guillochage ateliers decided they had no interest in, nor did they wish to work with guilloché. These men decided to make a living working elsewhere and left the older generation to look for help and hire employees from the cities.

This time frame was not a booming period for the popularity of guilloché, but there was a quantity of work that was too much for only one or two family members, so outside help had to be brought in, even if it was only one or two other people. This worked out well for all parties involved. The family had help and could reduce their hours a bit, and someone was trained in a new skill set that would become their permanent position. This lackadaisical attitude of heirs provided a new generation of guillocheurs. When the original owners retired or passed away the guilloché ateliers were bought by nonfamily guillocheurs. Once the ateliers changed hands the family style stopped. It would seem the new guillocheurs had other plans and decided that as the popularity of guilloché was slowly on the rise they would hire more than one or two other employees. Most ended up with nine to ten employees, creating yet another sort of generation that was larger and more production oriented.

While it may not seem like ten employees is a lot, let us remember that at the height of teaching at the École d'Art Appliqués there were ten students maximum at one time spread over four-year apprentice training. These ateliers were huge by any stretch of the imagination, and there was more than one. Once more guilloché work started to come in the ateliers ended up offering to work semi-exclusively for one or two larger companies. Stern Frères, an atelier of guilloché and enameling once based in Meyrin, near Geneva, Switzerland, is a good example. They were created in 1898 and were rescued by a holding group in the 1990s; then in July 2000, they were bought by the Richemont group and became industrialized:

> Richemont, the Swiss luxury goods group, today announced it has acquired the Stern Group from Orior Holding S. A.
>
> Stern Créations S. A. in Geneva, together with its subsidiaries Stern Manufacture and Stern Appliques in La Chaux-de-Fonds, in the Jura region of Switzerland, as well as a small French subsidiary, is one of the leaders in the manufacture of luxury watch dials.
>
> Since the creation of Stern Frères in 1898, the Stern Group has become one of the essential suppliers of watch components and has among its clients some of the world's most prestigious watch brands. Its vast range of products includes lacquered, precious metal, and jewelry dials.
>
> Richemont has expressed the wish for Stern to continue to create and supply dials to the Swiss luxury watch industry. Stern will retain a high level of autonomy within the Richemont Group to enable it to strengthen its partnerships with all its clients.[1]

There are many manufacturers that were small and once independent firms creating guilloché. Now they have been purchased by one of the two large watch groups to crank out pieces that are not generally very interesting or unique, but it is one way for people to make a living.

Another small atelier that is not entirely guilloché but definitely worth mentioning is Frères Rochat, in Le Brassus, Switzerland. They were once renowned for their singing bird pistol. They are now working on trying to recreate this piece from scratch in a small atelier that has enameling, guilloché, watchmaking, and other arts. The employees are few, and everyone wears many hats in the organization, but this is really how ateliers used to be, hopefully holding out against industrialization.

CHAPTER 5
Pattern Development

There are an endless number of patterns that can be created on the rose engine. While there are various parts and pieces that can be added to the machine, I will first discuss basic pattern development with just minor changes and adjustments to the most common equipment of a standard rose engine. You need to know there are between five and twenty rosettes mounted on a headstock and they all have different amplitudes (sine waves). The number of rosettes on a headstock depends on the make of the machine and how many could be physically mounted at one time. There are also additional rosettes for each make of machine that can be changed out one for one, but this is a bit time consuming. My suggestion is that before beginning, choose the rosettes you would like to work with or experiment with for a few days at minimum and just stay with them.

Extra rosettes to change out. *G. Phil Poirier*

Examples of rosettes. *G. Phil Poirier*

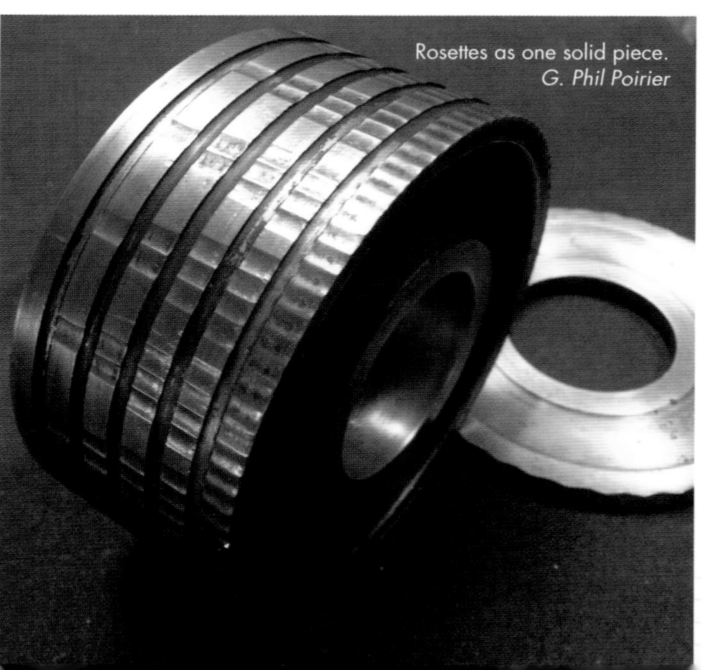

Rosettes as one solid piece. *G. Phil Poirier*

Straight-line pattern bars on a Plant machine. *G. Phil Poirier*

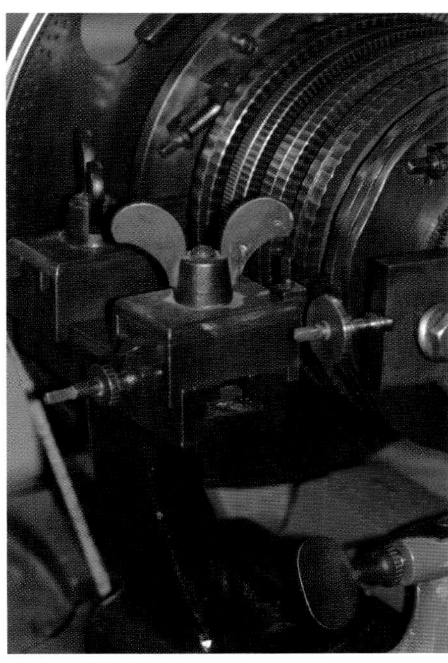

LANG rosettes of similar amplitudes. *G. Phil Poirier*

Assorted pattern bars in stock form. *G. Phil Poirier*

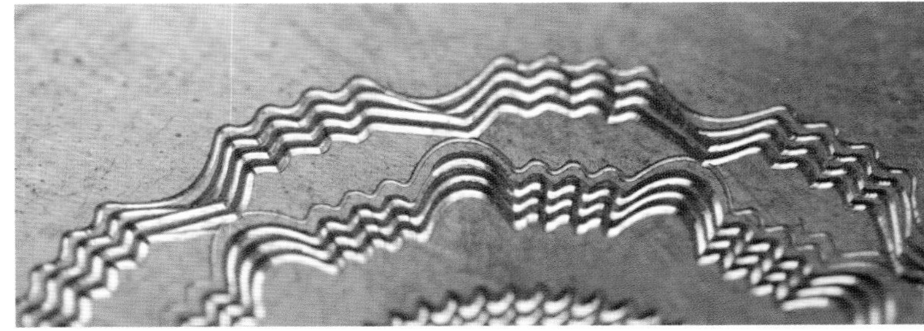

This is the starting block. From each rosette—without any major changes—there are three patterns that can be created. The first pattern is just the rubber/touch resting on a rosette on the left side; this is just basic engine turning—the norm.

It is often overlooked that the mirror image of a pattern can be made quite simply by moving the rubber/touch from its regular position on the left side of the machine to the right side (see below).

There is already a support built for the other side, although several companies are ignoring this and removing the support, or making machines where there is not a place on the right side

Rosettes of varying lobes. *G. Phil Poirier*

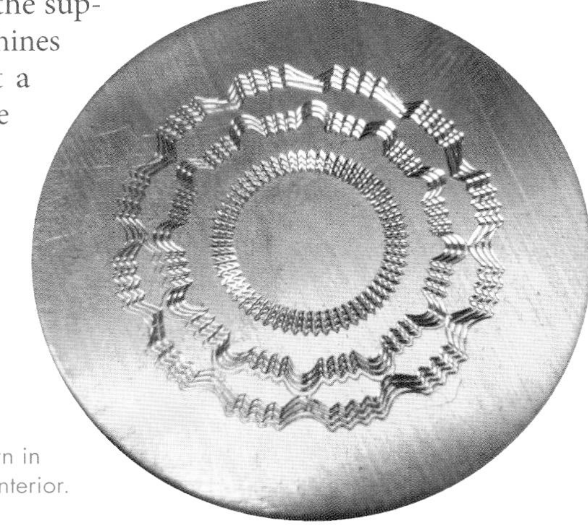

Mirrored pattern on the exterior, a regular pattern in the middle, and a filler interior. *Calina Shevlin*

FIG.05-07A

Illustration re-drawn from Lienhard Operators Manual 1895 by Calina Shevlin
This is a top view of a Lienhard rose engine that is set up to do a mirror image. The rubber is on the right-hand side.

1. Traversing Slide: This is what allows the cutter to move from left to right, as well as swing in an arc 180°. This is set up to do a flat piece.
2. Rubber Tool Holder: This is where the rubber is usually located, but everything has been moved to the right side.
3. Rubber Tool Holder: This is usually just a support waiting to receive the rubber. Now the rubber and holding set-up occupies it.
Calina Shevlin

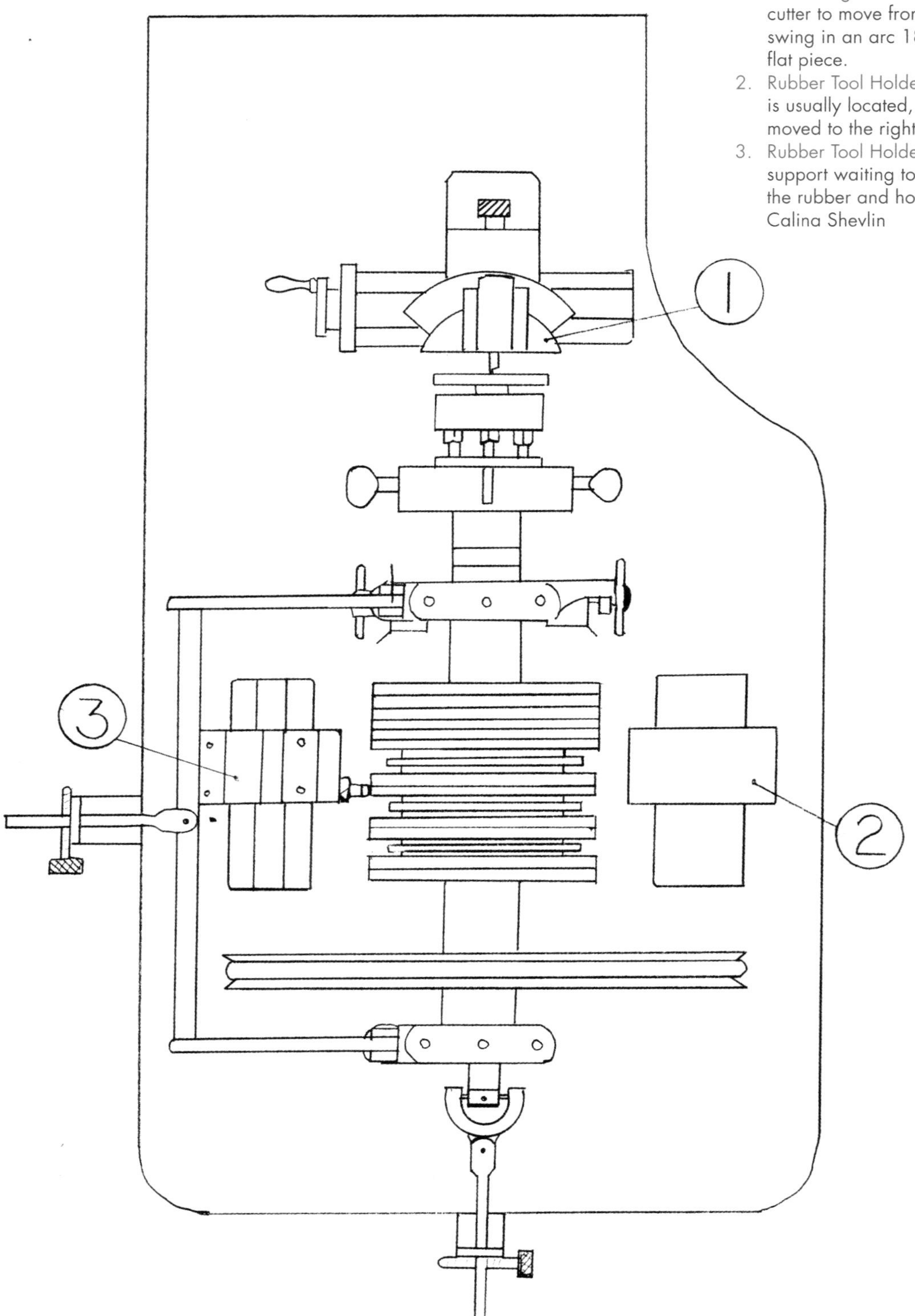

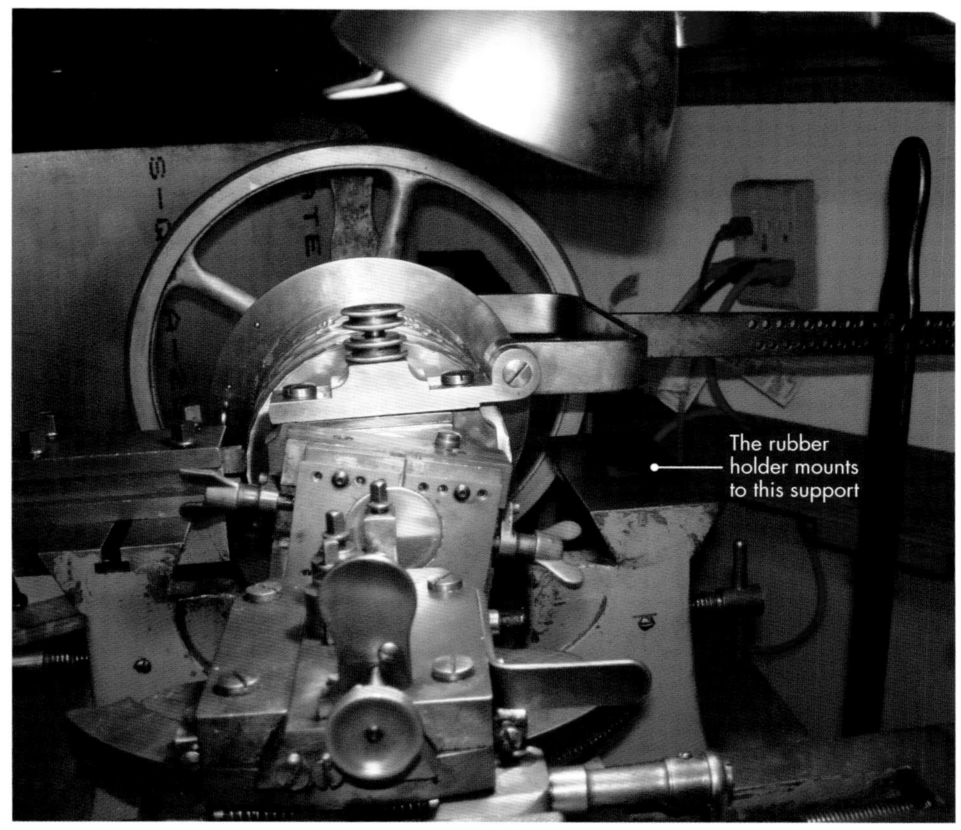
The rubber
holder mounts
to this support

Mirroring rubber mounted on the right side.

The leaf spring behind the LANG used to tension for pumping action. *G. Phil Poirier*

for a support. As it stands, a rubber holder can stay mounted to the right side all of the time so changing sides is even easier—only the rubber needs to move without other major adjustments. The resulting pattern is not a large change, nor entirely obvious, but it is a fresh take on an old familiar rosette or pattern.

Moving the rubber from the left edge of the rosette to the face of the rosette and going from a rocking action to a pumping action creates the third pattern. This pattern is similar for all rosettes, but the spacing is what makes it interesting. A handful of rosettes have the amplitude on the face for use specifically with pumping action, and this is often applied to three-dimensional works, or as a division between different sub-dials on watches. Changing the tension with the leaf spring is a simple action that takes the machine from side movement to forward and back movement.

This is the most basic patterning and can be practiced with a machine that has only a few rosettes, but allows the worker to create more interesting patterns than the classic eight. These three patterns I have just described are all made with the same rosette and the same rubber, but by moving the rubber around to different areas. Changing the diameter of the rubber can create even more patterns; some will be more interesting and some will completely fail, but the allure of guilloché is the fun of experimentation.

Pay attention to the rosette faces as they too are lobed; this is used for the pumping action of the rose engine. *G. Phil Poirier*

S12P
Experimental fun with modern rosettes. *Calina Shevlin*

With this basic formula a worker could potentially make between fifteen and ninety patterns—depending on how many rosettes are mounted on the headstock—with minimal effort. These will all be concentric diminishing patterns, and each one is simple and elegant. Someone sees the pattern and can tell

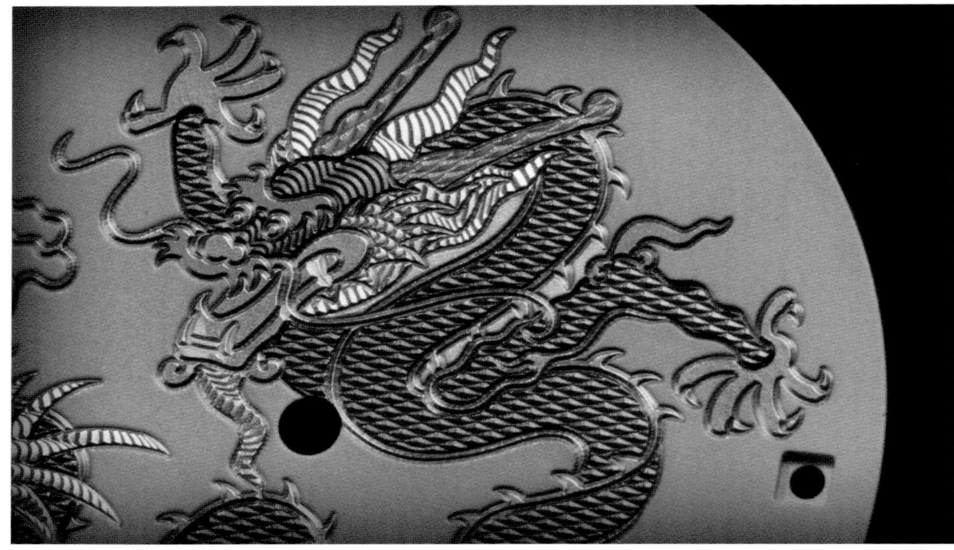

Vacheron Constantin branch of Richemont International SA

straight away how it was created because in simplicity creation is discernible.

Artistic Applications of Guilloché

Only one major watchmaking company has caught my eye due to their innovative and unique use of guilloché: Vacheron Constantin. They are in Geneva and have been for the last 260 years. While it was not Vacheron Constantin that pioneered guilloché technique on watch dials, they have decided to throw all caution to the wind and not play it safe. They do not use the classic eight patterns that other companies have worn out. They do not use a system to render the dial matte after guilloché work is finished, leaving the purchaser to wonder why

Vacheron Constantin branch of Richemont International SA

they did not just buy a machine made watch. What Vacheron Constantin does is innovate. They use new patterns, they use a few highly skilled workers, and they believe in the apprentice program to pass on knowledge. Their Métiers d'Art watches marry guilloché, enameling, and engraving. They add in tasteful stone settings, and these are no longer watches but masterpieces made in very limited editions, ensuring not everyone in the world will have the same watch as the purchaser.

It is clear there was a change in thinking about design at Vacheron Constantin around 2000. The designers created watches that were unveiled in 2005 as the Métiers d'Art collections. These collections included the series, Fabuleux Ornements, Florilège, and Univers Infinis. Each of the three collections was a marriage of perfect proportions between guilloché, enamel, and engraving; Fabuleux Ornements also included pierced work and some intricate stone setting. Vacheron Constantin also began thinking outside the traditional watch dial and created guilloché in the form of animals and plants.

This method of using guilloché not as the background but as the focal point urges the eye to inspect every little detail. This is the first time anything like this has been achieved commercially and it has been met with much success. One of the smartest moves for Vacheron Constantin is their ability to realize that the use of more than one art does not distract from the others, but rather enhances the properties of each one. Aside from Fabergé marrying guilloché and enamel not much experimentation had been explored. Many companies copied the Fabergé style of sifting or wet packing one transparent color over the guilloché. Vacheron Constantin has paid attention to detail and uses guilloché as a decoration inside the decoration, encased by many different colors of enamels to create a real feel to their guilloché dials.

I am neither suggesting nor hoping that other guillocheurs or watch manufacturers copy the work of Vacheron Constantin, but I do hope those aforementioned begin to think creatively about guilloché, instead of relegating it to a background texture. It should be celebrated and made the focal point, and get the attention it deserves. There is quite a lot of inspiration to be taken from the pioneering spirit at Vacheron Constantin regarding their artistic endeavors. This is one of the best examples that the possibilities really are endless. Vacheron Constantin also has enough guilloché work that they employ many independent guillocheurs and a few small ateliers. They officially only have one person doing guilloché for the company who has an apprentice. Vacheron Constantin has implemented a program for sharing information in the arts and is trying to preserve the knowledge for another generation.

Vacheron Constantin branch of Richemont International SA

CHAPTER 6
Practical Operational Knowledge

Parts of a Rose Engine and Straight-Line

The Division Plate

The second most common (popular) method of patterning is by way of the division plate/indexing plate/crossing plate. For simplicity I will refer to it as the division plate. At first glance, the division plate may seem to have copious amounts of random notches around its perimeter and a spring operated hand lever with a triangular tooth resting in one of these notches.

However, these notches are anything but random. The notches may or may not be numbered, depending on the time the machine was manufactured and the actual manufacturer. The notches are separated into groups; it is common to see between two and five sets of two notches.

These double notches correspond with the number of lobes on the rosettes. For example, if the rosette has forty-eight lobes we would choose twenty-four divisions, or anything divisible by the number, or that the number can multiply into.

William Mills division plate that is well marked; the notches are in great condition. *G. Phil Poirier*

John Bower division plate with large notches and clearly marked divisions. *David Wood-Heath*

Three different exterior rose engine patterns with only one rosette and three different factors changed. *Calina Shevlin*

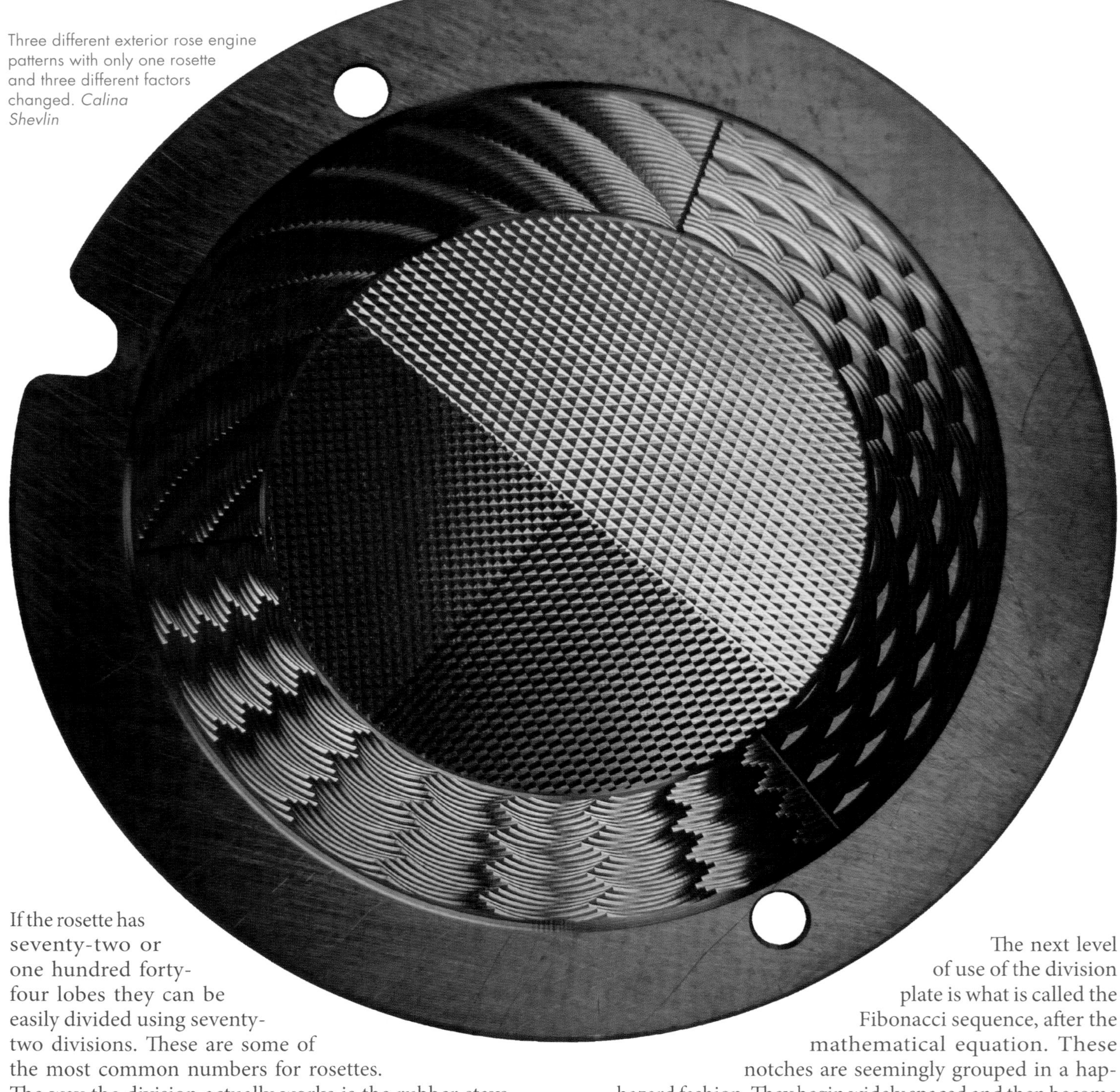

If the rosette has seventy-two or one hundred forty-four lobes they can be easily divided using seventy-two divisions. These are some of the most common numbers for rosettes. The way the division actually works is the rubber stays in place while the headstock with the rosette is rotated to half the distance of the sine wave. This is especially useful in making the basket weave pattern and any other overlapping woven type patterns, as well as a zigzag. These divided patterns in the basic category will vary greatly depending on the rosette and rubber relationship. While the divisions and lobes should go together, I do not want to stop anyone from experimenting with non-divisible numbers. I am a *huge* believer in experimentation. The patterns appear more intricate than they are and will often lead the eye to see a second pattern within the original pattern that does not actually exist. This phenomenon also works in mirror image patterning, but in a more subtle and surprising manner.

The next level of use of the division plate is what is called the Fibonacci sequence, after the mathematical equation. These notches are seemingly grouped in a haphazard fashion. They begin widely spaced and then become much closer together, almost indistinguishable from one notch to the next, but they are really precisely measured distances; moving the headstock just small degrees actually creates the Fibonacci sequence.

This helps in making a moiré pattern. The counting is definitely less of a mental challenge. The spacing takes up an area of around two and a half inches on the division plate per sequence. The notches act as the worm does, changing the position of the rosette in relation to the rubber. The movement is in fractions—small degrees—often difficult to see in placement, but they are perfectly clear in the patterning. If we think of a single lobe of a rosette as fifteen degrees, then each notch would change the rosette's position approximately

John Bower Fibonacci sequence, the first I have ever seen marked other than with the notches themselves. *Calina Shevlin, machine belonging to David Wood-Heath*

one-eighth to two degrees, depending on the sequence. Most Fibonacci type divisions are the "there and back" type, meaning you start at the first notch on the left, then advance through the notches to the last notch in the sequence on the right, and then reverse the action.

This would comprise one full cycle, but there are other options that result in the same patterns due to the precise spacing of the notches. For example, you could work from the left and go to the center notch and then reverse your action. Or you could start with the left notch and then go all the way through to the end instead of reversing, lifting the point and starting at the left again: going A to Z; then restarting at A again. The pattern remains the same no matter how you decide to tackle the Fibonacci notches; it is more about personal preference and how you concentrate or keep track of the actions than there being a "better" method.

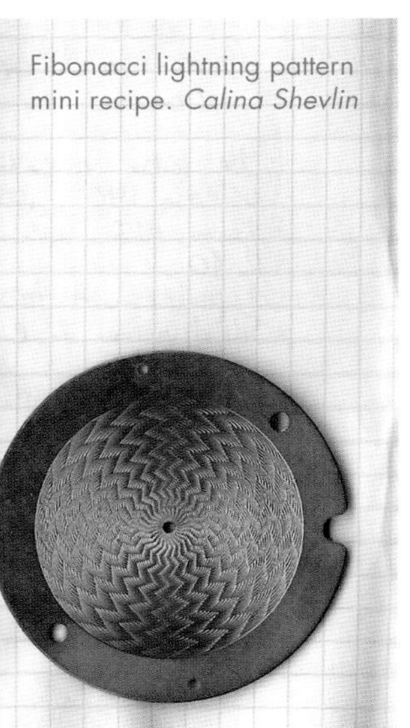

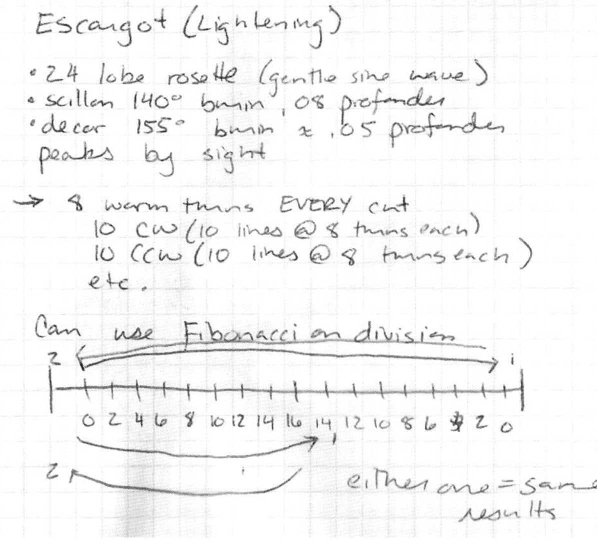

Fibonacci lightning pattern mini recipe. *Calina Shevlin*

The use of this division feature is an easier way to use the worm. This is the equivalent of one click clockwise, one click clockwise, two clicks clockwise, three clicks clockwise, five clicks clockwise, and so on. Starting out with the division Fibonacci is easier than the worm and provides instant gratification when beginning engine turning. There are instances where the worm allows for more varied work, but that is a different section. Even when I am using the notches I always keep a chart, because it is helpful to remind me where I am. The use of charts is certainly worth the effort whether just starting out or a veteran guillocheur (you can find charts to use in the appendix).

The hand lever on the division plate, to the left side of center, allows the work to rotate while the rosettes are blocked in place with some mechanism (which varies depending on the machine).

I have used a G. Plant and Sons machine that had a foot pedal that blocked the headstock. I have also seen a machine that used a pneumatically driven pump to lift up a brass stop of sorts to block the rosettes. One method that is simple to use on any machine is to put your right hand on top of the rosettes while you use your left hand to change the division. The blockage of the rosettes is necessary because it makes changing the division a bit easier; if using the hand method you will always know where to put pressure. The division is often difficult to change at first, but gets easier with practice and repeated changes.

The hand lever can be either to the left or right of the point, but is most commonly found on the left hand side to facilitate use of it. This enables the guillocheur to reach just an arm's length away to change the division, rather than over the entire machine.

The Worm

Vis-sans-fin in French means "screw without end," and this is what we call the worm.

Each small, slightly diagonal indentation in this medium size wheel is more or less three-quarters of a degree. The reason the French call this a screw without end is because it is round with endless notches; you can turn infinitely in one direction without damaging the part or machine. Advancing or retreating the screw can offset patterns according to the need or just the creativity of the designer or guillocheur. This method of patterning is best when using a chart to keep track of direction of turning if creating anything other than a basic spiral. If the desired decor is not equally spaced throughout, I also advise having an area on the tracking chart with the number of clicks, as well as the direction of worm movement (see the appendix for precise examples). For instance, if you want to off-set the pattern by twenty notches clockwise—more or less fifteen degrees—and you have measured the piece and decided on what spacing you need, you will be making approximately seventy-nine cuts, and you will need at least two passes to get clean bright cuts. This means you will cut from A to Z (exterior to interior), then have to return to the *exact* same starting point with *both* the worm and spacing for the pawl. This involves turning the worm twenty times per cut in a counterclockwise fashion and letting the tension off of the pawl to reverse the tool slide, bringing the total turns back to 1,580 turns! Without a chart this would be near impossible.

There is another way that I like to use: I launch into patterning like anyone else, working slowly and measured from exterior point A to interior point Z.

Then I reverse my actions and make the second cut from the inside to the outside, turning the worm twenty clicks counterclockwise every cut while moving my already measured distance with the help of a fixed micrometer on the tool slide. This has saved me so much frustration and ruining patterns. I find it is well worth the modification to add a fixed micrometer to your machine.

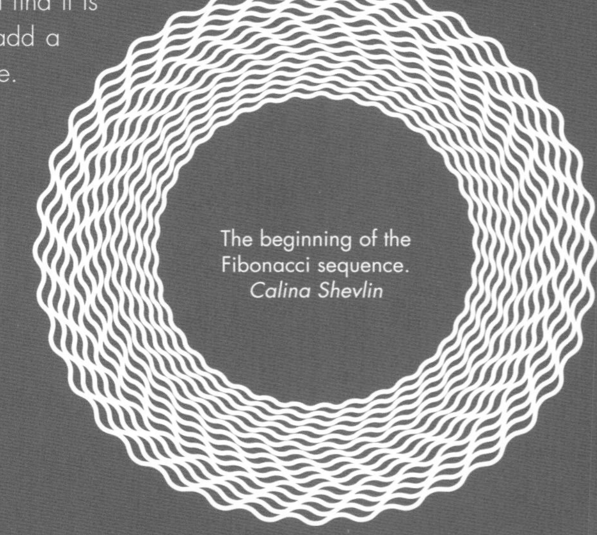

The beginning of the Fibonacci sequence. *Calina Shevlin*

The worm is the screw mechanism attached to the face of the division plate. *G. Phil Poirier*

The division for this Plant straight-line is the handle in the upper right-hand corner of the image. *G. Phil Poirier*

on your piece. As I have previously mentioned, I like to use a fixed micrometer on my tool slide so I know exactly how far—to the third decimal place—I am spacing between cuts. This also helps when I work in reverse for a difficult pattern: I simply write down the spacing there and then read it in reverse, and I am spot on every time. I am in a habit of working quite precisely, as I am often making dials and work for the Swiss watch industry, where precision is paramount. The pawl allows for close cutting or slight overlapping, depending on the intended pattern. While for the moment the pawl is only capable of being turned with measured clicks under tension clockwise, I have been working on designing a pawl with which is easy to change the direction, so that one may also work with the same advantages counterclockwise.

The worm is unique to each machine that was originally hand made, so every worm will be different from the next. This is a miniscule difference between each machine, but each worm will be a little different on the precise degrees between notches. This is not noticeable when patterning, but I mention it as my calculations are for my own machine. By employing the worm patterns such as zigzags, spirals, crossovers, moirés, and more can be created.

A new model and sturdier pawl. *G. Phil Poirier*

The Pawl

The pawl is on the right-hand side of the tool slide and is used to advance the tool slide with the cutter from left to right (exterior to interior) in measured increments.

The pawl has teeth that are angled slightly, allowing for the catch (which is adjustable) to rest at the selected position. There is a small slide with a screw to set the position of the pawl for repeated measured distances. If I want to advance ten clicks between cuts, I simply set the screw to stop the post after ten notches and then no longer have to count the clicks of the pawl; I pull the lever toward me and it will be ten clicks. It is the reverse motion (pushing it back to its starting position) that moves the pawl; for me this is such a relaxing sound—click, click, and click, to a sort of soft "shoomp" sound. Once you are in a rhythm the sound becomes almost hypnotic. This is good because if you forget it, you will notice right away. It is advisable to formulate a plan to move the pawl either before or after any other adjustments and stick to that every time so you do not lose track while working

An old model pawl. *G. Phil Poirier*

To return to the beginning and begin the second pass the pawl must be released from tension, wound the other way—past where the start is—then re-engaged and advanced one click at a time until in the same starting fillet. This is one of the reasons guillocheurs work from the outside in; the pawl is not currently capable of moving in measured clicks in both directions. The pawl is the most precise method of advancing the cutter in specific increments from as little as 0.02 mm (20 microns) to as large as the worker would like. With small adjustments and improvements—such as more teeth, more even spacing, and so on—to the pawl over time, guillocheurs were able to make more consistent looking patterns. If you look at old guilloché examples, you will often find that the patterning was not equally spaced. This is because the pawl started out with large teeth that were hand made, therefore creating a larger margin of play and allowing for more pressure changes, causing uneven spacing. From the 1920s onward, we can see more even spacing in works created on the rose engine, largely due to the improvement of the pawl.

Rosettes and Pattern Bars

Now that I have alluded to rosettes in every sense I will attempt to describe them in great detail. A rosette is what a pattern is taken from. I say "taken" rather than "created" because the rubber follows the rosette, and a smaller version of the exact contours is created from exterior to interior when working concentrically. The original rosettes existed in three different sizes, depending on the machine. The standard is nine-inch, but there was a seven-inch used by G. Plant and Sons for jewelry sized rose engines, and there was a fourteen-inch fabricated by G. Plant and Sons and a few other manufacturers. The applications were in a way dictated by the machine.

The material that was and is still the most common to make a rosette from is a bronze alloy that is very durable. Many of the rosettes that are found with original machines are also original, and while they do often show signs of wear, they are still functional and most are survivors from the mid- to late 1800s. The rosettes offer a myriad of decoration bases, and when coupled with other parts of the machine, such as the worm, division plate, double rubber, or mirroring, the patterns become infinite and incredible. The height of the waves cannot be too high, which is beneficial in ornamental turning, and they must be gently undulating. If the rosette has high amplitude waves the rubber will make a nice pattern on the ascent, but will be out of control on the way down, leaving the second half of the pattern in ruins. For ornamental turning the rosettes exist with waves that terminate at the top in actual points, more like a star.

Rosettes with pumping and regular action. *G. Phil Poirier*

Pattern bars have a different rubber that is shorter and more pointed, as the pattern bars are not as large or spaced out as a rosette. *G. Phil Poirier*

Ornamental turning rosettes given the extremely high amplitude. *Calina Shevlin*

A nice variety of original and new rosettes. *G. Phil Poirier*

While most rosettes for guilloché are gently undulating, they are not boring. Even the smallest change in amplitude lends itself to a new pattern. Rosettes are a fairly standard thickness (5/16), regardless of the diameter, which is from 4 in. to 7 in. They fit with the standard sized rubber coincidentally, or rather, not. The rosettes are sized to reduce vibrations because they fit the rubber so perfectly and are easily stacked (added) on to the headstock. There are between eight and twenty rosettes mounted on a headstock, depending on the manufacturer of the machine. The smaller the number the less vibrations, because the smaller the headstock (shorter).

As you can see from all of the different types of rosettes with different sized waves and crevasses, the selection of the rubber may not be as easy as simply grabbing one that is sort of close to size; the rubber needs to be a good fit with the entire rosette. You absolutely do *not* want to lose the detail of the rosette. That is the whole purpose of guilloché. Most rosettes have an even number of lobes, meaning most can be divided with the notches on the division/indexing wheel/plate. For the few rosettes that have an odd number of lobes it is difficult to use the division plate with satisfactory results. I find the patterns with odd numbered lobes are really quite interesting and do not need much tweaking with other parts of the machine.

Some rosettes are not only patterned on the outside but also on the face, which you might expect to be flat. This is so the rosette can be used with a pumping action (instead of

FIG.06-13A

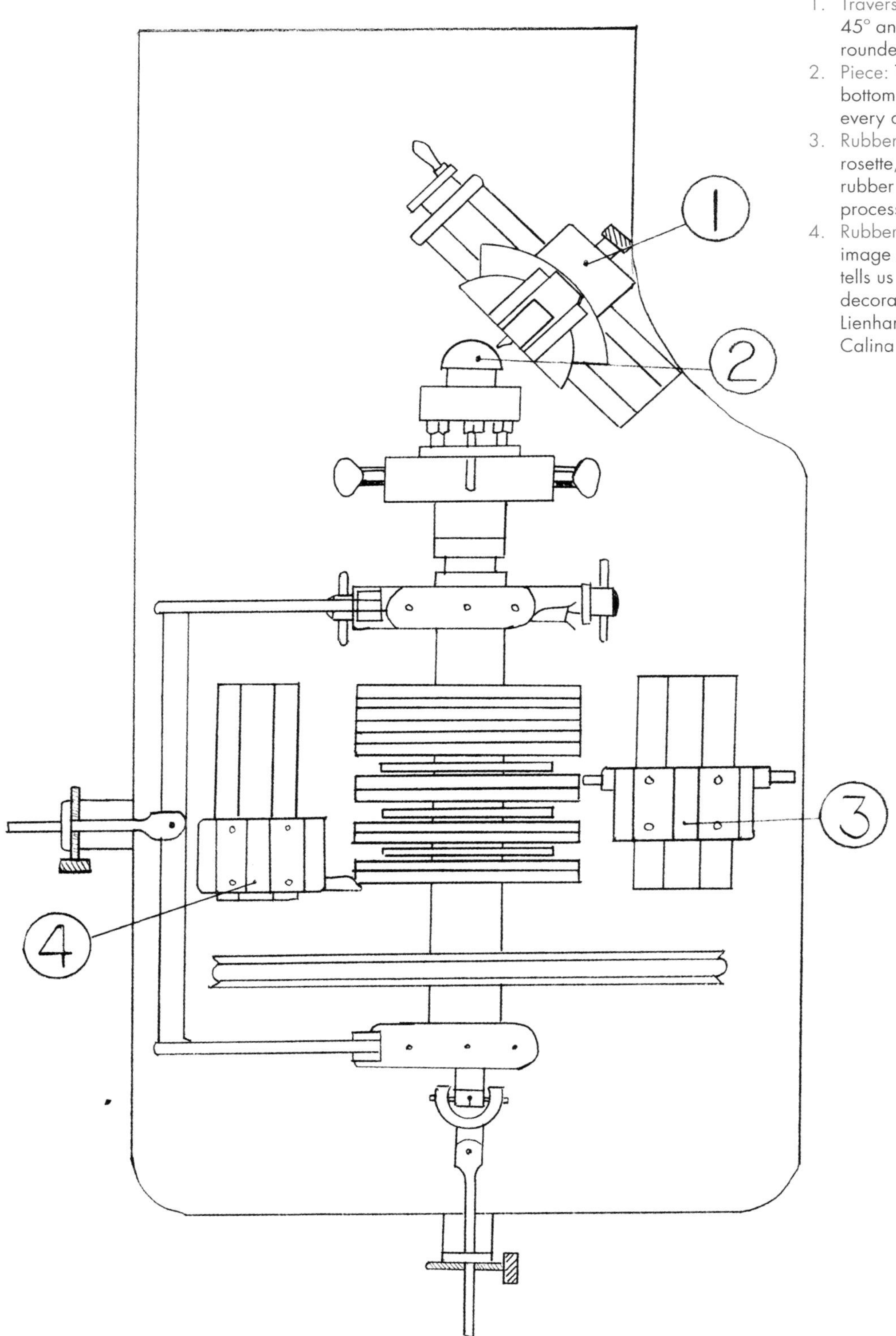

This machine is set up to do a three-dimensional piece; the traversing slide is at a 45° angle, ready to align with each angle of the surface (see pp 69, 73–74 for more information on alignment.

1. Traversing Tool Slide: This is set up at a 45° angle, ready to decorate only the rounded top.
2. Piece: This piece is much like an egg bottom, ready to be decorated on every angle.
3. Rubber: The rubber is against the face of the rosette, just like in regular guilloché. This rubber will not be used for the entire process of decoration for this piece.
4. Rubber: This rubber is set up on the mirror image side and for pumping action, which tells us the side of the piece will also be decorated. Illustration re-drawn from Lienhard Operators Manual 1895 by Calina Shevlin

rocking from side to side with the motion of the hand wheel the headstock will rock back to front). This means the rosettes with lobes on the face cannot be butted up as closely to their neighbors because you need room at least for a rubber, plus for the amplitude of the rosette. These rosettes have the same pattern on the outside as on their face—which makes for easy working. With a small change to the tension leaf springs from side action to front action the headstock easily changes its axis of movement. The pumping action is useful for a border pattern, usually found on watches around the different areas on the dial. The pumping action seems to have been relegated to the borders on dials, but is also really useful on three-dimensional objects.

When the tool slide is changed the pumping action transfers the pattern just like it would to a flat disc to the three-dimensional form. The eggs of Fabergé were created this way. This is also how pocket watchcases were decorated before modern technology stepped in (see Pumping Action).

Not all rosettes have patterning on the face as the originals were created; only about 50% were made this way. Rosettes were hand made (more so than today) with the technology of the day, and they were much more difficult to produce. This was also time consuming, because adding waves that matched the exterior with the same amplitude as the face was difficult. The stock not only had

A. Duguet rosettes; the divisions are squared rather than notched. *Calina Shevlin*

The pattern bars for straight-line machines can be either slightly wavy or flat, with small divots that the rubber falls into to make the pattern. These are the latter variety. *G. Phil Poirier*

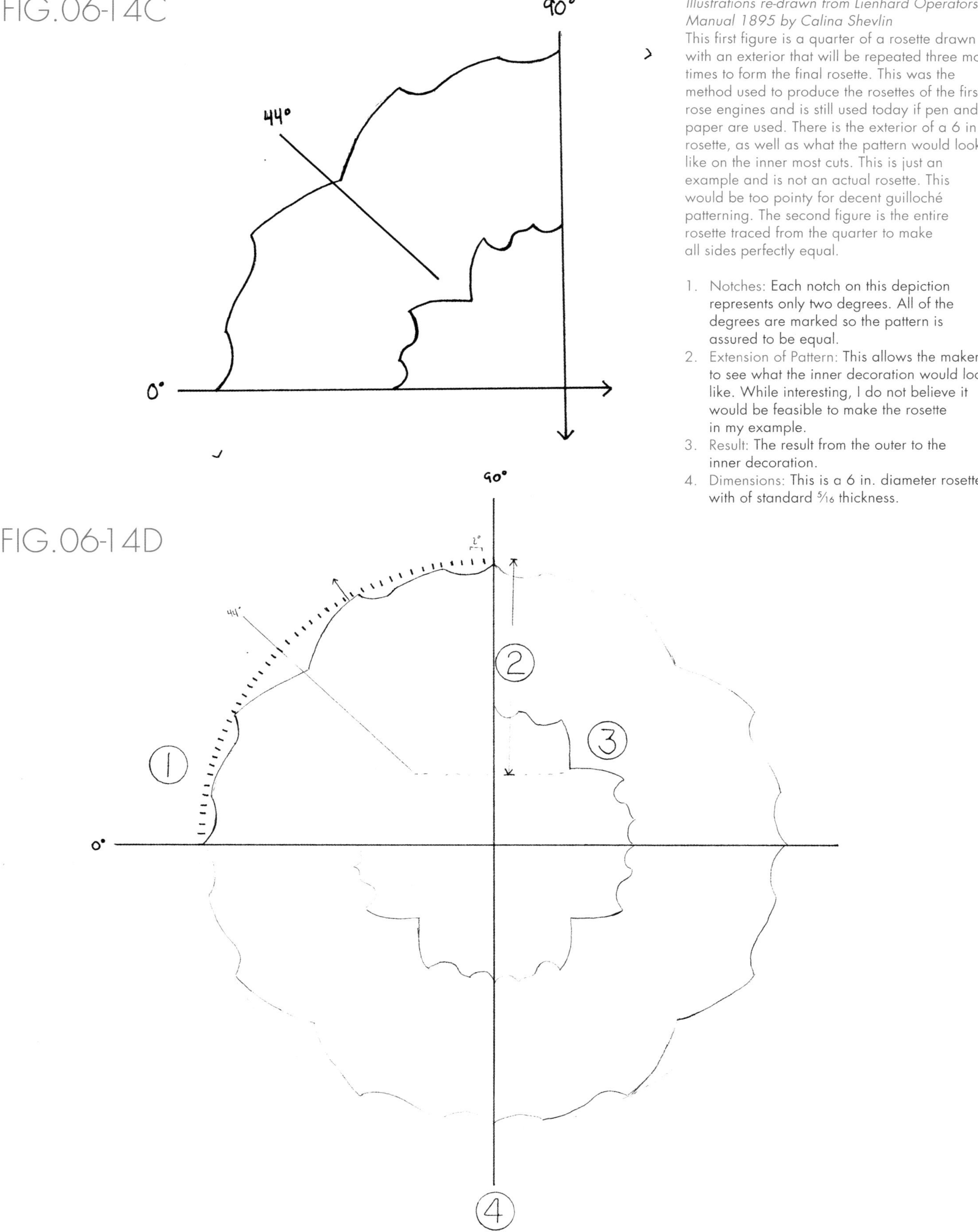

Illustrations re-drawn from Lienhard Operators Manual 1895 by Calina Shevlin

This first figure is a quarter of a rosette drawn with an exterior that will be repeated three more times to form the final rosette. This was the method used to produce the rosettes of the first rose engines and is still used today if pen and paper are used. There is the exterior of a 6 in. rosette, as well as what the pattern would look like on the inner most cuts. This is just an example and is not an actual rosette. This would be too pointy for decent guilloché patterning. The second figure is the entire rosette traced from the quarter to make all sides perfectly equal.

1. Notches: Each notch on this depiction represents only two degrees. All of the degrees are marked so the pattern is assured to be equal.
2. Extension of Pattern: This allows the maker to see what the inner decoration would look like. While interesting, I do not believe it would be feasible to make the rosette in my example.
3. Result: The result from the outer to the inner decoration.
4. Dimensions: This is a 6 in. diameter rosette with of standard 5⁄16 thickness.

to have a larger diameter that could be worked down, but also had to be thicker, with the material toward the center removed before the face could be worked. Even now with more advanced technology it is still quite difficult to get the face to match the side in terms of exact spacing and especially the finish. For the aforementioned reasons only the simplest rosettes were created with a patterned face.

Fabrication of the original rosettes was less advanced, with a lot of pre-planning and adjustment by hand until the rosette was just right. Then they were cast. This made a sort of rosette production much easier, but the quality of a cast rosette is lower than one that is cut from a solid piece of stock. The A. Duguet machine seems to have a headstock that was cast as one large piece instead of many individual rosettes.

The number of lobes desired divided the design of the original rosettes; then just one perfect portion was created as a template and simply applied to the entire piece. For example, a 12-lobed rosette—with one large and one small lobe being one entire lobe—will have had the small and large drawn and then rendered perfectly, and then cut out of wood. All of the other eleven lobes would be sized to it (below).

Rosette measured out 1⁄16, then the pattern is traced on to wood, cut out, and scribed all the way around the rosette, ensuring a perfect pattern. *Calina Shevlin*

After the layout was complete, the template was used to trace the pattern repeatedly onto a large piece of paper to see what the final result would be. Once the maker was satisfied they would lay the wood template on the stock of the bronze alloy and begin to sketch on the pattern that would be cut. Each 1/12—or however many lobes were present—would be traced, repositioned, and traced again until the entire 360° were completed. The rosettes were cut out with the aid of machines like the milling machine, then hand finished by sanding and scraping and taken to the polishing wheel. All the while meticulous measurements were made.

After years of use these often become misshapen. I believe this is due in large part to the incorrect use of the machine (i.e., the turning style of the operator). If a guillocheur is trained properly they would keep turning the hand wheel in the same direction at an even but slow and steady speed, never using only half of the rosette and then turning back over the same area. This leads to the rosette becoming misshapen on only one side and more difficult to fix. Many operators unfortunately worked in the ½ rosette manner, much to my chagrin. The old rosettes are obviously misshapen from years of misuse and it is clear there does not need to be any measuring involved. Learning guilloché, it is much easier to learn the correct way with an explanation as to *why* it is correct than to correct a bad habit. Fortunately, with technology it has become much simpler to input the desired measurements and completely resurface these rosettes. The diameter does unfortunately diminish, but that is part of the reason why the rubbers are so much longer than necessary at first; they

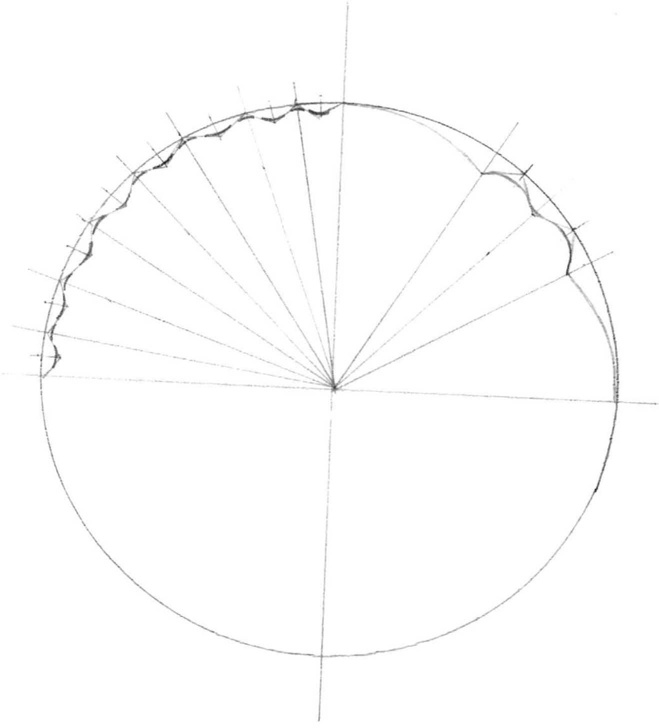

A multi-pattern rosette would save space and time, especially if working on small pieces that do not use the entire rosette. *Calina Shevlin*

compensate for this. Another cause of rapid wear and horrible work that is not even passable as work is spinning the hand wheel too exuberantly. This not only wears the rosette, but it also wears out the rubber.

I have long thought of the idea of multitasking with guilloché. If one is creating a production series and the pattern is only to be applied using ¼ or ½ of a rosette, why not create a multi-patterned rosette?

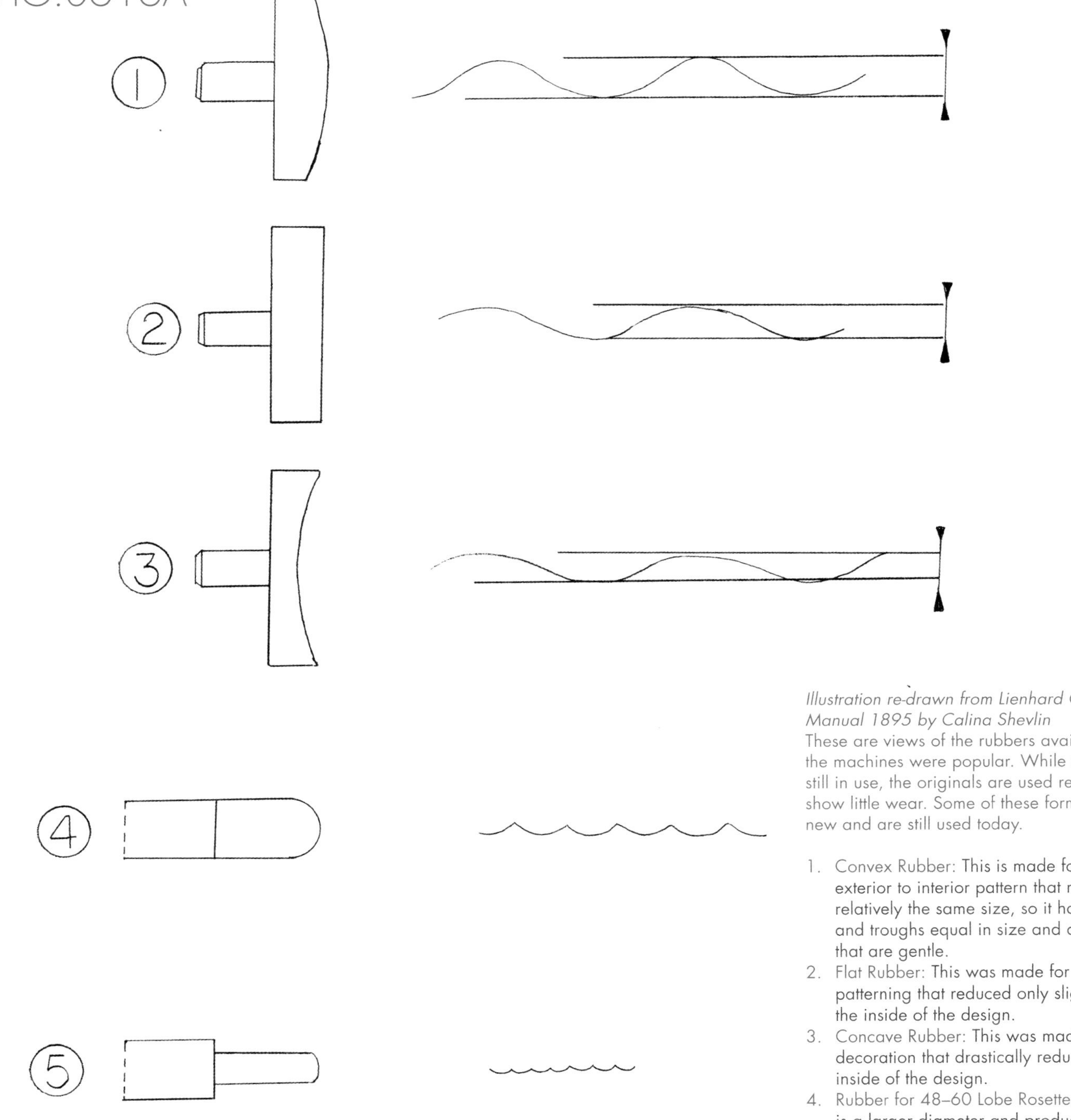

Illustration re-drawn from Lienhard Operators Manual 1895 by Calina Shevlin

These are views of the rubbers available when the machines were popular. While not all are still in use, the originals are used regularly and show little wear. Some of these forms are made new and are still used today.

1. Convex Rubber: This is made for a normal exterior to interior pattern that remains relatively the same size, so it has waves and troughs equal in size and diameter that are gentle.
2. Flat Rubber: This was made for normal patterning that reduced only slightly toward the inside of the design.
3. Concave Rubber: This was made for decoration that drastically reduced on the inside of the design.
4. Rubber for 48–60 Lobe Rosettes: This rubber is a larger diameter and produces peaked waves. This is one of the rubbers still in use and is replicated in slightly different diameters to fit all of the different rosettes.
5. Rubber for 80–200 Lobe Rosettes: This is a much smaller diameter rubber that produces very nice peaked waves. This is also still created today.

I like to think of it as a pie, easily divisible by two to eight and equal on every side. The possibilities of a multi-patterned rosette could open the door for smaller (think tabletop) rose engines. This could be for the beginning guillocheur or for the occasional hobbyist who does not have much space but desires beautiful patterns. The rosettes would make the machine less expensive, but the quality of the cut would never be quite as good as with a good old-fashioned rose engine. This is because the tabletop machine would not have the weight behind it to support vibration-free cutting. Even economizing and using half of a rosette for one pattern would help support many different things: first, innovation; second, it would cut down on the need to have a whole lot of different rosettes for small patterning needs; and third, it would enable hobbyists to explore guilloché in a more space-friendly environment. This downsizing and using multiple patterns on a rosette makes the rose engine transform from a machine into a tool.

Rubbers/Touches

Some types of rubbers came with original machines and are still in use today with slight variations (see p 61).

The *rubber* or *touch* (both terms will be used interchangeably) comes in many different forms, shapes, and materials. British and Americans often call the piece a *rubber* because it rubs the rosette and the Swiss and German often call the piece a *touch* because the rosette touches it; it is a matter of personal preference. The shape and size of each rubber corresponds with the inner sine wave of a rosette. For the optimal aesthetic pattern (or the consistent exact replication of the rosette) to be achieved, the rubber must be just slightly smaller than the internal trough of the rosette, with enough room for only the thickness of a piece of paper on all sides.

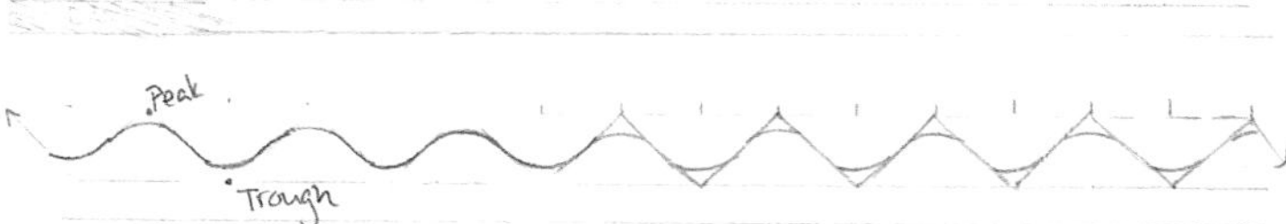

The peak and trough defined for sine wave (undulating) rosettes. *Calina Shevlin*

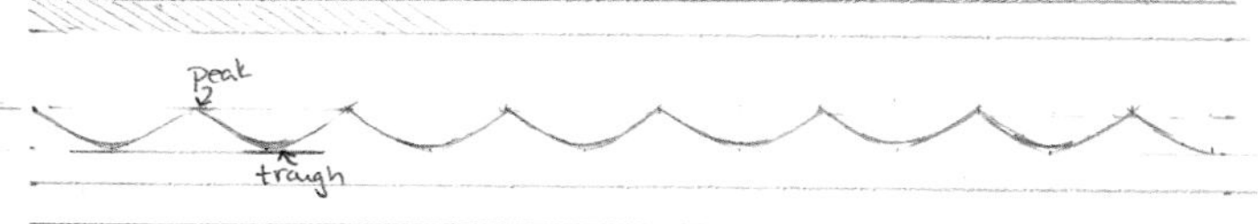

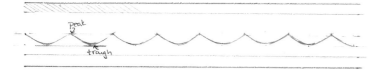

The peak and trough defined for pointed rosettes. *Calina Shevlin*

If the rubber is too large for the trough the pattern will be almost obliterated, because the rubber will only travel on the very exterior part of the rosette, losing the trough altogether. However, if the rubber is much smaller than the trough, the pattern will become exaggerated and the effect will be pointed rather than undulating. It is important to find the correct rubber for each of the rosettes (and any new ones you may have made). With some experimentation you can see the various pros and cons for what you are trying to achieve by playing around with the rubber to trough ratio. For the most clean and professional look, and the most exact reading of the rosette, the rubber should fit neatly into the trough with a bit of room to maneuver.

The material of the rubber is very important because the rubber is held in place with two large hex-head screws connected to the support arm attached to the table. This is important to know because the rubber takes all of the weight of the headstock as it rotates. The rubber remains fixed, much like the cutter, and the rosette pushes the headstock out and in along the waves, causing the piece to move—as it is attached to the headstock—in the formation of the rosette.

The material most commonly used for the fabrication of the rubber is a hardened tool steel. The rubber body (what is attached to the stand) is often square or rectangular, with a slightly larger girth than the rubber tip, because the tip is ground down from the stock slightly with minimal removal of material. The tip is shaped like a popsicle stick.

Think about gluing twenty sticks adjacently together—the tip shape of the rubber—but with variations in the radius. There are also some other materials currently in use depending on the type of rubber, whether it be a roller, mushroom shaped, removable tip, and so on.

The advantages of various materials depend on the desired outcome of the guilloché decoration. The roller rubber is often

A Delrin rubber—easier on the rosettes and easy to resurface—runs smoothly along the rosette without the need for much lubrication. *G. Phil Poirier*

Leather rubber is also more gentle on the rosette, but needs frequent changing due to the weight of the headstock. *G. Phil Poirier*

Steel roller type rubber and rubber for pattern bars. *Teri Jo Kinnison*

Plant rubber in the pattern bars. *G. Phil Poirier*

made of the same material as the body (steel) but is less durable, as it is hollow, allowing for rolling along the rosette. The main advantage to using this type of rubber is there is less wear on the rubber because it rolls and does not simply slide along the rosette. The roller can also be slightly more beneficial to the rosette in terms of wear. Rubbers with removable tips are usually made by the operator, or can be ordered from people who make rose engines and accessories, and offer benefits to the traditional steel rubber. The tips are generally a plastic such as super hard and slightly expensive PEEK plastic[2] or DELRIN[3], a white plastic often used for hammers for jewelers. These do not produce as crisp of a cut as steel but they are much easier on the rosette. Once the plastic or urethane is worn down from its original shape it can be replaced. The system is often a tap and die, where the all-thread protrudes from the body and the tip simply screws on. The replaceable tips are wonderful, allowing for one or two bodies with many tips that are fast and easy to change out. They also allow for uncommon rosettes to be used with uncommonly shaped rubbers specially made for each one at a fraction of the cost and time, which will cause much less wear on the rosette.

Old rubbers came in two standard shapes: the most popular was the one piece body and tip out of a rectangular or square stock with the tip radius ground down; the second and less common (but still able to be found) was the mushroom-shaped rubber. This was often coupled with rosettes that had fewer waves and more smooth areas. They are quite cumbersome for detailed work unless using a rosette with low amplitude points, but very few (i.e., square shapes, triangular shapes, etc.) and without much detail.

With advancements in machinery and technology filing and sanding of the rubber by hand to reshape it is no longer necessary, but is a good skill to have regardless. Every so often the rubber does need to be redressed. This means it needs to be reshaped due to wear, which is completely normal. There is really no preventing this because with time and use its shape will begin to change. If you do not have a lot of time to spend redressing your rubber, the quick option for a short time is to flip the rubber over so the bottom is the top. This will hold you over in a bind, but could be detrimental when redressing later, because the radius is so changed it could be much more work to return it to its original size. If you have the capability and skill to redress your own rubbers I applaud you. If not, it is really easy and fairly quick to send them off to an expert. Usually a machinist or technician can easily do this for you if you have the radii marked on the rubbers. Having the rubber professionally machined ensures even sides and radii. This will keep the diameter corresponding to what it was, thereby keeping the rubber relationship with certain rosettes the same. If you are willing to take the time and have access to a CNC machine you of course should learn to make and redress your own rubbers. This comes in handy, especially if you are making or having special rosettes made.

One last thing to consider is that it is possible to use two rubbers at the same time when creating a pattern. This creates a pattern within a pattern and is most commonly seen in older works but is slowly making a comeback. By using two rubbers you are concurrently using two different rosettes. The two rubbers must be fitted to their respective rosettes to achieve optimal results. When using two rubbers/rosettes, one of the rosettes needs to have larger amplitude and the other generally a more multitudinous pattern. If the possibilities were infinite before, they have just doubled.

Double rubber patterning creates a pattern within a pattern. *G. Phil Poirier*

FIG.06-22A

This is the top view of a rose engine set up for double rubber use.

1. Traversing Slide: This is set up to do flat work. The slide and cutter are centered.
2. Work: Flat and ready to be decorated.
3. Double Rubbers: The tool support is equipped with two holders and two rubbers so the piece can be decorated with a pattern that does not exist solely on one rosette.

How the double rubber use works is there are two different rosettes: one having high amplitude and one with low amplitude. The rubber of the low amplitude rosette rides along and transmits the pattern until the high amplitude of the other rosette is reached, then the low amplitude rubber is lifted off the rosette. *Illustration re-drawn from Lienhard Operators Manual 1895 by Calina Shevlin*

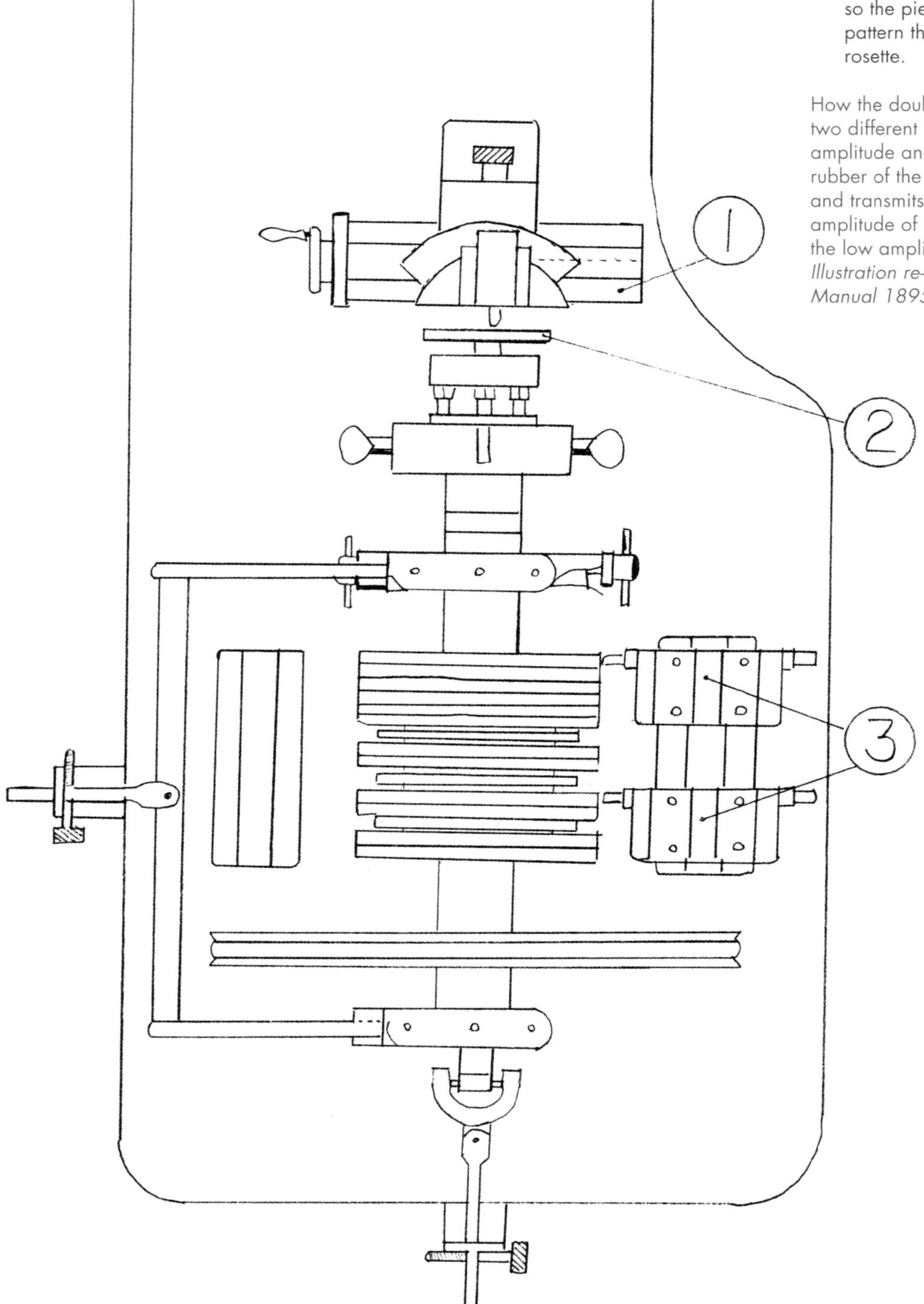

Calina Shevlin

Most machines were equipped with two rubber holders on the side stand and today are often used one at a time for convenience, using whichever one is closest to the rosette desired for use.

These were intended for double rubber use. The rubber holders are both movable, meaning the desired combination of rosettes is easily achieved. If there are a few double rubber patterns that you find you enjoy immensely, I suggest you set up the headstock to facilitate the use of the rubbers with minimal readjusting. While it is a fair amount of hassle to do this, in the long run you will save time and perhaps your sanity.

I hope that with the advancement of new machines will come new and curious people who wish to find innovative advancements or alternatives to the rubber. It should be fairly easy in the DIY world that we now live in. Or perhaps the rubber does not need to be changed because it is the best design for the machine.

So far I have described the rosettes and rubbers for the rose engine and want to assure you that as the chapters progress I will also describe the parts of the straight-line engine. Keep in mind the principles are much the same for both machines.

This is the type of cutter I learned on: a lathe cutter repurposed for engine turning. They are often HSS, and once they are sharpened a few times and low they are tossed in the trash. *G. Phil Poirier*

The Cutter or Burin

The cutter exists in many different shapes, forms, and sizes, and while the sizes and materials have varied over the years, the forms have relatively remained the same. While there is always room for improvement, the form was already perfected and needed no alterations. An entire chapter of George Daniels' book *Watchmaking* is dedicated to the decoration of watches and cases and gives a brief but thorough introduction to guilloché, but more importantly, to the fabrication of tools and how to be self-sufficient and also sharpen cutters.

This cutter is from Diametal. I use it to cut the area around a space to be left blank. It is 40° one side and 20° the other side. The 40° side goes toward the blank space and the 20° goes toward the side to have guilloché. *Calina Shevlin*

I use this Diametal cutter to cut clous de Paris and grains d'orge (barley corn) patterns. It is a nice wide cutter with 12.5° each side. This is only good for shallow, wide cuts. *Calina Shevlin*

A goniostat, still used in most guilloché shops for sharpening cutters with precision. *Calina Shevlin*

Somewhere around 50% of current guillocheurs still use the method outlined in Daniels' book to sharpen their burins, while the rest opt for using Agathon or GRS lapidary machines with adjustable angled stands for precise sharpening. I find the two methods work equally well. The Agathon is more for cutting the initial form from a blank, so if you are only sharpening cutters that are already the form you wish to use, the GRS horizontal lapidary wheel is all you need. If you are cutting square, rectangular, or other shapes (e.g., to stamp a brand name afterward), then you will also need to have engraving cutter tools. These are always made by hand by the the operator become comfortable with constant realignment of the machine. This is because not every cutter will be shaped exactly the same. With each new burin introduced the machine must be realigned to the new piece being decorated to ensure the burin is perfectly perpendicular to the work and centered. With practice this becomes a breeze. I remember my first time trying to align the machine and center something: I took about forty-five minutes and it still was not very good—now it takes about thirty seconds. What I like about Diametal holders and cutters is that with the turn of two small screws the cutter can be slipped out and another inserted and aligned straight away.

This is a Diametal cutter with a 90° radius. The tip is parallel with the work piece and is used only for pumping action. *Calina Shevlin*

guillocheur to best fit their hands and needs. I keep the following shapes on hand so I can connect corners seamlessly and have them seem to be one guilloché line that turns at 90°. I use a microscope and steady hand to achieve this effect.

When it comes to types of cutters there appear to be two schools, but the older method seems to be moving over to the new one quite rapidly. The first is using old lathe cutters (small ones) and shaping them to the needs of guilloché, while the second, introduced by Georges Brodbeck of Saignelegier, Switzerland, is to use a universal tool holder fitted with miniscule removable high speed steel (HSS) blanks that come in two different widths and one length and are 100% customizable by the operator. This second method is more expensive to start out but is much cheaper and produces much less waste in the long run. A Swiss company called Diametal makes these and the holders under the DIADEC name, and I find they are worth the initial investment—good tools lead to good work.

I know these tools are finding their way to Americans who are doing guilloché, as a friend has purchased a pack and is happy with them. This product is also great for extremely tiny work, which often requires the use of a movable binocular or permanent mounted binocular.

When sharpening these new burins a binocular set up near the lapidary machine is a huge help, ensuring that the sides are equal and guaranteeing the best possible cuts.

Both of the cutters I have mentioned are made of high speed steel (HSS). I know there are some people who have used carbide steel and other materials, but I have no personal experience with them. The most optimal use of the cutters would be to make a few watch-sized pieces—depending on complexity and size—and then re-sharpen the cutters. Watch-sized is not the rule, but for the best looking cuts it is a guide. Changing the burin often helps two-fold: it allows for the optimal cut surface, but it also helps

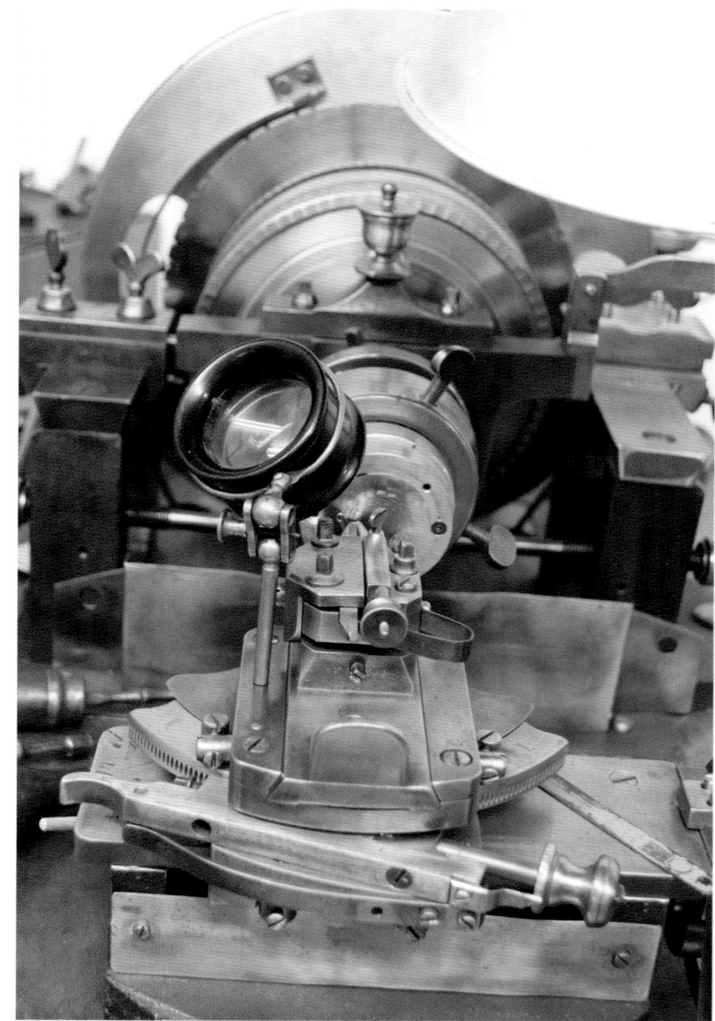

This mounted loupe is how guillocheurs used to work in less than ideal lighting conditions. *Georges Brodbeck*

FIG.06-29A

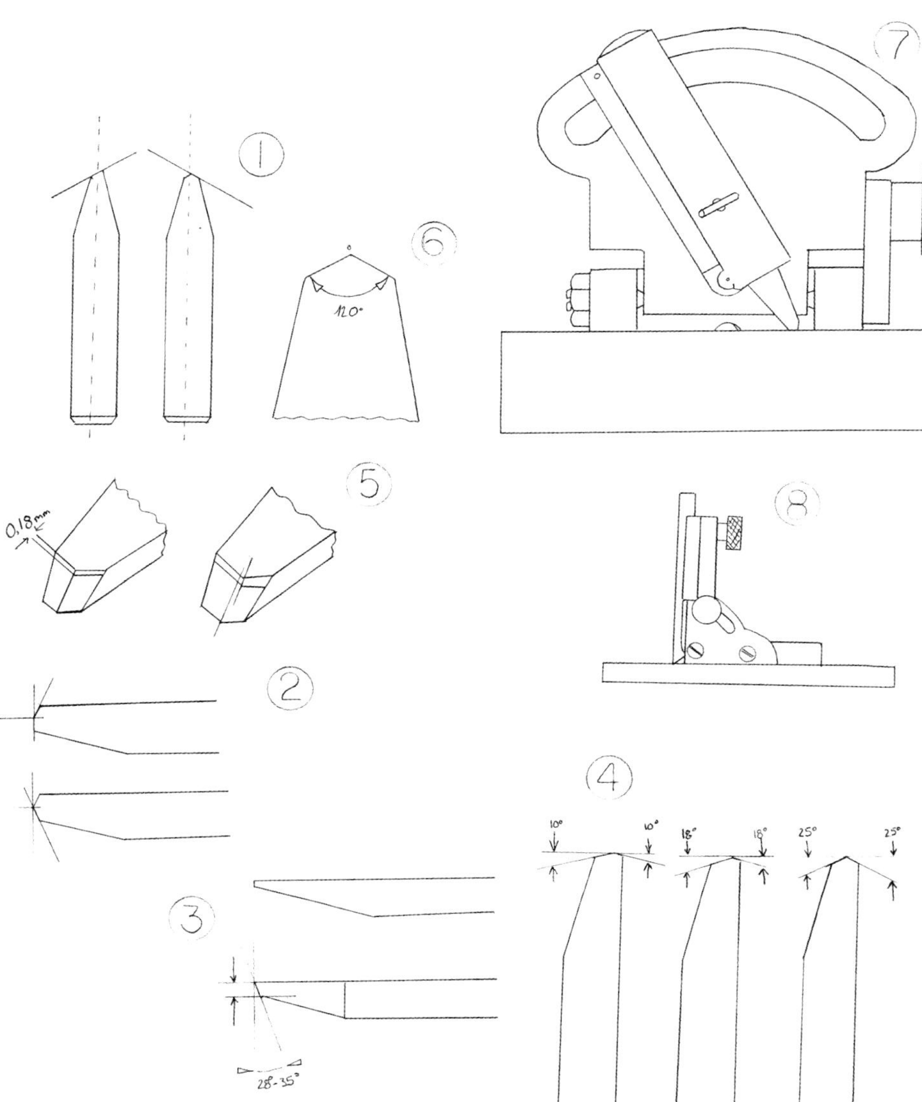

Illustration re-drawn from Lienhard Operators Manual 1895 by Calina Shevlin
These are drawings showing cutter sharpening and ideas for different degrees of cutters.

1. Shaping the Cutter: The image on the left shows the first cut made; the image on the right shows the second cut for starting from a blank stock.
2. Shaping the Cutter: This is again the first and second cuts, but for a cutter with less of an angle, so for barley corn or nail head decorations. To make the first angle, you would attach the cutter to the goniostat and set the tool to a 20° angle with the butt of the tool to the left and the area being sharpened to the right. For the second angle you would attach the cutter opposite, with the butt at the right and the area being sharpened to the left. Move the goniostat to 20° and make the second angle.
3. Throat Angle: The cutter needs to have the throat ground down so that, when creating the decoration, the cutter does not drag the bottom half into the piece. By leaving only the point foremost the work will be clean and in no danger of being damaged. The rule of thumb is to leave 3 mm top to bottom of cutting area and a 28–35° set back at the throat.
4. Cutters: This shows different angles of cutters that are commonly used. The left cutter is for barley corn and nail head decorations because it is very shallow but wide, lending itself to nicely aligned peaks. The middle cutter is medium depth and width. It is not centered so the smaller angle is toward the work that has not been cut to avoid damage. The right cutter is very steep and is used for making deep cuts, such as the circle I make around all of my patterns before starting with the rose engine.
5. Polished Faces: This shows the correct alignment of the 0.10 mm polished face on the tip of the cutter. On the left the point is equal to the center, whereas on the right the center is not aligned with the point. The cutter on the right cannot be used.
6. Rounded Tip: For this cutter the tip is ever so slightly rounded with a white stone or ceramic before starting work.
7. Goniostat: This is for specifically finding the correct angle and grinding the cutter lightly to find the sharp cutting edge. The assembly rests atop an Arkansas sharpening stone or something similar.
8. Goniostat: Side view.

Now most guillocheurs work with mounted microscopes. Georges has one on each machine. *Georges Brodbeck*

A Diametal cutter (all come unformed—the guillocheur makes them to their own specifications). Form is important, so it is best to have a microscope by the cutter sharpening area. *Calina Shevlin*

It is essential the cutter not be changed while working on a piece if it can be avoided. As I have stated, cutters are never exact copies, and this is quite evident if changing out the cutter on a piece. I know that sometimes a burin can chip at some point and you must change out the cutter. Although this happens when it is worn out! If this is the case there is a way to blend the two cutters. Align the machine as closely as possible to the last burin by using the last two to three cuts to match with the current burin and continue the work at the same depth. Then go over the piece with a second pass and ultimately a third pass, all a bit deeper than the last, generally around 0.1 mm deeper than originally planned. This will generally disguise the change, but may not be a desirable depth; if you are making samples just throw in a new one and realign as usual.

It is beneficial to guillocheurs to learn as many of the sharpening methods as possible, because one may not always have access to their own personal preference and it would not do to arrive somewhere to teach, help, or learn guilloché and not know how to sharpen one's own burins. Pages 69 and 71 show some basic forms and rules of cutter sharpening.

Burins come in different forms for different types of work, and when I create recipes, I always include what type of cutter I used so I can replicate something exactly. When starting with guilloché, it is really beneficial to be able to play with the machine and discover its secrets, especially with cutters. It is important to know that slightly different shapes can produce slightly different patterns or facilitate more minute work. Each cutter lends itself to a certain pattern or multiple different patterns.

The difference in degrees may not seem large, but for a decoration it can make or break a beautiful pattern. The cutters are not just cut on the sides, but also on the belly.

If the burins were simply cut on the sides the belly would drag along the work and leave a mark (cut) that would ruin the pattern. While most burins have a pointed tip with only the angle changing, there is a flat burin that is quite popular and used with the pumping action to create rings on watch dials to separate the different parts of a dial and allow for multiple decorations. This burin is not pointed, but is sharpened so it is parallel with the surface to be cut. Special care must be taken with this burin, as it is more susceptible to breakage due to its parallel angle to the work piece.

The most common angles are 12.5°, 40°, and 20°, but there are more for specialized and less frequent work. The operator is left to decide what angles and tips are best for their needs. When sharpening the cutter, I personally use a lapping wheel from GRS in the bed formation (horizontal) to rough cut, and then change out the diamond wheel (which removes material quite quickly, so care must be taken) and put on a polished ceramic wheel with a diamond spray to give it a smooth mirror finish that will transfer to the facets of the cuts for guilloché. It should be noted that even the tiniest pit in the cutter—from a grain of sand, to a dust sized ding, and even a small bit of rust—if not corrected immediately

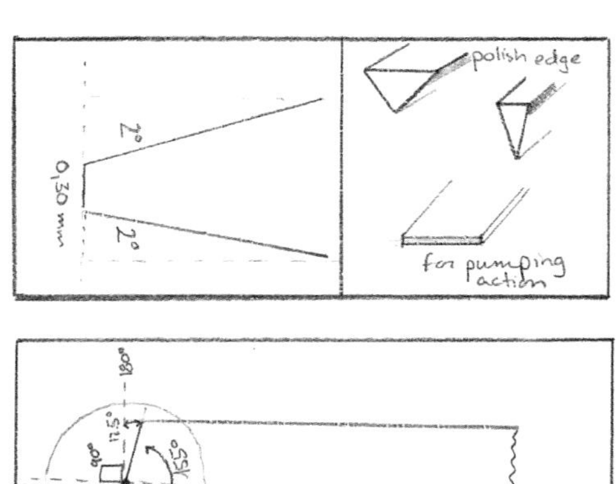

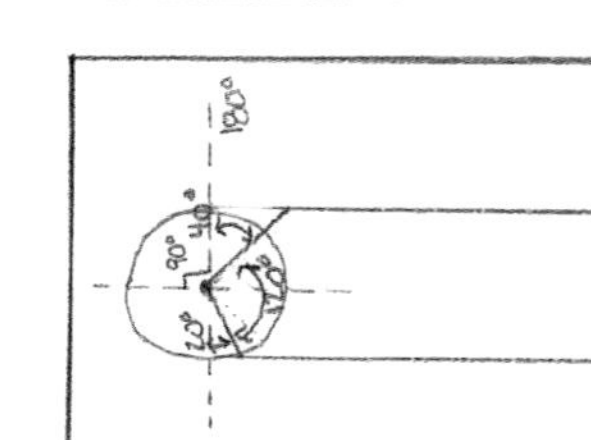

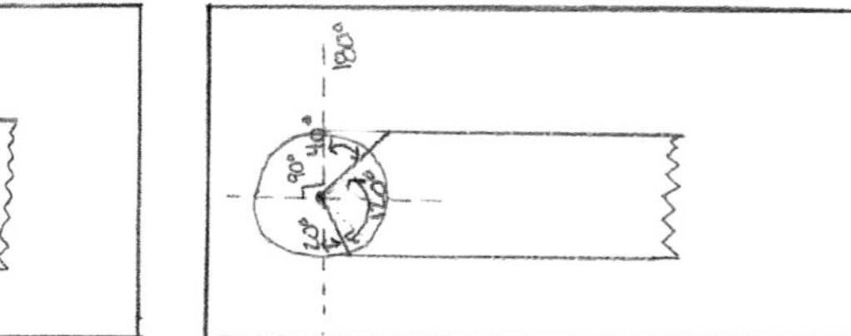

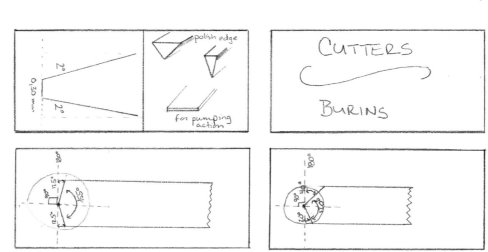

Some math pertaining to cutter sharpening and sensibility. *Calina Shevlin*

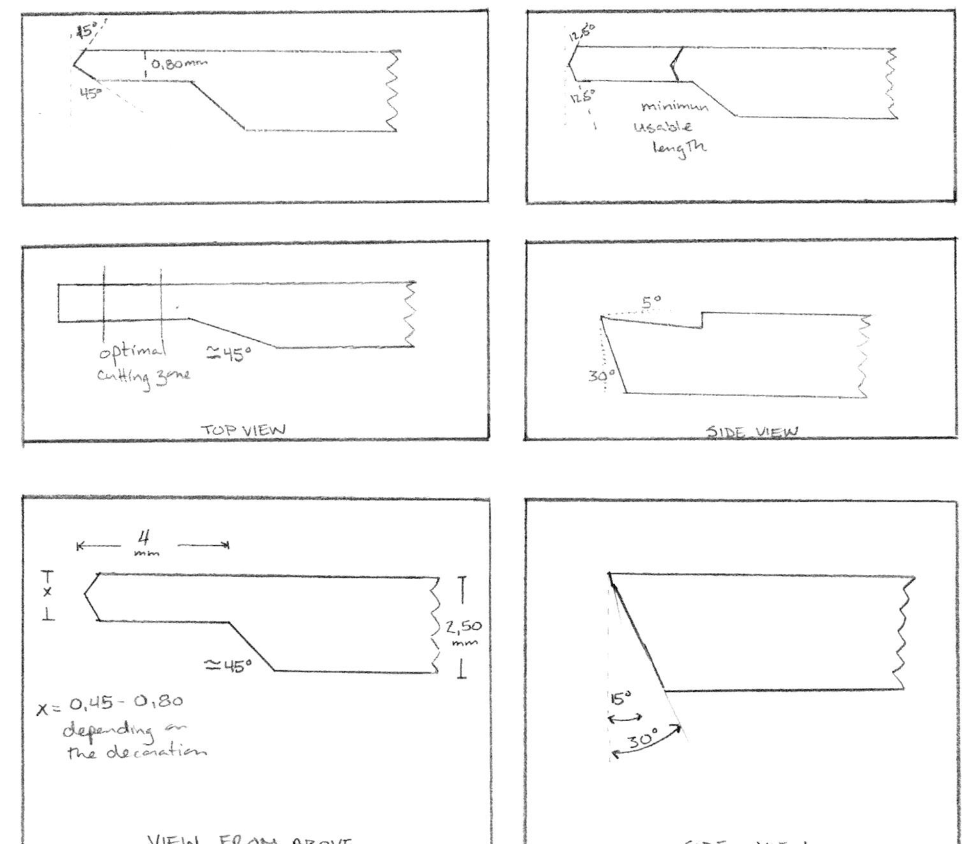

Common cutter shapes and radii. *Calina Shevlin*

will be a glaring scar once cutting begins, so due diligence is of the utmost importance. As stated previously, the object of guilloché is to incise lines into a metallic surface that act as facets that reflect and bounce light off of them, producing a pattern that does not actually exist. I also use a binocular for sharpening; I stop frequently and check my angles and finish on the highest power possible.

I find it best practice to sharpen many different cutters of a low quality just to get the feel for what you are doing; these are not throwaways, but rather test cutters you can try out to see what went wrong or really succeeded well, so it becomes muscle memory or habit and is easier to do in a short amount of time with future sharpening. As for practice sharpened cutters, I recommend using red or yellow brass until you are comfortable with your newly acquired skills, preventing the destruction of a precious metal such as silver, gold, or platinum.

Now let us turn our attention to the angles of cutters and their importance to the cut. I will start with a 90° parallel cutter and move to a 35° cutter. The flat cutter is for use with the pumping action. This is sharpened like a knife point and still has a mirror finish.

This is mostly used to make borders; I have not seen any other innovative uses, but have designed several samples using this method while using more than one rosette. It is a trying experiment, but I am hoping to eventually find a beautiful new pattern. This 90° cutter is used in conjunction with the rosettes like any other cutter, the difference being that the pumping action requires the rubber to rest on its face, rather than the normal side. This limits the patterns available from the original rosettes, but there is hope for current rosettes with endless possibilities.

While this type of cutter is the most prone to breakage, it is also the easiest to sharpen because you do not have to have two equal length and angled sides—just one. The toughest part is holding the cutter perfectly straight; with the aid of the goniostat or an angled stand it is easier, but also not perfect every time. Perhaps you are looking to make a decoration that is widely spaced with a shallow and wide cut. Some patterns that fit this description are the clous de Paris and clous de Dallas, as well as the clous de triangle.

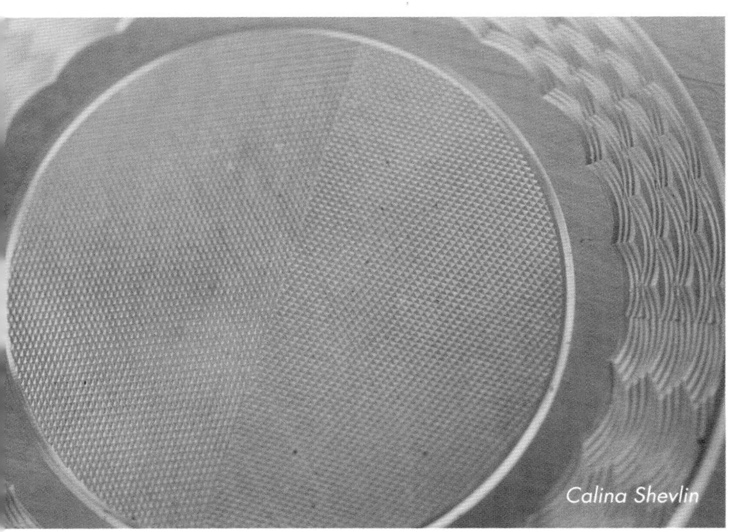

Calina Shevlin

Using just the tip of the 12.5° cutter yields an extremely fine pattern almost indiscernible to the naked eye. *Calina Shevlin*

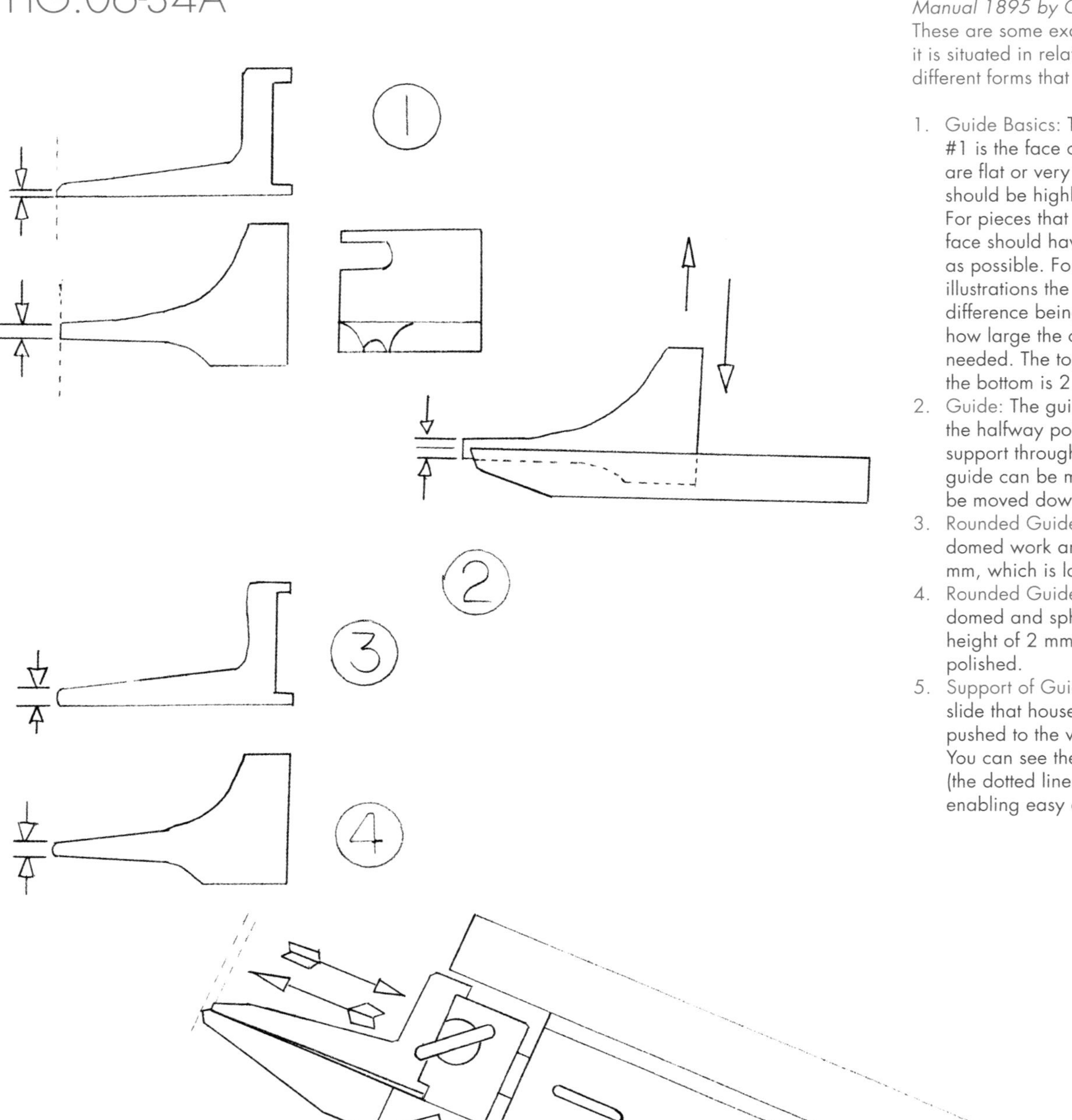

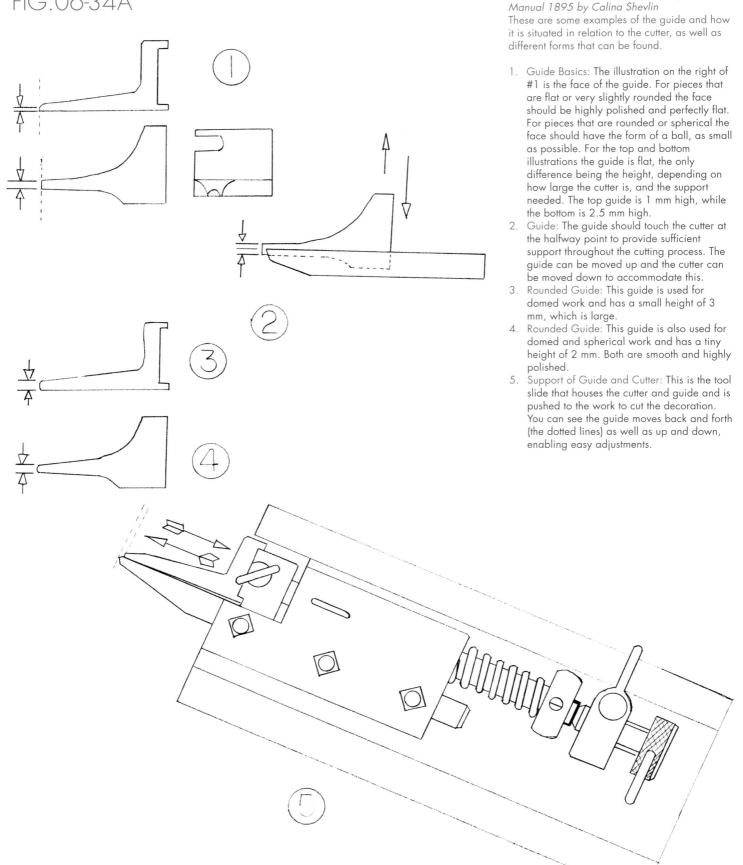

Illustration re-drawn from Lienhard Operators Manual 1895 by Calina Shevlin

These are some examples of the guide and how it is situated in relation to the cutter, as well as different forms that can be found.

1. Guide Basics: The illustration on the right of #1 is the face of the guide. For pieces that are flat or very slightly rounded the face should be highly polished and perfectly flat. For pieces that are rounded or spherical the face should have the form of a ball, as small as possible. For the top and bottom illustrations the guide is flat, the only difference being the height, depending on how large the cutter is, and the support needed. The top guide is 1 mm high, while the bottom is 2.5 mm high.
2. Guide: The guide should touch the cutter at the halfway point to provide sufficient support throughout the cutting process. The guide can be moved up and the cutter can be moved down to accommodate this.
3. Rounded Guide: This guide is used for domed work and has a small height of 3 mm, which is large.
4. Rounded Guide: This guide is also used for domed and spherical work and has a tiny height of 2 mm. Both are smooth and highly polished.
5. Support of Guide and Cutter: This is the tool slide that houses the cutter and guide and is pushed to the work to cut the decoration. You can see the guide moves back and forth (the dotted lines) as well as up and down, enabling easy adjustments.

Another example of shallow but fine cuts: clous de Paris and clous de Dallas. *Calina Shevlin*

These all require pointed peaks at the top, and a wide cutter aids in taking off just enough material; with successive cuts this becomes exact, leaving just a point. If you are looking to make a pattern that is more complex or the rosette/pattern bar is deeper than a divot (as with the toile patterns), you may want a much finer cutter with a point that is deeper on the cutter and can produce deep and angled cuts, or use just the very tip to create very fine patterns.

Changing of the burin for up-keep, rather than a break or other accident, should happen as soon as you notice cuts becoming less brilliant as you continue with your work. I have heard people change the cutter after one to two pieces (consisting of one pattern on an entire watch dial), but there are also those that almost never change it unless absolutely necessary. I strive to be a little closer to the obsessive side of things and change the burin just before it dulls. I know this sounds difficult, but each cutter has its own life-span per sharpening, and with lots of repetition you start to get to know the cutters you sharpen and can estimate about how many pieces, what patterns, and so on, and can gauge the need to change before its too late. A guide is next to the cutter and helps prevent the cutter from digging in too deeply. The guide can be flat or slightly rounded and is always highly polished.

One of the fastest ways to dull a cutter is to cut steel and not change the cutter, and then continue on to a softer metal. Often steel has guilloché applied to it to create a stamp (usually to the end of quality bar stock) that in turn will be able to create hundreds of guilloché stampings. To tell the difference between stamped and real guilloché look for facets. The "facets" from stamped guilloché are the same texture as the base metal—not facets at all. Not only will steel dull the cutter and make it undesirable for cutting a soft metal without sharpening, but now the cutter will contaminate the softer metal, leaving traces of cut steel on it. This is mostly a problem if enameling afterward or doing any kind of heat treatment such as soldering.

Alignment of the Work Piece

I cannot emphasize enough that if you change the cutter, you absolutely must remember it is essential to realign the machine. If needed, write a note on a piece of paper and stick it to the machine, or the box of cutters, or wherever you need. Good cutter care and regular sharpening will keep your tools going longer; therefore, this is better for production work. When I say "production work," I do not mean to simply imply mass quantities of the same thing, but rather a piece that is *produced*.

To adjust the headstock (and thus the piece attached to it) after changing a burin you need to know where the four screws on the sides of the headstock are.

These four screws will center the work up and down and left and right, along the x and y axis. When centering I find the center of the work first and make a tiny mark with a thin punch; this helps rather than just eyeballing the piece and going from side to side to see if it is even. I have seen people

This shows the screws used to align the work with the new cutter. *G. Phil Poirier*

FIG.06-35A

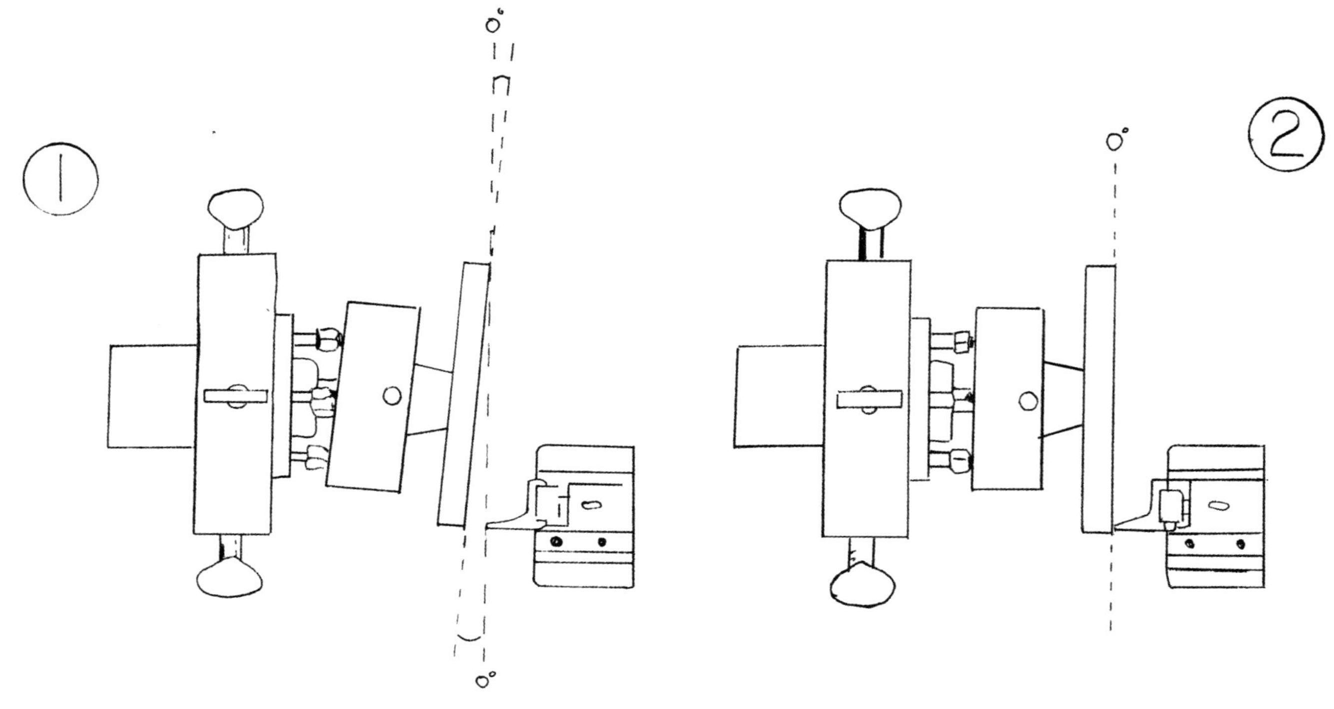

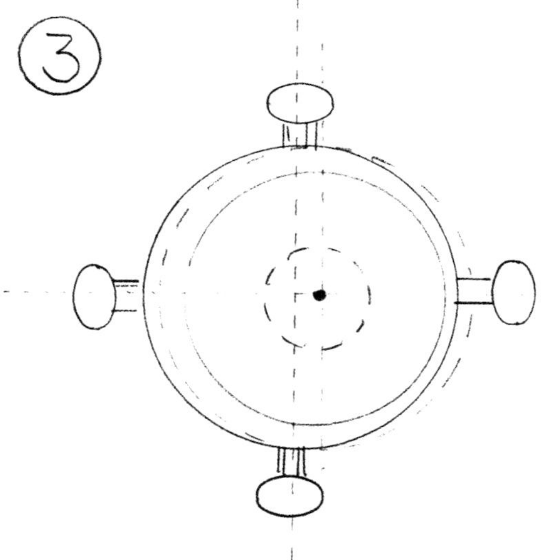

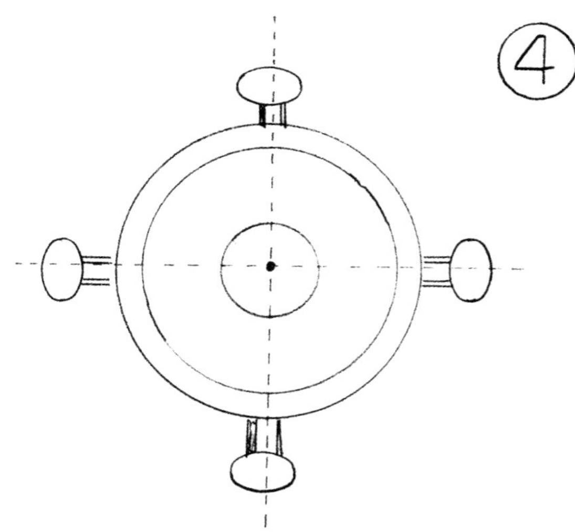

Illustration re-drawn from Lienhard Operators Manual 1895 by Calina Shevlin

These images depict the tilt of the headstock on which the flat work is attached. If the stock is not flat the cutter will not touch the bottom and will touch the top, so if the piece is rotated the pattern will only appear on roughly ¼ of the piece. This is why it is very important to use the cutter to center and align the headstock with the cutter, as some pieces may not be as flat as you believe.

1. Tilted Headstock: This is the depiction of an out-of-true headstock with the cutter not touching a good portion of the work piece.
2. Aligned Headstock: The headstock is well aligned in this depiction.

Not only is the tilt important, but also the alignment of left to right and top to bottom.

3. Misalignment: The work is not centered in the ring. The four screws can be changed to remedy this problem. To lower the piece, tighten the top screw and so forth. If you need to move left 1 mm you would tighten the right screw 0.5 mm to make up the difference between the two sides. This can sometimes be challenging at first but becomes easy with practice.
4. Aligned: This shows the work centered with the four screws.

use tools that mount to the headstock like a regular piece to be worked and have a point (much like an awl tip) protruding from its center. This is really tops in centering, but care must be taken to back the tool slide up before starting, or you will tap the point (usually steel) with the cutter and need to change it before you even start to work (see opposite).

What is nice about the point is that once you decide how you would like the piece to be you can mount a point off-center so you can center the machine to other areas (using an eccentric chuck of course) to start the pattern elsewhere. You could even make a movable point to quite easily change the area of centrality for the point. This tool (which does not yet exist) would be really good to make to ensure supreme accuracy. Now, sometimes the angle of the newly sharpened cutter is slightly lopsided (pointing more upward or downward so the degree of elevation is off a bit). This will affect the work to be cut, so this also needs to be taken into account. To adjust the machine on the z axis, the four screws *behind* the headstock need to be located. This is the same for any straight-line. There are four screws behind the main plate for the Güdel, and for other straight-line machines there is one screw that tilts the plate forward or backward on a centerline.

This is the screw for tilting the headstock on a straight-line to align with a new burin, or to accommodate a form that is not perfectly flat. *G. Phil Poirier*

These screws are quite sensitive and need very little pressure to change considerably. These essentially push the top or bottom of the work out in small increments until the piece is flush with the cutter. This involves checking the top and bottom distance to the cutter with the naked eye (aided with an optical device), as well as rotating the piece 45°, then another 45°, and so on, and checking to make sure the distance top to bottom is equal all around. This is a bit time consuming, so ensuring the cutter is aligned well when sharpening is a big time saver in the long run. I like to live by the measure twice (or thrice) and cut once rule. Once one of these four screws is tightened a miniscule amount the opposite must be loosened an equal miniscule amount. This requires lots of work and patience, but the finished piece will be fantastic.

While making all of these adjustments the cutter remains fixed and should only be moved along the x and y axes while tilting the work to ensure accuracy with distances and so forth.

Pumping Action

Pumping action refers to the machine's direction or axis of movement. For regular engine turning, a pattern is cut into a flat or three-dimensional piece of metal with a fixed tool and the piece is rotated on the x axis. For pumping action, a leaf spring or some sort of tension device is changed over from holding tension on the x axis to holding tension on the z axis. This means instead of the headstock rotating with the rubber on the side and creating side movement the rubber will be resting on the face of the rosette, creating a front to back movement.

The pumping action is used to create patterns on the side going up to the curve of three-dimensional objects, as well as a more pronounced texture on two-dimensional surfaces. This is mostly seen on watch dials, the rings that separate

Plant rose engine set up for pumping action. *Calina Shevlin*

patterns, or the different parts of the dials called sub-dials. The cutter for two-dimensional pumping cutting is different than a regular cutter: for the regular cutter, the end is triangular for cutting a fillet type shape, but for the pumping action the cutter has a flat tip that is parallel with the surface being cut and can be thought of as more like a gouging in and out action. This type of tool is only effective on a two-dimensional surface such as a watch dial, because the cutting of an egg form or other surface entails the use of a regular cutter.

For the creation of three-dimensional pieces the angle of the tool slide must be rotated 90° and slowly returned to the

FIG.06-36A

Illustration re-drawn from Lienhard Operators Manual 1895 by Calina Shevlin
Top view of a rose engine set up for pumping action.

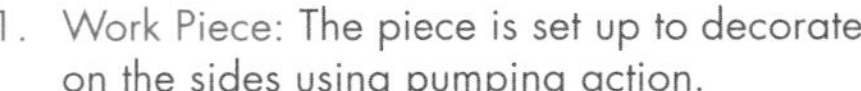

1. Work Piece: The piece is set up to decorate on the sides using pumping action.
2. Tool Slide: This is moved 90° to accommodate the pumping action that will allow for the decoration on the side of a box, cylinder, etc.
3. Leaf Spring: The spring on the side of the rose engine is engaged for pumping action while the leaf spring at the end of the headstock is disengaged to take away the rocking action.
4. Rubber: The rubber is positioned on the side of the rosette created for the pumping action.

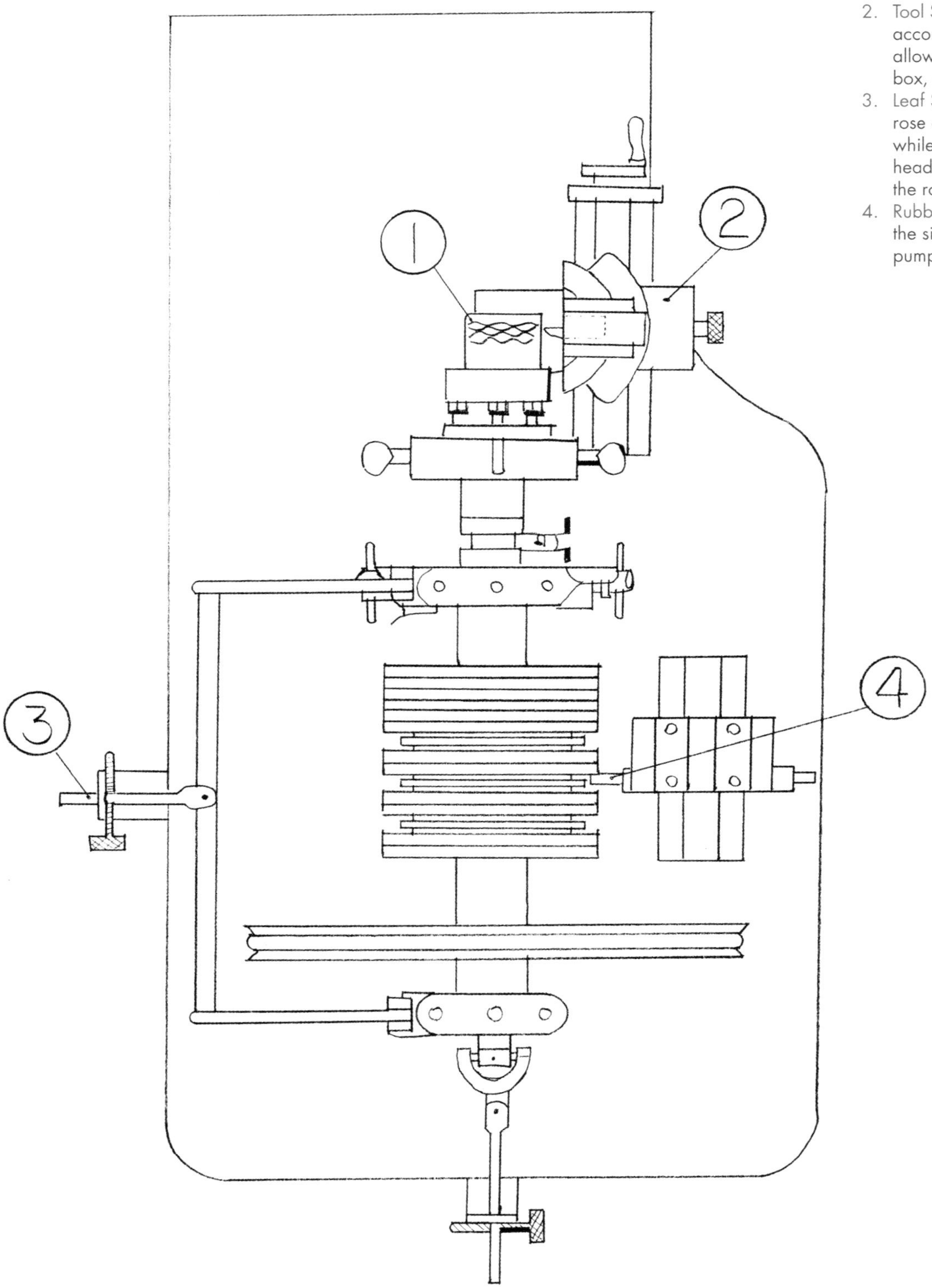

FIG.06-38A

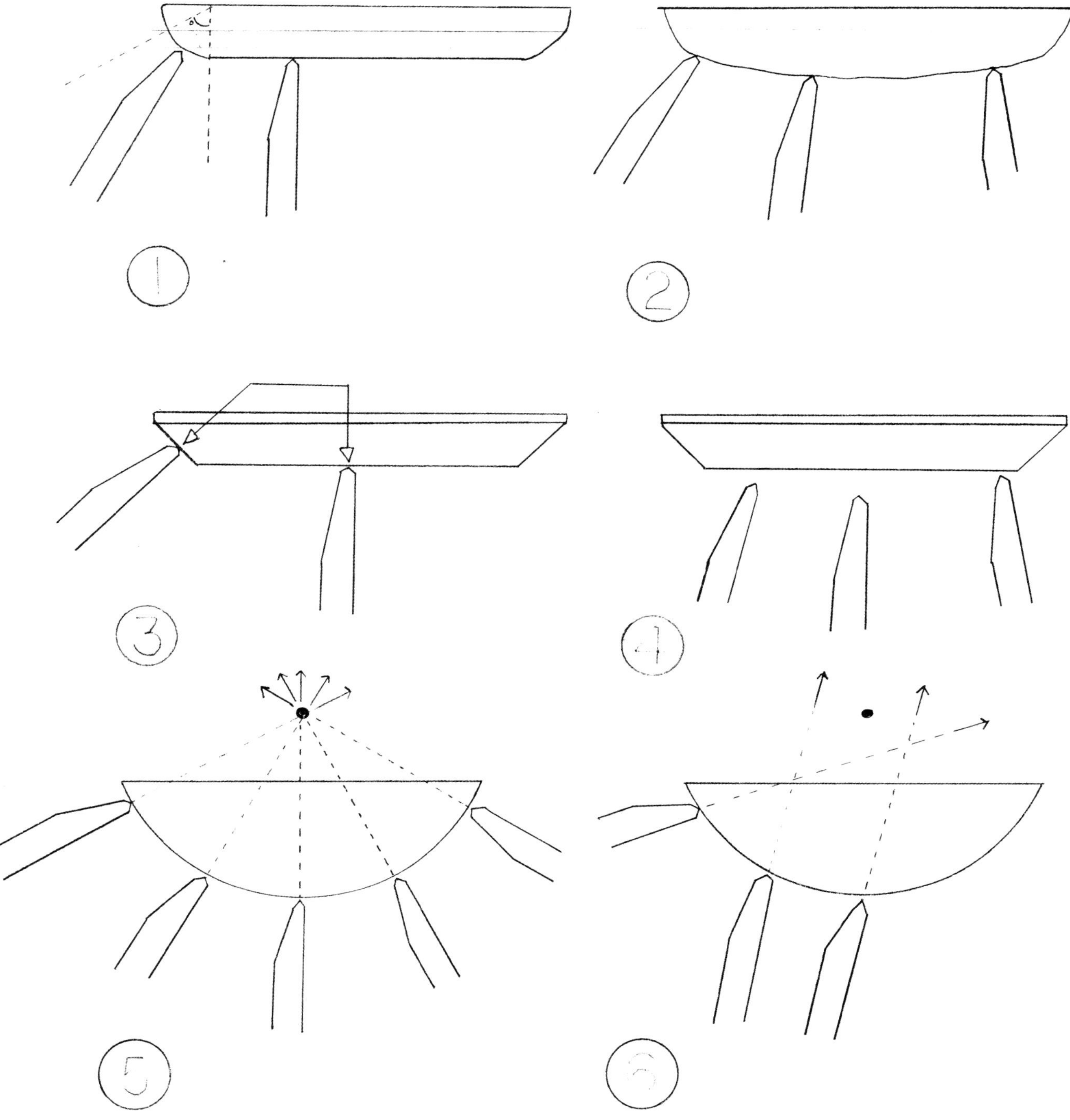

Illustration re-drawn from Lienhard Operators Manual 1895 by Calina Shevlin
These illustrations show the ratio of work piece to cutter centering. With a well centered cutter the work will have even cuts throughout.

1. Curved edges: It is important to make sure the cutter is aligned at the corners, as well as the flat work.
2. Rounded edges, Rounded surface: The cutter will need to change for each part of the surface.
3. Flat with Beveled edges: The cutter will ultimately have two positions for this piece: the bevels and the flat. This is an easy three-dimensional piece to start out with.
4. Flat with Beveled edges: Cutter centering through each portion.
5. Rounded: Well centered at every step.
6. Rounded: Misaligned at every step.

When working on three-dimensional pieces make sure to take your time and really center the cutter; this will save countless hours of heartache.

FIG.06-38B

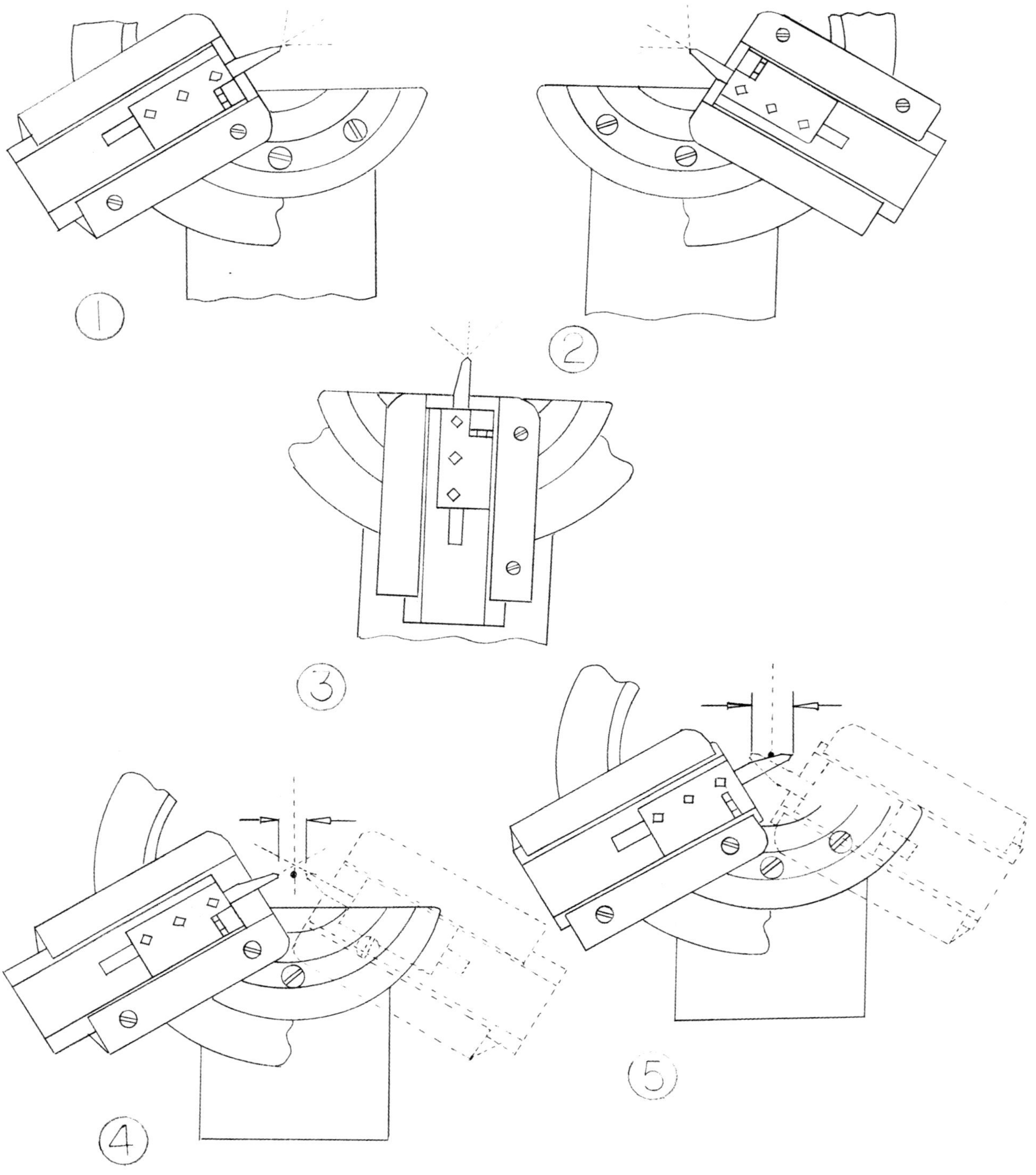

Illustration re-drawn from Lienhard Operators Manual 1895 by Calina Shevlin

Position of the tool slide when trying to center the cutter for any type of work. This is a fantastic beginning skill to practice until it feels natural.

1. Left: With the tool slide to the left work on centering the cutter to a center point that can be drawn on, punched in, drilled out, or an attached literal point.
2. Right: With the tool slide to the right, center the cutter.
3. Center: Center to the center as well as to the sides; the more you practice the easier it is.
4. Short of Center: If the cutter does not reach the center on the right side it will not reach on the left side. The sides are equal.
5. Over shot Center: If the cutter overshoots the target on one side it will be the same on the other side.

The differences in distances will be the left plus the right; if the left side is off by only 0.5 mm then the total difference from the center will be 1.0 mm. This does not seem so big, but in guilloché it is huge.

The areas being cut and around the dial and sub-dial were created with pumping action. This pattern is often called Liseret. *G. Phil Poirier*

starting point. This tool slide must be moved and aligned by hand along the exterior angle of the piece that is being decorated with guilloché. As can be seen (p 73), the cutter needs to align perfectly with a central imaginary point at each position or the piece will not turn out with even guilloché.

This is never an exact science and relies heavily on good vision, judgment, concentration, and above all else attention to detail and the changes needed to ensure an evenly spaced decoration. The change of each degree is accomplished entirely with the use of the pawl and eyeballing the angle change. There is a component on the tool slide that is similar to the worm, but it does not have a 360° radius, only 180°. With this tool slide it is necessary to center the tool at every angle before beginning, allowing for the piece being worked on to have a nice even pattern. The following are tips on centering (p 74), where you can see common problems in centering.

The division for this Plant straight-line is the handle in the upper right. *G. Phil Poirier*

It is with this component that one is able to turn the tool slide to accomplish work on, say, an egg form. There is also a component used to fine tune the angle, but it has limited capabilities, for one must already be close to the location of the cut.

If decorating a ring, napkin holder, or side of a box, one would need to move the tool slide 90° and then use the smaller radius to make finer adjustments or to fine tune the setting if the piece was not 100% evenly surfaced and could then begin cutting.

The old rosettes—the original rosettes for any given machine—are limited in what can be created with pumping action, but new rosettes are beginning to appear with pumping action and now the possibilities are becoming greater. Something to think about is that pumping action on a flat two-dimensional surface is not terribly varied from one rosette to the next, but is simply closer together or more spaced apart. When creating decorations on a three-dimensional surface, the patterns are just as can be seen with a rosette on a regular flat surface, but the cutter will be different.

Up to this point all patterns have been created with the standard and most basic equipment found with old rose engines and the standard chuck attached to the headstock directly, with no bells or whistles.

Standard rose engine headstock. *G. Phil Poirier*

Methods of Attaching Pieces to the Headstock or Chuck

There are various tried and true methods of attaching a piece of work to the headstock or chuck. There are important factors, such as the type of work and whether it is three-dimensional or two-dimensional. Most, if not all, of these methods are employed today by the remaining practicing artisans. The machines on which I was fortunate to learn were equipped with a headstock with circular plate and four screws to hold the (flat) work in place by squeezing it down. This wonder used tension to hold the piece, and while there was

This is a chuck for holding the work by placing it between an outer ring and a flat base and screwing it down. This sometimes leaves marks, so it is best if you are not using the entire piece and can spare the outer edge. *Calina Shevlin*

This is a chuck for holding the work in place with tension. Many different shapes of plates can be made to accommodate anything from hearts to discs to diamond shapes. The worker chooses the shape and makes a tension plate to fit under the four main screws on the face. *Calina Shevlin*

This straight-line uses wax to securely hold a large plate of brass. Wax is heated slightly with the thinnest coat on the headstock, then the piece is pressed firmly down and allowed to cool; to remove you do the opposite. *Teri Jo Kinnison*

little chance the piece would move, I find I now prefer this method to all of the others I have seen, mostly for its ease and lack of clean-up. With this tension it is easy to secure and release the work, and it is also easy to center the piece securely in place in the tension ring. This method may sometimes leave a small mark around the screws that has to be accounted for, but it is best if the outer regions of the piece of metal are not the highlight of the piece, or they will later be removed or covered up.

The second method is using shellac, wax, or pitch (jet plastic) to hold the work securely in place. This method is good if you want a piece that will not have extraneous marks on it and also helps ensure that the hold is maximum benefit with minimum risk. This is great if moving from engraving to guilloché, as most hand engravers also use these products to hold their pieces in place. Therefore these are good uses for long-term work, with multiple steps and guilloché as one of the last. Each of these substances is heated until it is pliable but not completely melted and boiling. Once the substance cools a bit (so you do not burn your hands) you can press the piece into the substance, being careful to ensure it is flat. The pitch, wax, shellac, or plastic is really just the thinnest layer. For example, when I use wax, I heat the tool that will hold the work to be decorated just a bit, and then touch it with the wax, keep it heated, press on the piece, and let it cool in a horizontal position.

Once the substance has cooled the work is securely attached and ready to mount on to the headstock. The down side to using these materials is that although flat, they may not be

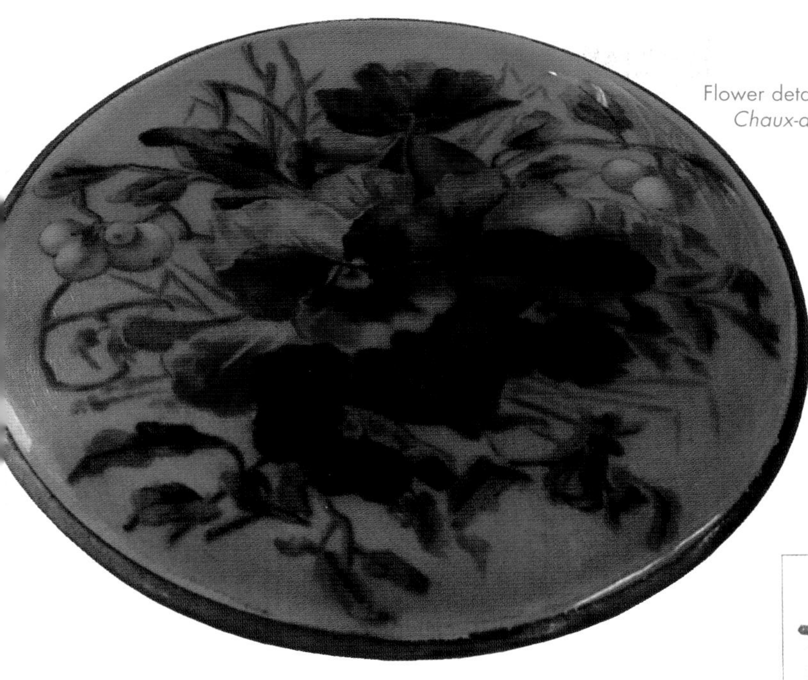

Flower detail. *Collection D'Arts Industriels De L'École D'Arts Appliqués, Ville de La Chaux-de-Fonds*

The guilloché on pocket watchcases was often two-fold. There was one pattern where the painted enamel would be applied, and then there was the pattern where the clouds, or even sometimes the lightest enamel with little painting over it, would be applied. The more interesting or difficult patterns were utilized for the more intricate areas—the areas where more guilloché would be visible—while the easier or more basic guilloché was applied to areas that were covered with more opaque or painted enamels.

Both of the axes are adjusted independently using something like a worm that moves in clockwise and counterclockwise fashion. If you would like to start a pattern in the bottom corner and come up, creating a sort of clamshell pattern, you would use the eccentric chuck. This was especially popular with watchcases and enameled decorations that involved scenes with clouds that were frequently enameled with an opalescent white, allowing the guilloché to appear faintly in the cloud formation.

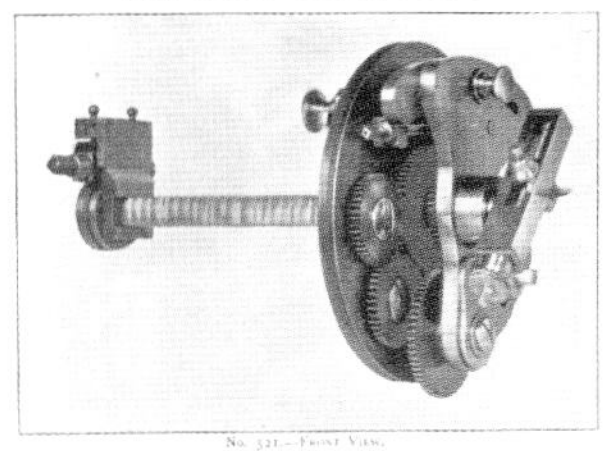

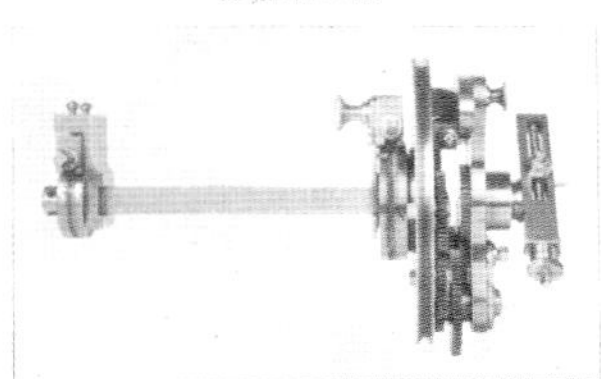

Epicycloidal cutting frame (first stage of the geometric chuck). *Calina Shevlin*

Epicycloidal Cutting Frame and Geometric Chuck

This brings us to another attachment and the most complex—the epicycloidal cutting frame. This chuck is the first stage of the geometric chuck and can create geometrically complex patterns in guilloché. This was the tool initially employed to create patterns on

Painted enamel flower over guilloché. *Collection D'Arts Industriels De L'École D'Arts Appliqués, Ville de La Chaux-de-Fonds*

William Britton Geometric Chuck. *David Wood-Heath*

money, but then countries moved to using other machines that were fabricated for just that purpose.

If the epicycloidal is added to the rose engine the possibilities are infinite. This attachment is what led people to liken guilloché to a Spirograph. This is a gross misstatement, but the Spirograph is a good learning tool for the interaction of gears, where there are 144 gears that can be used in conjunction for the entire geometric chuck. The story I have heard is that J. J. Ibbetson invented the geometric chuck and gave the prototype to John Jacob Holtzapffel to see if he had a chance of having this marvel manufactured, as Holtzapffel was the leading manufacturer in England at the time.

It is rumored Ibbetson was told it could not be manufactured, but then Holtzapffel proceeded to recreate the chuck in its entirety and produced it in

Geometric Chuck. *G. Phil Poirier*

Geometric Chuck. *G. Phil Poirier*

Geometric Chuck. *G. Phil Poirier*

Geometric Chuck. *G. Phil Poirier*

Geometric Chuck. G. *Phil Poirier*

his own name. As can be seen, this is a monster and was quite difficult to produce en masse at the time, so there were few originally manufactured—around eighty is the going estimate.

On the fully assembled geometric chuck not all of the gears are used together at one time; all 144 gears are

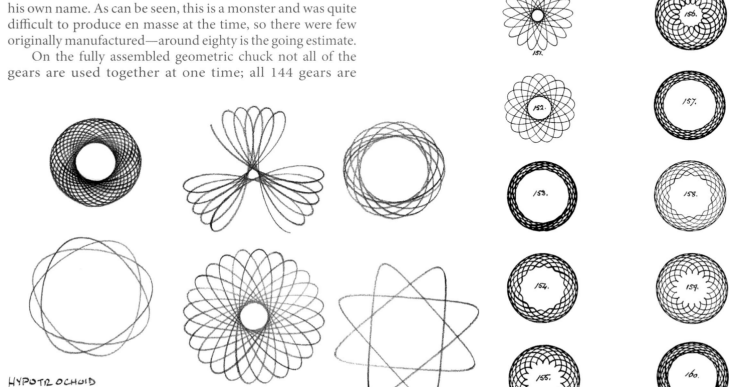

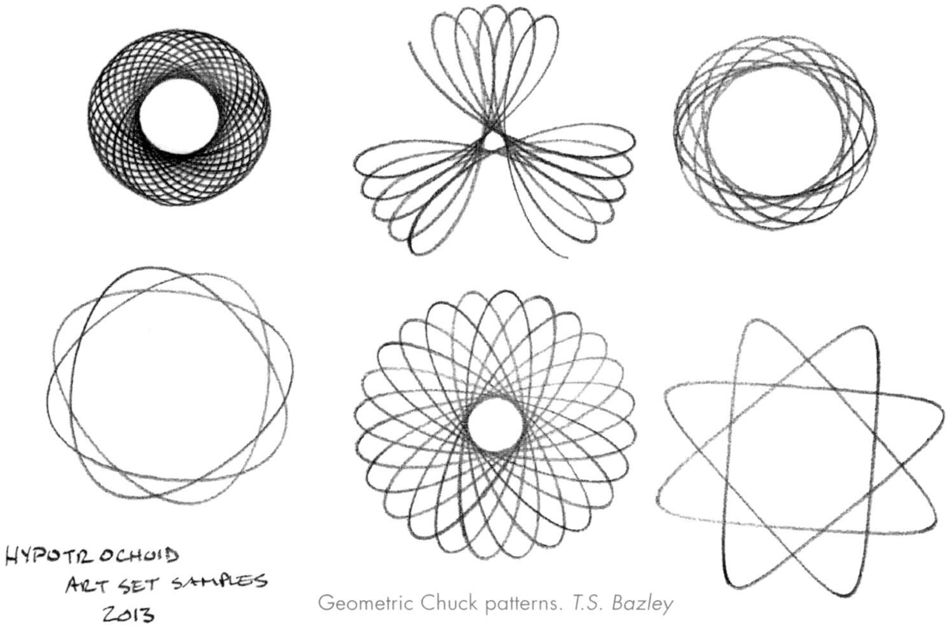

HYPOTROCHOID ART SET SAMPLES 2013

Geometric Chuck patterns. *T.S. Bazley*

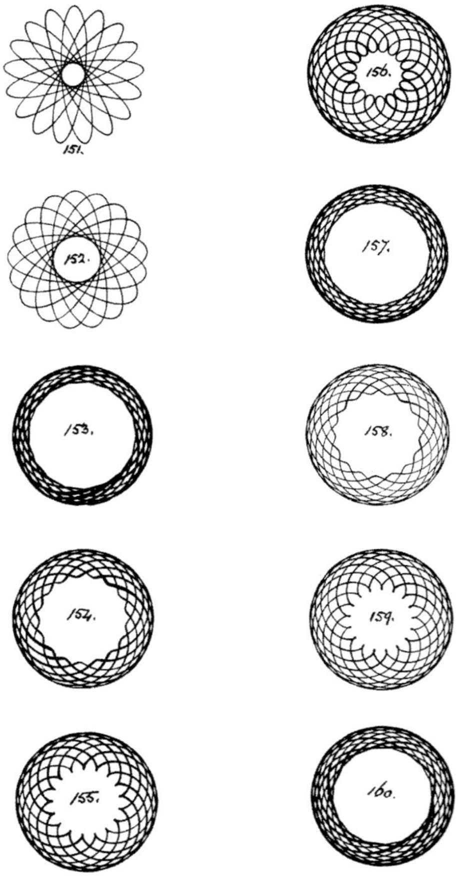

151. 152. 153. 154. 155. 156. 157. 158. 159. 160.

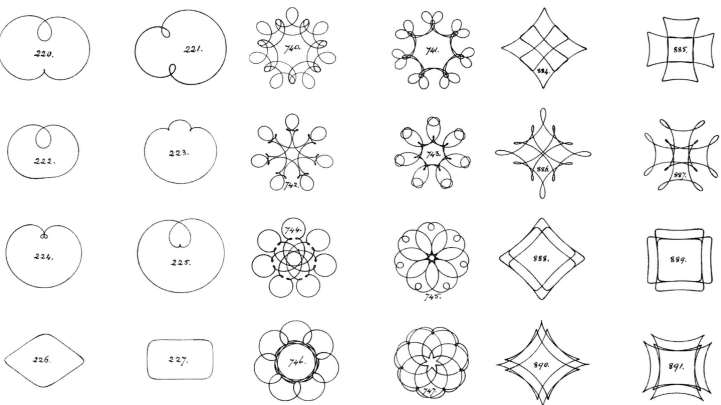

Geometric Chuck patterns. *T.S. Bazley*

interchangeable, depending on which part or parts will be put to use. There are several places on each of the stages of the geometric chuck where gears can be attached and fitted together to create the desired pattern. There is a book by T. S. Bazley that chronicles the various patterns (he includes pen and ink samples on paper made by holding a pen in place of the cutter) and gives examples of 3,500 different patterns. These are not all of the patterns that can be created—only what Bazley put to pen and paper. The book gives a sort of recipe section with a gallery of patterns to create a plethora of geometric patterns where you can choose what final décor you would like, and then look up the gears and their placement and how many stages you need. Personally, I find the book difficult to follow since it was written in 1875, with antiquated wording and lots of math I am not able to wrap my head around.

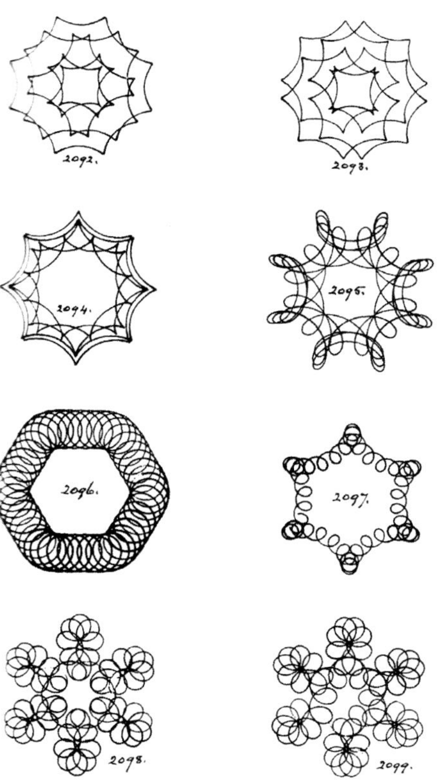

I have not seen a lot of patterning in guilloché with the geometric chuck from yesteryear or even now. This chuck is not a common or plentiful attachment for the rose engine. I know several people who own geometric chucks and who have made their own, but they do not utilize them very much for guilloché. What I *have* seen is people in the ornamental turning community using the geometric chuck to create beautiful designs in wood. Aside from the Bazley book, the information on geometric chucks and their stages was not widely available or passed down orally from master to apprentice; it was all self-learning and experimentation. As it is today, many people simply remembered the gears and ratios and when they died no one else knew the exact recipes to recreate certain patterns, so the patterns were again accidentally discovered. All of the people who have created or are currently creating geometric chucks are inadvertently repopulating the geometric chuck stock and I hope to see the innovators add new tweaks here and there to facilitate its use, and perhaps even exploit the capabilities in other fields—most notably ceramics. I name this field because it is rumored that Wedgewood used a rose engine to cut into his vases and bowls before firing. I have seen images at the Wedgewood museum, and I am not sure it was a rose engine that was used, but it must have been an ornamental turning lathe or some bastardization of one.

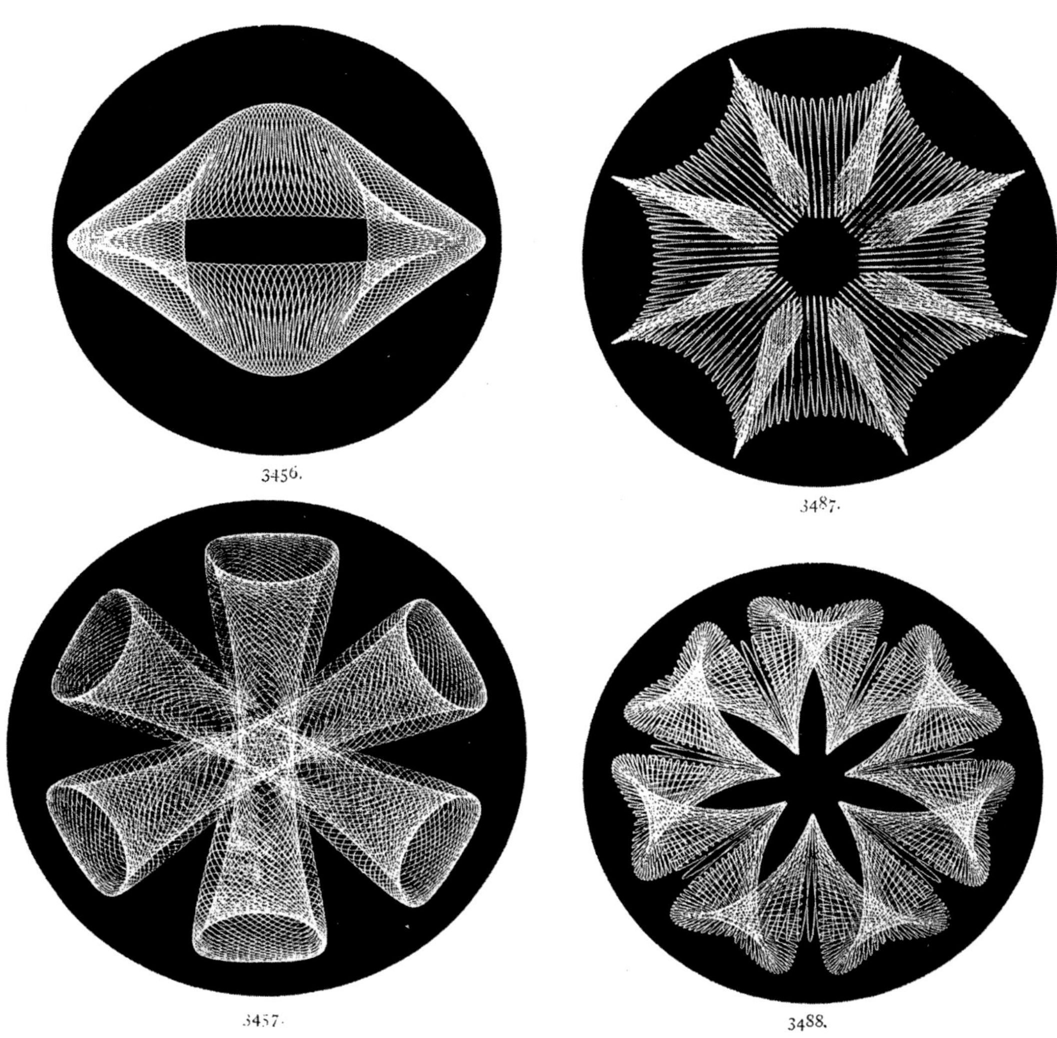

Geometric Chuck patterns. *T.S. Bazley*

CHAPTER 7

Pullout Map of a Rose Engine

Rose engine map with labeled parts. *Calina Shevlin*

A Leaf spring tension for regular action

B Rosettes

C Rubber/Touche holder

D Division plate

E Screw to relieve the weight off the rosettes and make simple circles (no pattern)

F Traversing tool slide

G 180° rotating tool slide (for domed or 3-D works)

H Cutter/Burin holder

I Work piece holder

J Worm

K Pawl

L Leaf spring tension for pumping action; and the drive train

CHAPTER 8
Pullout Map of a Straight-Line

The pattern bars of a straight-line machine are what the rosettes are to a rose engine. The original pattern bars for straight-line machines were cast as one piece and usually had six different patterns. These patterns could be used in conjunction with one another or individually for many different effects. There were pattern bars that were singles, doubles, and so on after the initial blocks. This means sometimes a bar is smaller than the support and extra steel is needed to block the pattern bar into place.

The pattern bars also have limitations, like the rosettes, as to the size of the rubber. When too large the pattern is scalloped like fish scale, and when too small it becomes elongated and scaly as well. The right rubber, which is 3⁄4 of the size of the trough, is the perfect size. We use 3⁄4 as a general rule because the rubber needs room to easily move from trough to trough, but not so much that it moves for some time in the trough before reaching the peak. If the rubber is too large it starts out touching the peaks and the pattern is not defined. You can find drawings of the perfect size in the following illustration (numbers 1–3).

The rubbers are not always rounded. They are often ground flat on the top and bottom and remain only slightly rounder at the end. Think of this as a sort of duckbill shape. This is because the pattern bars have much smaller diameters in the forms than a rosette (see numbers 6–7).

The headstock of the straight-line machine is capable of turning 360°, which lends itself to making a sunray pattern. There are several knobs and levers involved, but releasing the headstock from fixed straight up and down to the ray capability is relatively easy. You can see the headstock in its fixed position (opposite) and beginning to turn (p 95).

FIG.08-01A

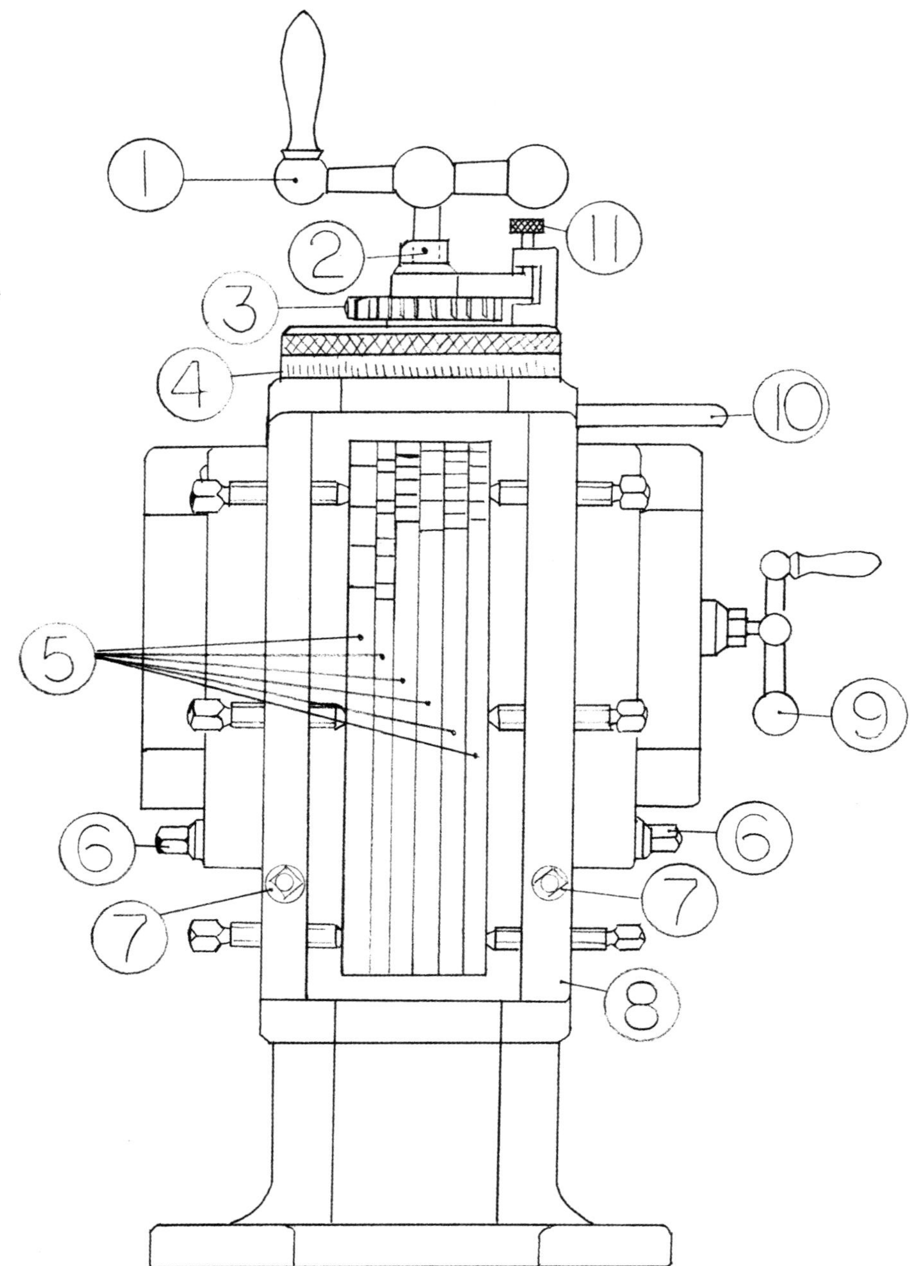

Illustration re-drawn from Lienhard Operators Manual 1895 by Calina Shevlin
View of the pattern bar support on a Lienhard straight-line machine.

1. Hand Crank: Used to turn the counter to displace the pattern bars up and down for indexing.
2. Nut: Used to block the hand crank.
3. Counter: Used for measuring the distance turned by counting the clicks.
4. Counter: Used to measure the distance of turns.
5. Pattern Bars: This is a typical six bar stock made from one large piece of steel.
6. Screws: These are used to block the bar support in place and prevent slippage and tilting of the frame.
7. Screw: Used to perfectly align the frame with the pattern bar.
8. Frame: Used to block the pattern bar to reproduce certain designs in guilloché. This piece is lightly inclinable and allows the pattern bars to be perfectly vertically aligned.
9. Hand Crank: Used to displace the pattern bars horizontally, usually if there are different sizes being used (i.e., you have five individual bars: one is taken away, so the other four need to be centered horizontally).
10. Broche: Used to tighten or loosen the mount for the pattern bars.
11. Stop Pin: Used to block the counter in place for patterns that do not need it.

FIG.08-02

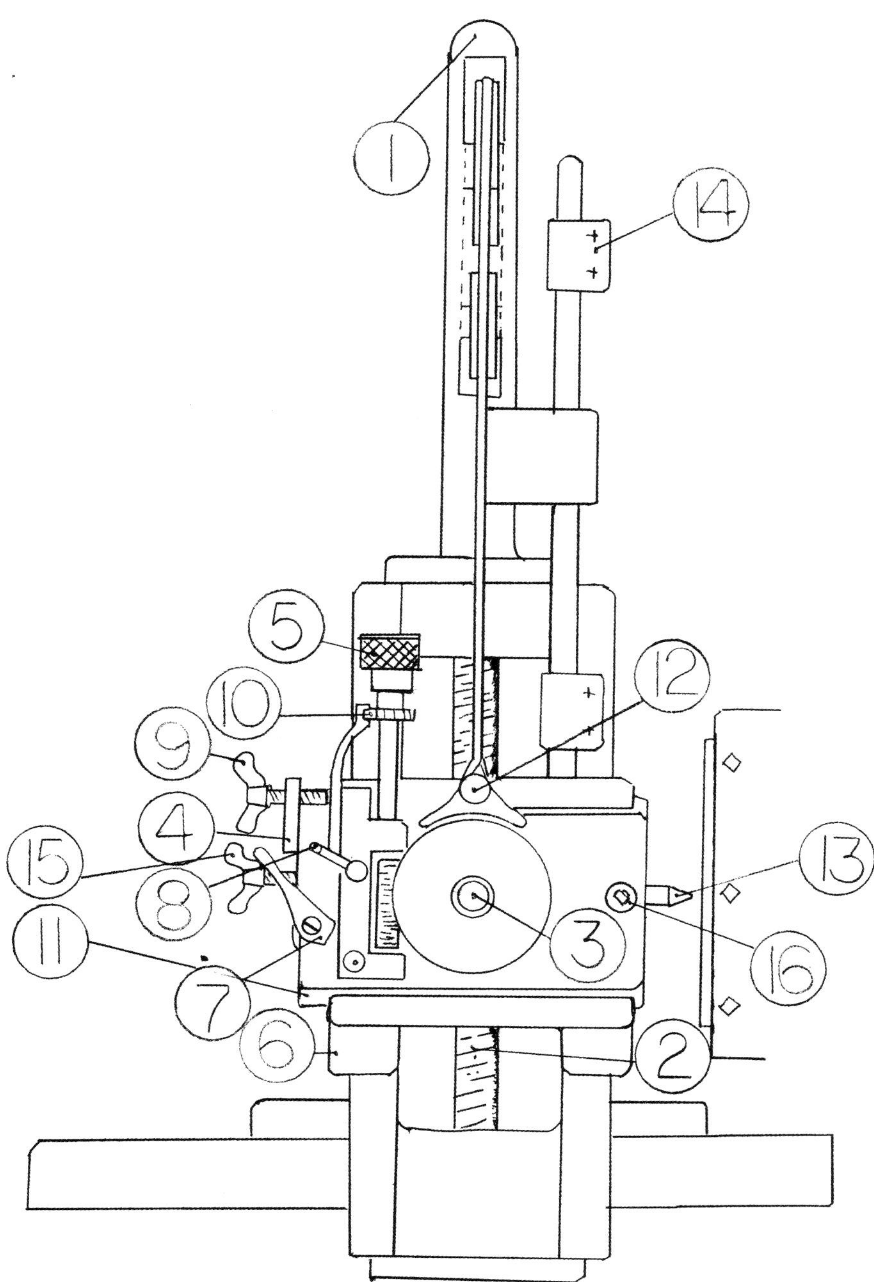

Illustration re-drawn from Lienhard Operators Manual 1895 by Calina Shevlin
Here is a front view of a Lienhard straight-line machine.

1. Roller Bed: This supports the two rollers (pulleys) that pass the cords with the counter weights.
2. Screw: This meshes against a bronze nut and is intended to move the slide upward; it is the screw that drives the pulley.
3. Pulley Throat: This operates with screw number 2 and is connected to the groove of the pulley and the cranks by a round cord.
4. Support and Block: Supports and blocks the stop screw #9.
5. Worm: Allows re-dressing the guilloché objects and is desirable in obtaining parallel lines with small incremental adjustments. The cutter is aligned with the desired cut and the worm is turned until the cutter is re-aligned with the cut.
6. Rising Slide: Displaced with screw #2, where we find the pulley throat. It acts the same as a crank.
7. Lever: This lever meshes with the worm. To block the worm the lever is pressed down; to unblock it is simply lifted. When the worm is free the piece is able to move freely.
8. Screw: Serves to block the piece supported by the worm.
9. Stop Screw: Permits the traversing slide to be lifted from the pattern bars so the rubber does not rub, allowing for straight lines with no pattern.
10. Counter: Serves principally to vary the cuts in the Sunray patterns. A set of these types of counters can be found with each machine.
11. Traversing Slide: Should always be free moving with regular maintenance. This is what allows for patterns to be reproduced following the pattern bars.
12. Screw: Supports the counterweight.
13. Rubber: Runs along the pattern bar to create the decorations. It can be blocked in the raised position (to the left) by tightening screw #16.
14. Stops: Used for the desired length of the beginning and end of the decoration. If you wish to stop each line on a horizontal line adjust the stop to block the vertical movement where you want.
15. Screw: Gives the spring tension to the traversing slide against the pattern bars, ensuring a constant contact. This tension should always be regulated to a medium force—not too much and not too little.
16. Screw: Blocks the rubber #13 and prevents it from returning, under spring tension, to the pattern bar. This is employed when making straight sunrays, striped patterns, and any other patterns where the pattern bars are not used.

FIG.08-03

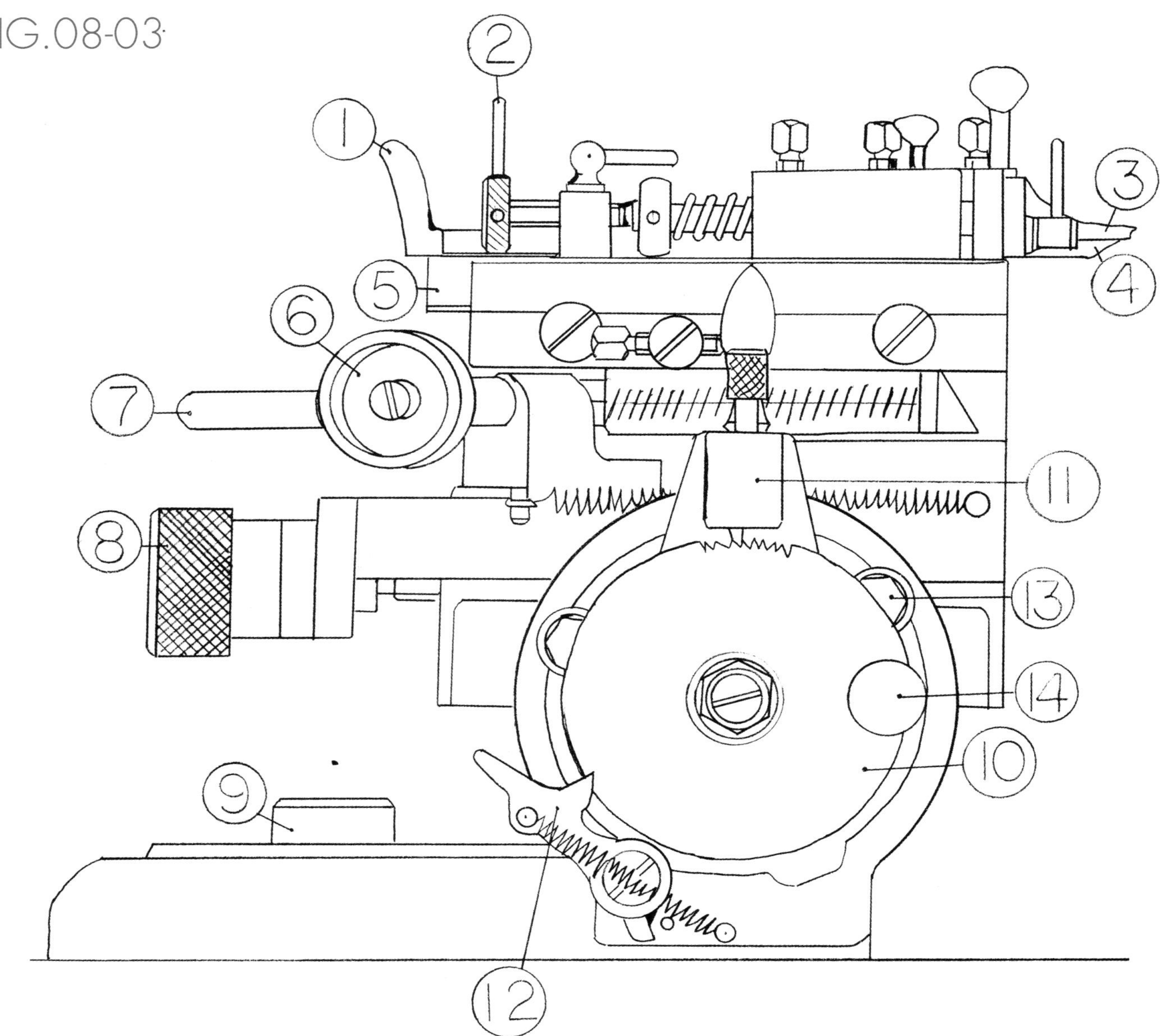

Illustration re-drawn from Lienhard Operators Manual 1895 by Calina Shevlin
This is the side view of the rubber/guide and pawl pieces of a Lienhard straight-line machine.

1. Pusher: Pushes the cutter against the work to create the necessary pressure. It is operated with the right hand and needs to have a very regular pressure. This comes with experience.
2. Screw: Serves to displace the guide, allowing for shallower or deeper guilloché on a piece. These are often replaced with modern screws like those on micrometer calipers. The new screws allow for very precise depths, but as with all things can be over-ridden with too much pressure as the machine has give.
3. Guide: Often pronounced in the French manner "geed"; a steel piece that can be straight or rounded and is highly polished (see p 72). The guide rubs the work piece and leaves a polished mark called a black mark. This should lightly rub the work and not disfigure it, as its purpose is to guide the cutter and give support to avoid vibrations in the cutter.
4. Cutter: This cuts the metal. It is fixed while the work turns. There are different types of sharpening produce cutters used for different patterns (see p 67).
5. Half-Moon Slide: Serves to move the superior part of the slide to center the cutter to the work. It is operated with worm #6.
6. Worm: A small worm with the sole purpose of moving the half-moon slide and centering.
7. Brooch: Withdraws the worm, allowing the free displacement of the half-moon to find the center. This is used when there is a large distance to find and the worm to refine.
8. Centering Screw: Advances and pulls back the half-moon to find the exact center of a cutter.
9. Nut: Blocks the support entirely.
10. Toothed Wheel (of the Pawl): Divided into 120 teeth, generally with each tooth equaling 0.0125 mm. This allows the distance between cuts to be exact and also helps recreate patterns exactly.
11. Pawl: Allows for exact displacement of each cut of guilloché.
12. Counter Ratchet (Pawl): Frees the pawl from connection and can be turned freely to return to the starting point easily to start another piece; for the nail head pattern, it allows return to start to begin the second portion of the pattern.
13. Screw: Can be loosened and allows the worker to set the pawl at the desired number of clicks. If I mention moving the pawl fourteen clicks, instead of counting fourteen tiny clicks this screw can be set at the fourteen clicks and then the operator knows one pull of the pawl is fourteen clicks.
14. Hand Crank: Used to operate the pawl.

FIG.08-04

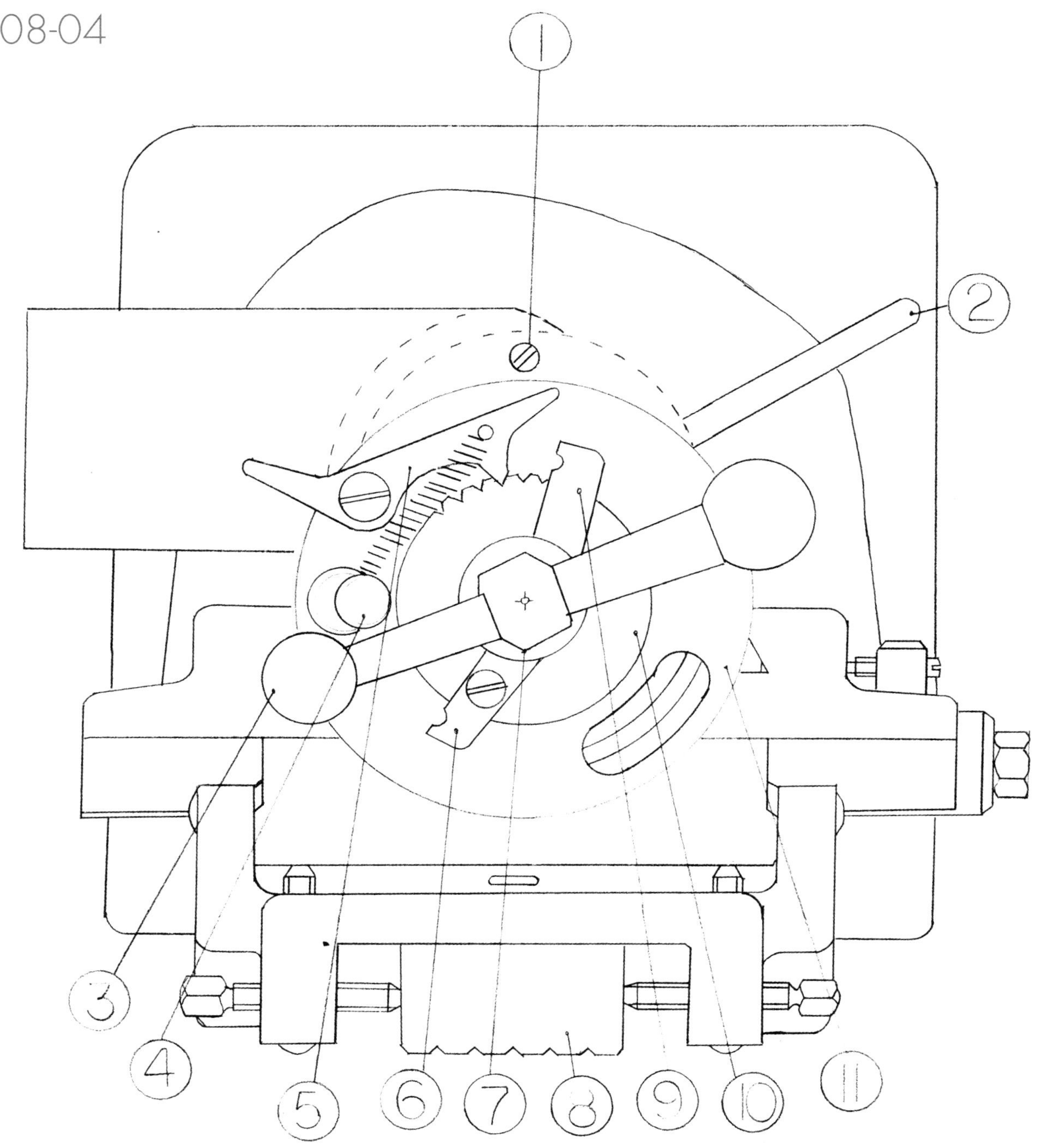

Illustration re-drawn from Lienhard Operators Manual 1895 by Calina Shevlin
Top view of the support for the pattern bars.

1. Grease Receptacle: Where the grease is applied to keep the support running smoothly.
2. Brooch: This lever is what blocks the counter, #11.
3. Hand Crank: Displaces the pattern bar vertically.
4. Stop Pin: What the stops (#6 and #9) butt against.
5. Ratchet: This is used to count the teeth of the counter. It is under a tension spring and works much like the division counter.
6. Fixed Stop: Tightened at the start to regulate the stopping point in advance.
7. Nut: Used to block the adjustable stop in the position desired (#9).
8. Pattern Bar: This can be anywhere from a single bar, a medium bar with three separate patterns, or the standard in the 1800s of one large block of steel with six individual patterns.
9. Adjustable Stop: Moves at will to get the exact coordinates needed for some designs, often in the middle of the pattern bar.
10. Counter: Divided in fifty parts, where one part is equal to 0.06 mm displacement. This acts much like the pawl.
11. Counter: Divided in 100 parts, where one part is equal to 0.03 mm displacement. Again, much like the pawl.

To find a crossing point, the brooch (#2) blocks the pin (#4) and the fixed stop is pressed against the stop pin. The nut (#7) is loosened. You can count the number of teeth necessary using the counter (#10) by means of the pawl (#5). Then we can press against the adjustable stop (#9) pin (#4) and re-lock the nut (#7). The space will thus be fixed between the stop and the adjustable stop will be crossed.

Straight-line map with labeled parts. *Calina Shevlin*

- A Screw to lift off pattern-bar
- B Screw to rotate headstock for radial patterns
- C Division screw
- D Tilt for the headstock
- E Rubber
- F Cutter and guide
- G Pattern bars
- H Winder for multiple bars
- I Depth screw
- J Tool slide
- K Pawl

FIG.08-05

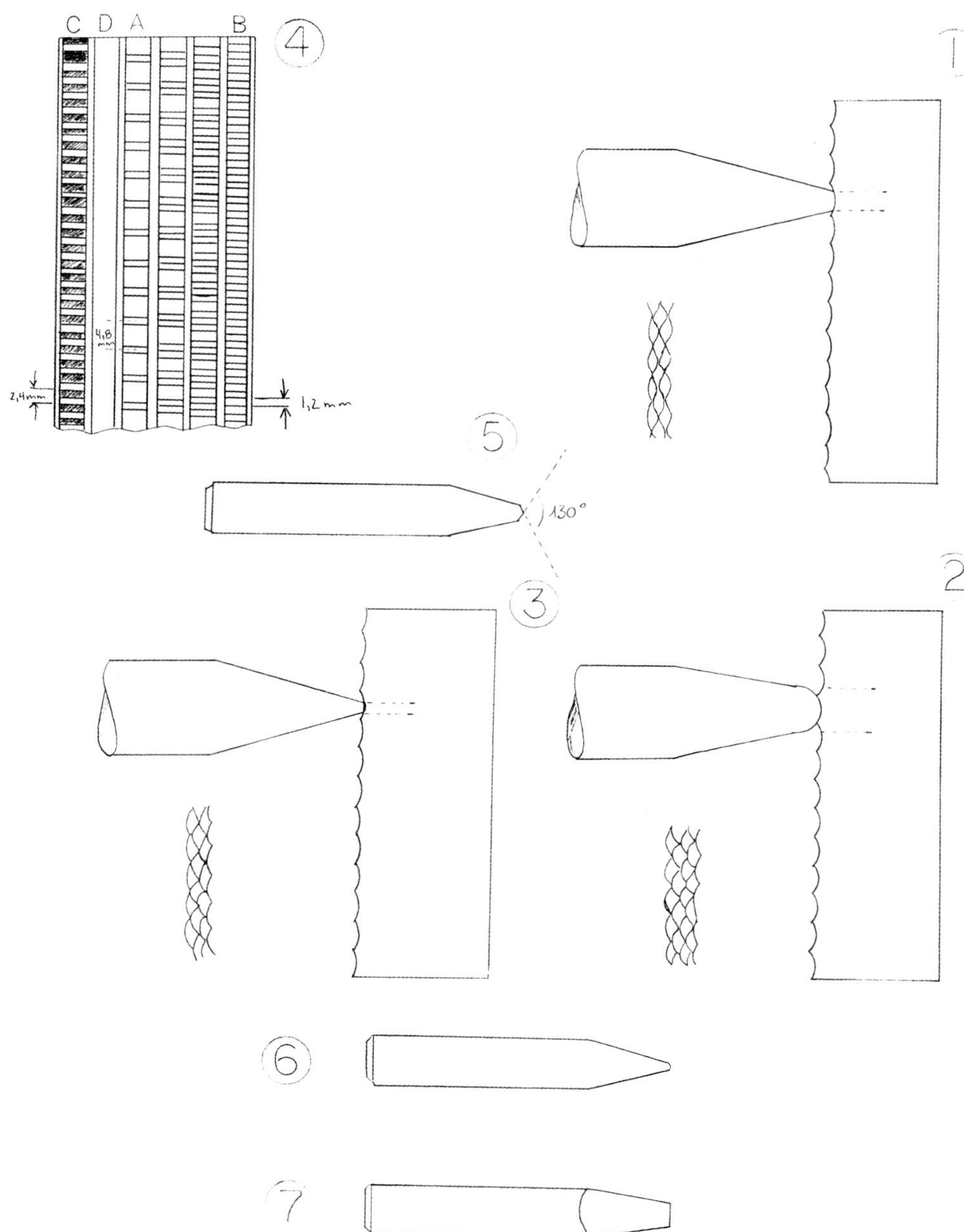

These drawings depict the rubber in relation to pattern bars, as well as what they look like "sharpened."

1. Just Right: The rubber to pattern bar ratio is perfect. The rubber is 3⁄4 the size of the trough, meaning it will produce waves that are even. If doing a barley corn pattern this will turn out perfectly.
2. Too Large: This rubber is much too large; the pattern will not be undulating and will have stiff starts and stops.
3. Too Small: This rubber will produce a fish scale like pattern; it has too far to travel in each trough and because it is so small it will just want to jump over the peaks of the waves.
4. Pattern Bar: This is an example of a traditional and common pattern bar set made out of one piece of steel.
   4a. The size between the middle to middle of the indentation is 4.8 mm, meaning if you were to use the division you would only need to move 2.4 mm.
   4b. The size between middle to middle of these indentations is 1.2 mm and the division would only be a 0.6 mm. This pattern is particularly good for making barley corn as it is really even in its spacing.
   4c. The size between the middle to middle is 2.4 mm, making the division 1.2 mm.
   4d. This pattern bar is smooth (no indentations), making it easy to make a straight cut in conjunction with patterning without having to move the headstock away from the pattern bars when working on one pattern.
5. Sharpening: When sharpening the rubbers it is wise to keep 30° angles at the sides, much like making a cutter. This is because the pattern bars are much smaller patterns and #4 has only lines cut in, so no waves are being followed.
6. Side View: Side of a sharpened rubber. The tip is still rounded ever so slightly.
7. Top View: This is the top of a sharpened rubber; it is not only made square, but ends in a taper.

Making the rubbers yourself for the pattern bars can be rewarding, as you will always have the diameter and form you need at hand. It can be a bit challenging in the beginning, but if you can sharpen your own cutter this will come quickly and is less finicky. *Illustration re-drawn from Lienhard Operators Manual 1895 by Calina Shevlin*

FIG.08-06

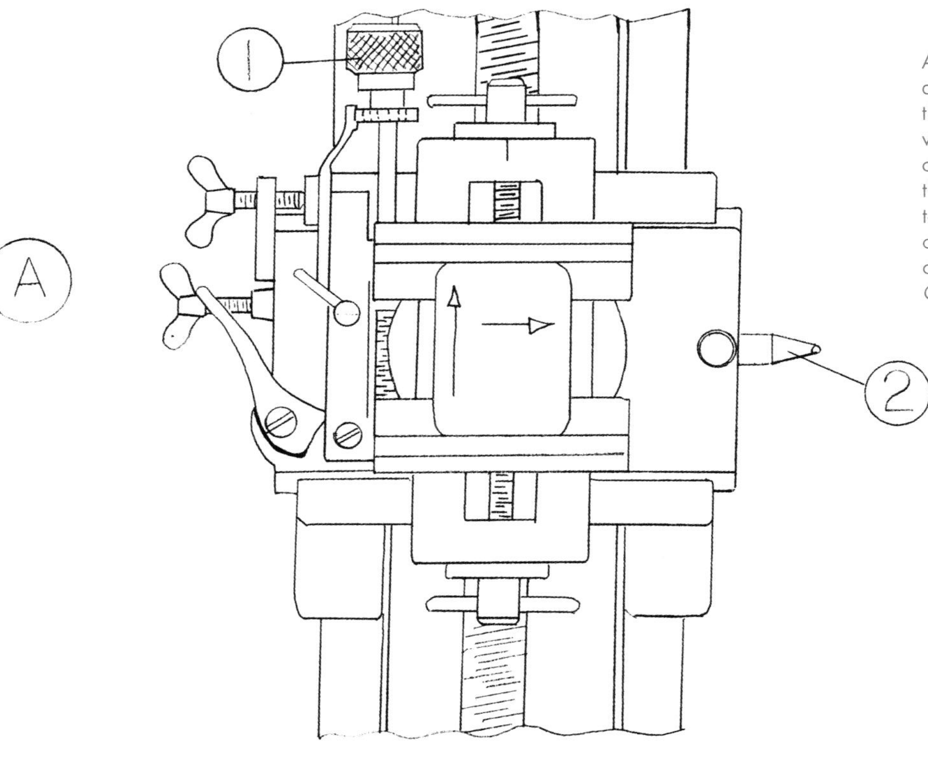

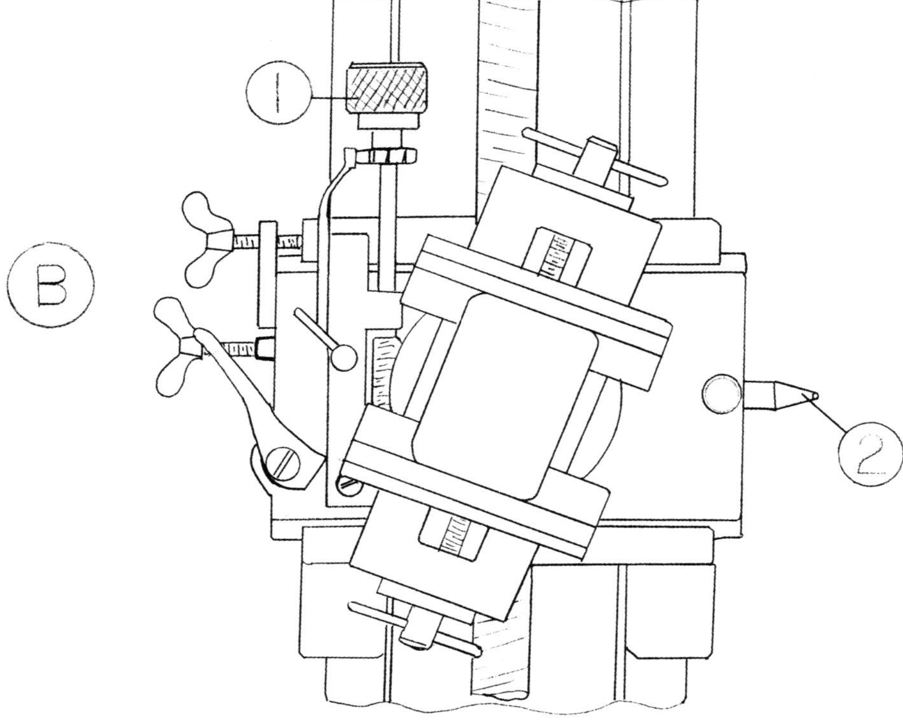

These are views of the headstock that holds the work pieces from the operator's view on a Lienhard straight-line machine.

1. Worm: This is used to slowly turn the work piece from vertical to horizontal and 360°.
2. Rubber: This stays static and can either be touching a pattern bar or free.

A. This is the work piece and headstock as it is aligned for most straight-line patterns, but with the turning of #1 the worm, headstock, and work piece begin to turn either clockwise or counterclockwise. This function is used for all of the sunray patterns. The pattern does not have to be centered in the center; it could be coming out from a corner, a side, or be slightly off-center. *Illustration re-drawn from Lienhard Operators Manual 1895 by Calina Shevlin*

CHAPTER 9
Thoughts on the Free Dissemination of Information

While I feel that everyone should have free access to information about guilloché and the machines that can produce these decorations, such as libraries, the Internet, conferences, atelier visits, and the like, not everyone feels the same way. For example, I attended a lecture where a gentleman whose family had been in the guilloché business for more than fifty years was speaking about guilloché to a group of watchmakers. I had met this gentleman a good six months before the talk and he offered me a job before letting me see his atelier. Secrecy was of the utmost importance to him. He said in the talk that he felt it was a shame that older guillocheurs (he was in his mid-forties) did not want to share their knowledge with new people interested in the art. He stated to the group that he feared the art would soon cease to exist because many practitioners were so unwilling to share their knowledge and personal experiences that they had learned through apprenticeships. The old method, and still the most prevalent today, was teaching by practice, practice, and more practice. I laughed softly, and he just stared at me with complete confusion on his face. I then asked in the public question session if he had any images of machines or his atelier, rather than the many photos of patterns that he proudly displayed. He told the group that he unfortunately could not show any images of his machines or atelier because it would pass out proprietary information. He had made some modifications to the machines, and he did not want to show people who might then steal the ideas and use them. This is the most obvious example I have of secrecy and hypocrisy all rolled into one neat package. I anticipated his response based on my previous experiences meeting him on several occasions. He had offered me a job not only without showing me the facilities but also without asking me to do test pieces; I could have made up that I knew how to do guilloché. He felt a test of my skill would compromise his "modifications" and that I would copy or sell the information of his atelier, and he would somehow miss out on some unnamed thing.

I find it interesting that the modifications and improvements people make to their machines have often been made elsewhere. Necessity is the mother of invention. The modifications are usually obvious things like compressed air close at hand to blow away the bur that is freshly cut. Almost everyone I know, and almost every atelier I have visited, has something of this style on or near their machines, but if people believed in the free transmission of information to begin with we could be moving on with better modifications and inventions.

The unwillingness to share, give, write down, or pass on the information necessary to continue guilloché will be the complete obliteration of the decorative art. Ornamental turning is freely passed on and talked about. Ideas are exchanged and conferences are held, ensuring the longevity of the ornamental turning art form. Guillocheurs need to form something like this, along with demonstrations and small hands-on classes to ensure guilloché does not die out. My final thoughts are that if the knowledge is available to everyone everywhere, there are only going to be a handful of people who are really interested enough to do deeper independent research. And of that handful of people there will be about 2% who will *perhaps* pursue guilloché even further, and will look into learning and rise up from this point. This is exactly why I do not see a danger in the transmission of free information, or in building a bench top model of a rose engine. Many will want it, few will take a vested interest, and fewer will succeed. But I want to get the information out there to the few who may want to continue, but maybe do not even know about the existence of guilloché—yet.

CHAPTER 10
Artistic Applications Emerging

With the knowledge and skill of guilloché comes a great responsibility. I realize this sounds a bit strange, but one must have taste when applying guilloché to an object. The goal is not to overwhelm the piece or detract from other elements, but to sparingly create complementary patterns. There is no need to try every single pattern you can think up on one piece. It is commonly believed that in the Victorian period (1837–1901), ornamentation on top of ornamentation was quite popular. People were adding guilloché on top of already elaborate decorative objects. It was a bit too much to take and guilloché began to go the way of all things Victorian—on the way out.

Guilloché is beautiful and timeless when applied with a discerning eye. Since the popularization of guilloché it has been used in a classic fashion, without overuse coming into play. Parure sets for vanities including a hairbrush, mirror, and small boxes were popular. Other applications varied from car dashboards decorated lightly with guilloché to watch dials.

I have only seen the "classic" watch dials first introduced to the world by Abraham-Louis Breguet in the late 1700s. Recently watch manufacture Vacheron Constantin (Geneva, Switzerland) has begun to think a bit differently about guilloché. They saw an opportunity to combine several different techniques, including guilloché, and the Métier d'Art line was born in 2005.

Calina Shevlin

Fabergé used tasteful patterns of guilloche under the enamel, but the patterns were mesmerizing nonetheless. The innovation of decorating with guilloché and then forever preserving it under glass and adding more decoration on top was a purely Fabergé invention.

Now, concerning the future of guilloché and engine turning—it is happening right now! On the whole it would seem to be on the up and up, and that has heavily influenced this book. I want there to be as much information avail-

Silver boxes with guilloché. *G. Phil Poirier*

able to as many people who want it so this will not only be another temporary surge and revival. I want to help guilloché stay for the long term, and yes, I do have a vested interest in it. I would like to exploit the talents of young craftsmen that are emerging and putting their innovative thinking to work while also incorporating guilloché.

First, I would like to start with G. Phil Poirier. Phil is a jewelry artist, teacher, and inventor in New Mexico. Phil is my mentor and taught me all of the basics I could learn about guilloché. He sent me off into the world and I landed a job as a guillocheuse in Switzerland, and I owe it all to him. It was Phil who encouraged me to make a book out of a graduate school paper and six long years later I have arrived. Phil makes beautifully enameled pieces that showcase his guilloché work and do not detract from the design. They are clean and simple, and extremely well executed. Phil has also created steel plates that have been cut with guilloché patterns so people can roller print them on to soft metals. These plates can be found at Rio Grande Jewelry Supply under the Bonny Doon accessories. Most impor-

Anodized titanium belt buckle with guilloché. *G. Phil Poirier*

Fine silver guilloché box tops with enamel. *G. Phil Poirier*

Rutilated quartz, agate, and guilloché necklace. *G. Phil Poirier*

tantly, Phil is passing on his knowledge with full disclosure and will help anyone who wants to learn. He is perpetuating the profession, ensuring there is a future for guilloché and that it does not die out. I think since he is educating a younger generation there is more hope for the longevity of guilloché. In the past people who found a love of guilloché were retired and it became their hobby. I am glad when anyone is even remotely interested in guilloché, but there does also need to be a younger generation to keep it going. Phil picked up guilloché while living and working in the United Kingdom in the late 1970s and has not stopped since.

Celia Kudro is a jewelry artist from Colorado who came to guilloché in the midst of a career change. She has been creating jewelry for a few years and takes a great interest in the collection and restoration of original rose engines and straight-line machines. Celia has begun working with guilloché in an interesting manner, as most of it is hidden on the backs of her rings. She has started branching out to include guilloché under rock crystal as ornamentally turned wood for the focal point of the ring, created with the same rosette she uses for the back guilloché pattern.

Frieda Doerfer is a German-based artist who discovered guilloché only a few years ago while doing a residency at a museum. Her school happened to have a straight-line machine, as did the museum, and she began to think creatively about how to exploit the detail of guilloché while making it into large, wearable, light jewelry forms. She came up with careful planning and soldering ever so gently on the inside seams. The hollow jewelry is lightweight and really moves into the jewelry world on a grand three-dimensional scale not attempted before. There have been uses of guilloché in jewelry before now, but nothing that crosses into the art jewelry area, and this really speaks out.

Silver ring with guilloché. *Celia Kudro*

Assortment of silver and guilloché rings. *Celia Kudro*

Necklace with guilloché under quartz. *Celia Kudro*

Silver rings with guilloché, ornamentally turned African Blackwood, and Cabochons. *Celia Kudro*

Copper guilloché necklace. *Frieda Doerfer*

Gold plated guilloché necklace. *Frieda Doerfer*

Brass guilloché necklace. *Frieda Doerfer*

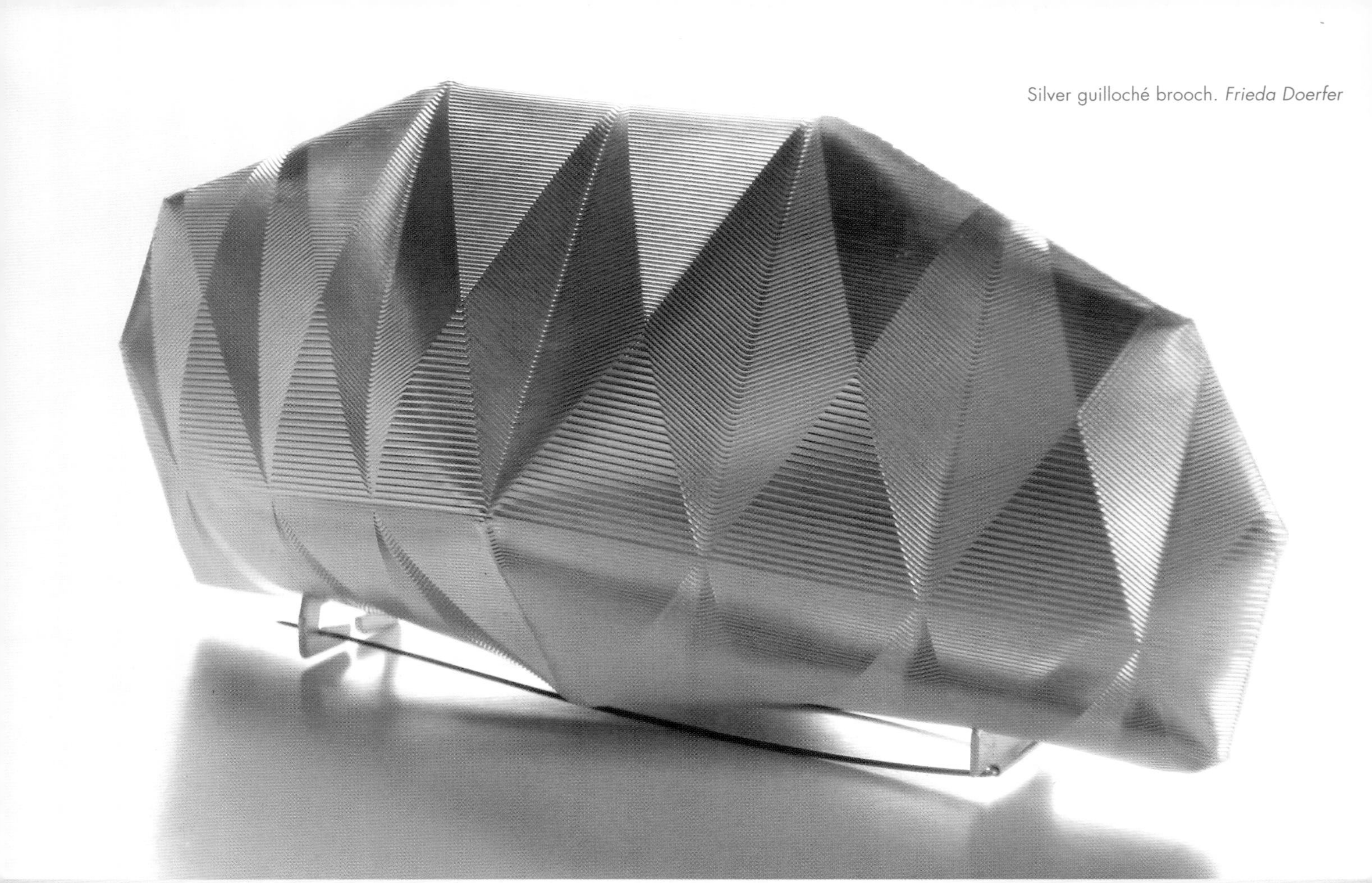

Silver guilloché brooch. *Frieda Doerfer*

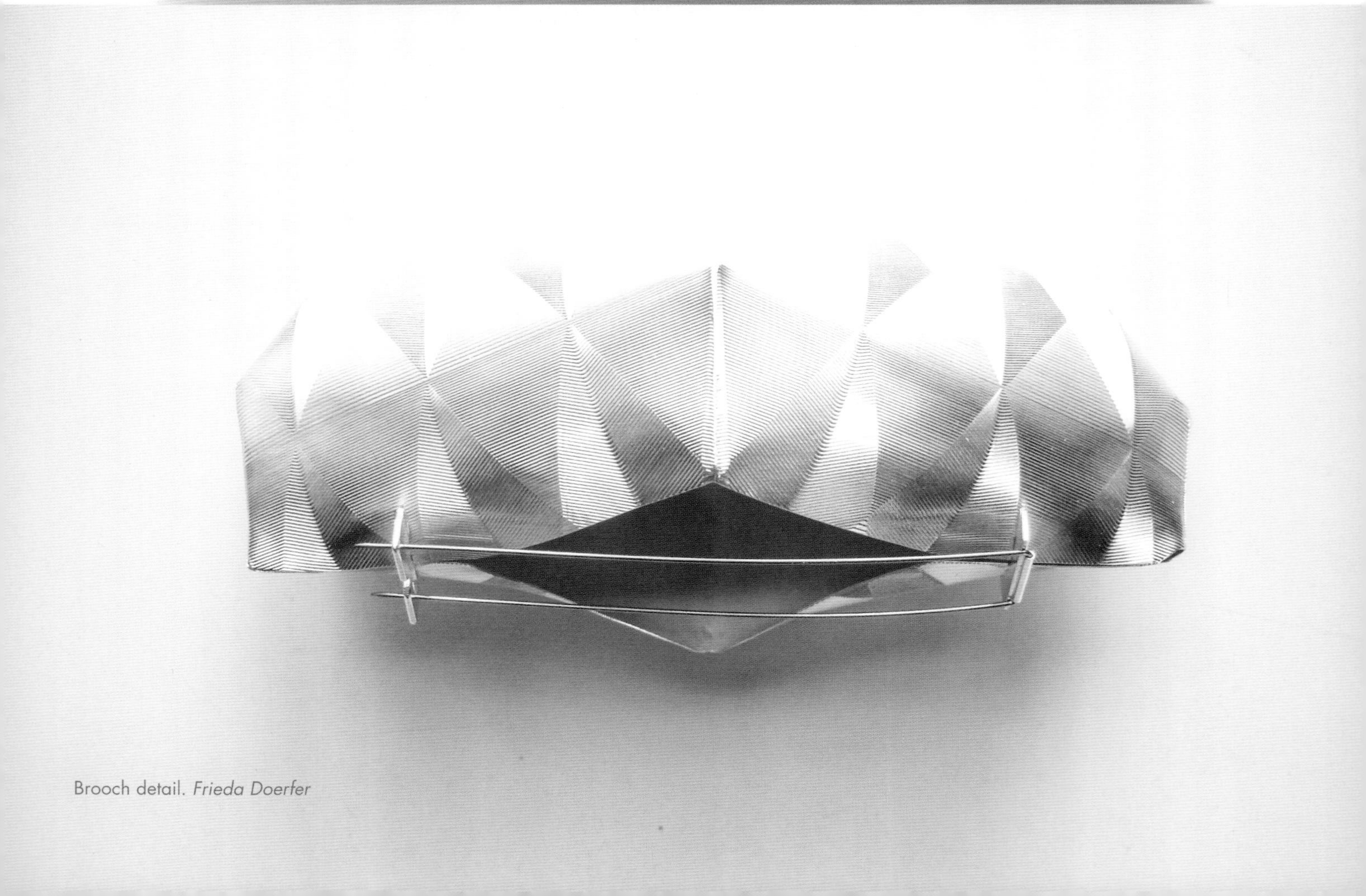

Brooch detail. *Frieda Doerfer*

Silver guilloché pen. *Chris Manning*

Chris Manning is a metal artist based in Ottawa, Canada. He has been creating custom fountain pens, men's accessories, and pendants. Chris discovered guilloché at a Fabergé exhibition in 2007 and has fallen in love with guilloché and enameling, and the way the two interact. His work is very meticulous, and he plans to continue with guilloché indefinitely. People need more bespoke items in their lives, and he will be there to facilitate that need.

Silver iPhone 4 case. *Chris Manning*

Silver and sapphire pendant. *Chris Manning*

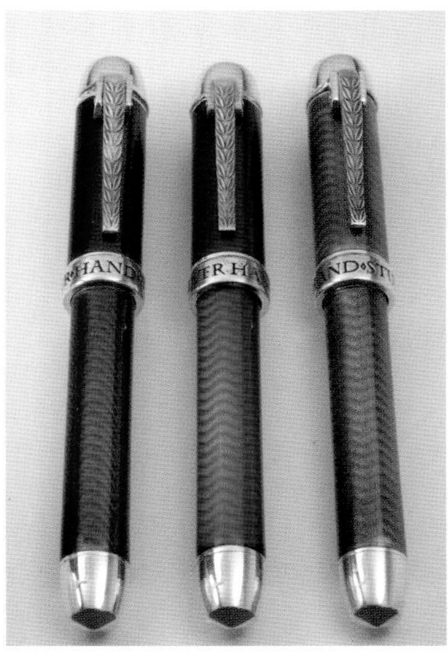

Three straight-line guilloché and enamel pens. *Chris Manning*

Teri Jo Kinnison is a silversmith artist from Mesa, Arizona. She bought a rose engine from the Robert Whiteside estate many years ago and has not stopped experimenting on it since. Teri Jo also teaches classes at the Mesa Art Center and would like to introduce students to guilloché in a class setting.

Copper and enamel samples. *Teri Jo Kinnison*

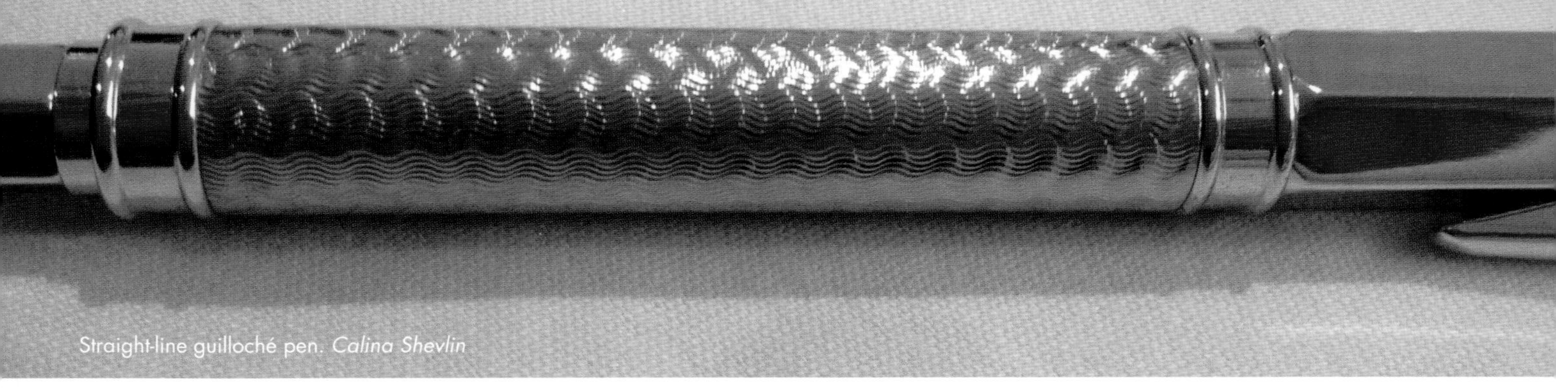
Straight-line guilloché pen. *Calina Shevlin*

I am including some photos of my own work as well. I have been practicing guilloché since 2009, and I currently only make professional work. In my spare time I like to run samples to see what looks good and what does not. These are just some fun images to think about.

Spiral sample. *Calina Shevlin*

Multi-patterned dial sample. *Calina Shevlin*

CHAPTER 11
Examples and Collections

There are a good deal of places around the world that have excellent collections of guilloché items. These items were quite popular in the late 1700s to early 1900s, and they have been preserved, unlike many of the machines. Museums often label guilloché pieces as simply guilloché; I would like to travel to these places and also add the name of the pattern to the description.

One of my favorite places to visit on a fairly regular basis is the Patek-Philippe Museum in Geneva, Switzerland. This museum is filled with old pocket watches and table clocks that are abundant with guilloché nicely preserved under enamel. This museum has well-lit vitrines with a good amount of pieces with guilloché (around 200–275). They also have the singing bird pistol made in Le Brassus, Switzerland, as well as a video showing it in magnified detail. The video is not specifically focused on the guilloché, but it does highlight it well.

The Musée des Arts et Métiers in Paris is well stocked with rose engines and straight-line machines, meaning they have some. They also have a nice collection of guilloché and ornamentally turned items.

The Musée International d'Horlogerie in La Chaux-de-Fonds, Switzerland, has many interesting watch pieces and some with guilloché. They also have a rose engine on display under Plexiglas so people can see what kind of machine made the guilloché. The machine at this museum looks to be from around 1785.

Another place I have heard of is the Providence Jewelry Museum in Providence, Rhode Island. Peter DiCristofaro, who has a vested interest in keeping the old tooling and machinery, currently runs this museum.

A grand collection of guilloché, although not open to the public and not on display, is at the École d'Art Appliqués in La Chaux-de-Fonds. If you ask nicely they will let you look at and handle the pieces with gloves. I find these pieces beautiful and well executed, and to think you are holding something made by the first students of guilloché is an amazing feeling.

This is by no means a definitive list, and I know that there may be even more places to visit. These are the places I am familiar with, either by personally visiting or by hearing great stories of fantastic visits. I am sure any collector of rose engines and straight-line machines has more than one, and it is more than likely they have more than five. Most of the people I have met in this situation have been gracious and allowed me incredible access to see, touch, and even try out these machines. I will not give their names here, but if you happen to come across one of them you will be more than pleased.

I will share some wonderful images of a collection that resides with an acquaintance in the United Kingdom. These plates were used to press into a colloid plastic and make designs in things from clock faces, to car dashboards, to picture frames. The plates are each about eighteen square inches and each element of guilloché is hand turned; some of these have 120 circles on them. Enjoy!

AMERICAN
INTERMEDIATE
FOREIGN

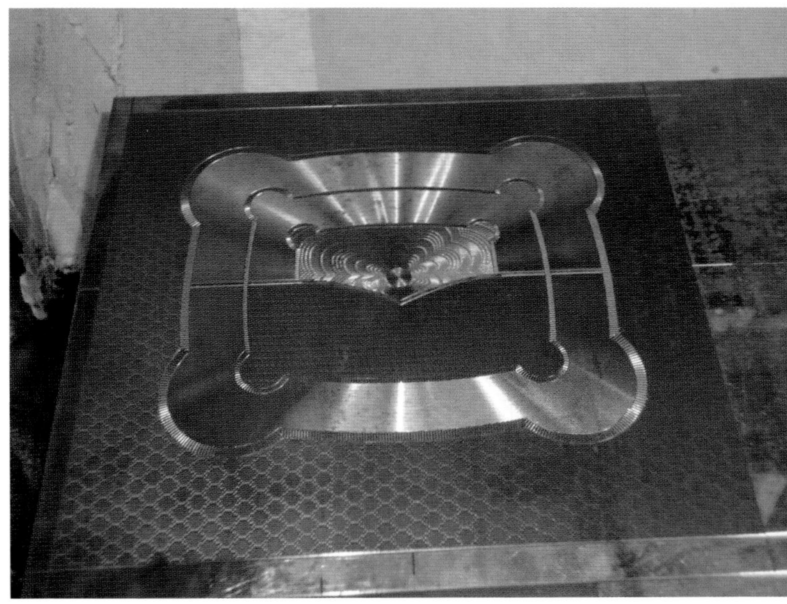

CHAPTER 12
The Future of Guilloché

When thinking about the future of guilloché, I am hopeful—maybe more than some—but what I have seen over the last few years has been really eye-opening. There are young people, eight and nine years old, becoming interested in guilloché. There seems to be a movement away from technology and more toward the handmade, as well as hands-on learning. These are the things that really matter, and a move toward the past is in no way a regression. There are new ways of using guilloché, new methods for working with it to benefit the operator, without simply making bland dials for watches. I think dials could be so much more, as proven by Vacheron Constantin, and jewelry could be more than smooth forms in three dimensions: it can be angular and with seams, and it does not lose its beauty. From all of the people I have met in the past six years, my guilloché family, and ornamental turners moving into guilloché, I can see that the future is bright for guilloché, just like its facets.

Incorporating Guilloché

Guilloché can be easily incorporated into jewelry, and not just as a focal element that covers the piece. It can be used as a background, or a small secret detail, as seen with Celia Kudro's pieces. It can be the decoration to more mundane, everyday household items, such as drawer knobs, spoon handles, and so on—little bits of decoration that personalize the things we use every day.

The pens I have seen are fantastic, and they are certainly things that we use every day. Having a metal pen with a beautiful decoration is not only supporting a local craftsman, but is also ecologically sound. Guilloché can be used on the outside of rings and also on the inside, as shown by David Lindow.

Before moving too far into the past there needs to be a marriage of past and future to find the perfect combinations and applications for guilloché. It will be easy to incorporate into life, especially now with so many talented people doing things differently with guilloché.

New Instructional Formats

With a new generation of guillocheurs comes a new opportunity to teach. The first actual classes since 1917 will be held in 2015 in New Mexico, to introduce a group of interested people to guilloché. Some already have machines and some are completely new to the field, but they are all excited and will hopefully use their resources to pass on the information. This is the first official class in nearly one hundred years. The art was almost extinct due to trade secrecy and a lack of interest. Sometimes I am convinced that to spark interest in something in a niche world one needs to do a lot of marketing and advertising of their skills and why others should want or need to learn them.

The more people who are interested—not necessarily practicing—the more exposure guilloché will have. Even if people are simply interested, they may not want to take up guilloché for whatever reason, but they might pay someone—hopefully an independent worker—to make them guilloché and to get that out into circulation. Phil Poirier, Phillip Bedford, David Wood-Heath, and I are the group informing, writing, and teaching guilloché currently, but there is always room for more. Phillip and David are both based in the United Kingdom and take their machines around in a trailer to museums and engineering conferences, not only demonstrating guilloché, but letting people try it out. They let children have a go, and it is the children that have the most curiosity and willingness to learn, and practice until they succeed at even a small task. There will soon be another generation of guillocheurs upon us. Phil is based in the United States and I am based in Switzerland, but teach classes in the United States and Switzerland.

The instruction does not have to become complicated, as the machines allow the student to self-explore and create freely with really no wrong way to go about pattern discovery. As long as people understand the basics they should be free to experiment. With as much hands-on experience as possible more people will talk about guilloché, and perhaps even know how valuable it is in time and skill.

The giving of information is a great idea, but it is the hands-on experience that really makes that idea become a reality and stick with an individual. I could lecture all day about guilloché, and in the end nothing would be gained unless I had photos and videos, and even that would not do justice for this subject. Guilloché really requires a hands-on approach to the subject. Guilloché is really a hands on approach of a subject. There is no getting around that fact. One cannot learn how to gauge the depth without seeing the work and touching the machine. I hope that through hands-on instruction in the United States, Canada, United Kingdom, and Switzerland a much younger generation will become interested and willing to do what this generation is trying to do and disseminate the information in an easier to understand format with verbal, written, and demonstrated instructions.

We must all remember that ideas we form about what jobs we would like often begin to take seed at a young age. I remember when I was much younger, all I would do was make house plans; I really wanted to be an architect or engineer because all of the precise details and measurements really appealed to my personality. If I had the opportunity to have a few introductory classes, I would have decided then whether or not I definitely would or would not become an architect. It is like this with guilloché. If a young person has the possibility to learn hands-on guilloché in a fun and noncritical environment, they may decide that is what they would like to do.

I believe learning should be in a calm and non-threatening environment when getting the basics under one's belt. Once the basics are understood gentle corrections are needed to continue exploring pattern development and machine operation, pressure sensing by hand, and hand wheel speed. Once progression is shown then it is time to critically look at pieces and give feedback to help students realize what kind of work makes a successful guillocheur. In this digital age we have access to all sorts of photos, charts, information, and forums that often provide support. We need to exploit all of the materials available to us to delve into a subject and learn or teach it optimally.

CHAPTER 13
Recipe Formats

Recipes are what I call the notes that I have made so that I can repeat any patterns I make while making samples, playing, or just not paying attention. I am a bit obsessive about note keeping, and I have made several tracking sheets, as well as base recipes with areas to fill in other ideas as they occur to me. The basics that I find are necessities are laid out here.

Recipe Layout

What the piece is: a bowl, watch dial, egg, pen, etc.
The name of the pattern: grains d'orge, basket weave, or spiral
What rosette was used: 96 lobe, or 12 lobe with 3 divisions each lobe
What division was used, if any: 96, 124, or 48
What diameter rubber was used: #3, #10, or #6 (I number mine in ascending order.)
The spacing for the pattern: 0.30 mm, 0.20 mm
The cutter used for the pattern and its exact angles: 12.5º/12.5º, or 20º/40º
The angle of the cutter: the upward angle at the point
The angle of the tool slide, if any
The depth of the pattern: 0.01 mm, 0.05 mm
If you used the worm, how many turns and in which direction were they each cut (clockwise or counterclockwise, and which direction was first)?
Did you move the tool slide, and if so, what was each of the angle intervals?
How many passes did the pattern require?
What is the depth of the outlining lines, if used?
All of the information for each cutter used, including the widths.
What medium was used to adhere the piece to the headstock?
How much time did the pattern take?
Who is the client of this particular piece, and do they want a bespoke?
Was a special chuck used, and if yes, which one?

If the process is complicated I often write step-by-step directions and revise them afterward to find the most efficient method to perform the tasks.

Ideas for Creating Recipes

To create your own recipes, you must simply write down what is important to you, and what you do not think you could remember in six months. I used to keep sloppy notes when I was starting out, abbreviating everything, and when I went back to try a pattern I had absolutely no idea what some of my own abbreviations were. Now I keep the previous list in a spreadsheet, where all I have to do is fill in the blanks. It makes life and pattern tracking so much easier to do.

Recipe Sheets and Instructions for Basic Patterns

Barley Corn (Grains d'Orge)

Rose Engine
For this pattern the goal is to not leave any spaces between the "grains".
Rosette/ Pattern Bar: 96-lobe rosette
Amplitude: Medium
Cutter: 10°/10° angles and 0.80 mm wide.
Maximum depth: 0.075 mm
Number of passes each cut: 2
Division: 96
Pawl: 25 clicks (0.50 mm) to the stop

I like to start about 1 mm inside from the edge, and I generally add one plain circle without the rubber touching the rosette. This is deeper than the decoration to prevent nicking the side, so I cut it at 0.085 mm using a 140° cutter that is 0.60 mm wide.

Any rosette with medium amplitude and a corresponding division can be easily substituted. There is no standard, and experimenting allows you to choose your favorite. With the depth I recommend a minimum of two passes, with the first taking out 0.05 mm and the second an additional 0.025 mm for a total of 0.075 mm. Again, experiment.

Cut one line with the starting division on I or II (I like to mark my machine with permanent marker to keep track of I versus II).
Advance 1 pull of the pawl.
Change the division from I to II.
Cut one line.
Advance 1 pull of the pawl.
Change the division from II to I.

Continue with the above instructions until you arrive just before the center. You can cut a straight circle near the center at the end without the rosette touching the rubber.

BARLEY CORN RECIPE SHEET

Set your stop to 25 clicks (0.50mm)	mark 96 division with I on the left and II on the right	Cut at a depth of 0.075mm
Cut one line	Cut one line	Cut one line
Pawl 25 clicks	Pawl 25 clicks	Pawl 25 clicks
Division 2	Division 1	Division 2
Cut one line	Cut one line	Cut one line
Pawl 25 clicks	Pawl 25 clicks	Pawl 25 clicks
Division 1	Division 2	Division 1
Cut one line	Cut one line	Cut one line
Pawl 25 clicks	Pawl 25 clicks	Pawl 25 clicks
Division 2	Division 1	Division 2
Cut one line	Cut one line	Cut one line
Pawl 25 clicks	Pawl 25 clicks	Pawl 25 clicks
Division 1	Division 2	Division 1
Cut one line	Cut one line	Cut one line
Pawl 25 clicks	Pawl 25 clicks	Pawl 25 clicks
Division 2	Division 1	Division 2
Cut one line	Cut one line	Cut one line
Pawl 25 clicks	Pawl 25 clicks	Pawl 25 clicks
Division 1	Division 2	Division 1
Cut one line	Cut one line	Cut one line
Pawl 25 clicks	Pawl 25 clicks	Pawl 25 clicks
Division 2	Division 1	Division 2

Barley corn. *Calina Shevlin*

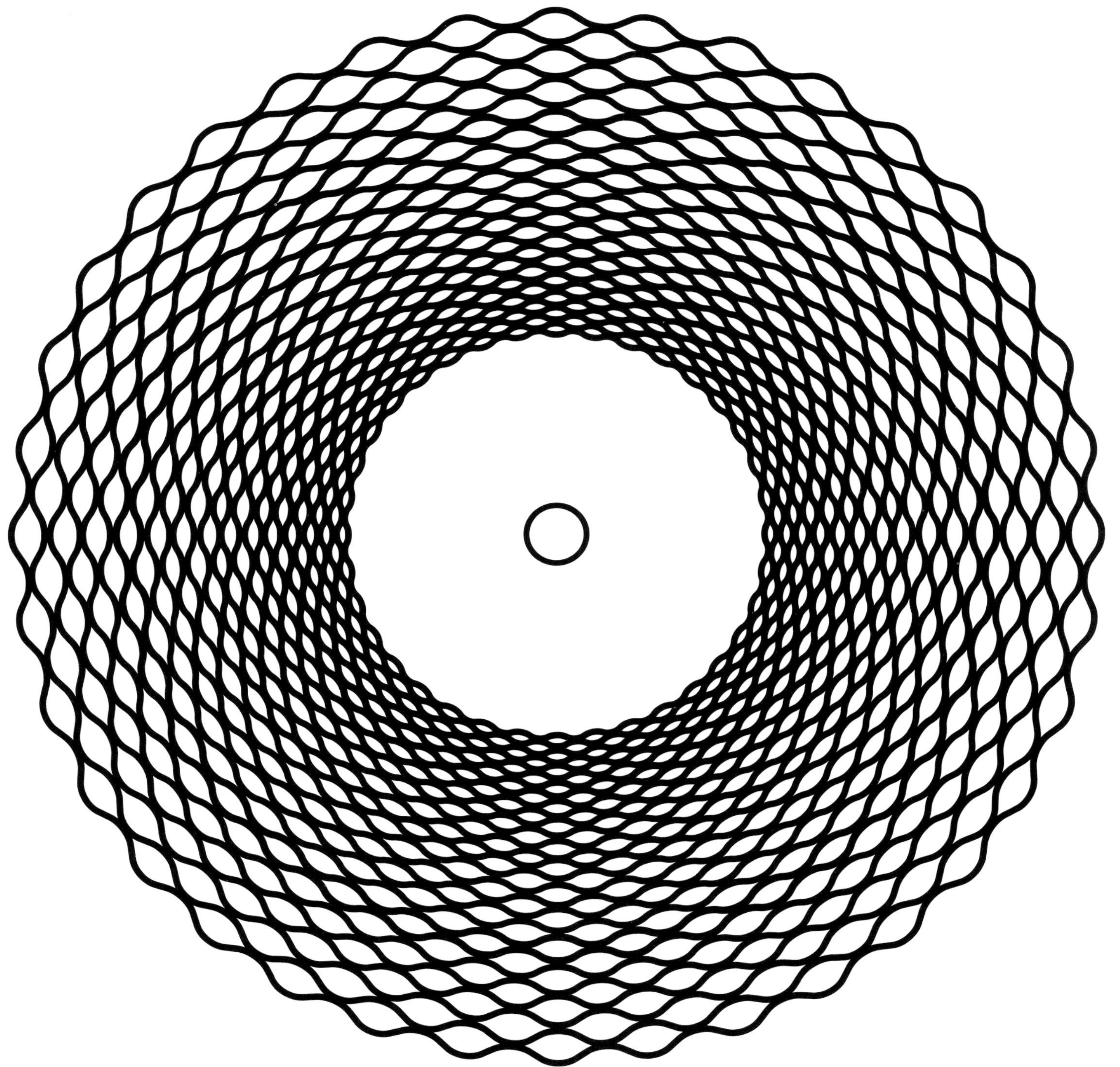

Barley corn recipe. *Calina Shevlin*

Basket Weave (Panier)

Rose Engine

For this pattern, the goal is to create a pattern that gives the illusion of being interweaved.

Rosette/Pattern Bar: 24-lobe rosette or 12 × 3 lobe

Amplitude: Low

Cutter: 12°/ 12° angles and 0.80 mm wide.

Maximum depth: 0.05 mm to 0.06 mm

Number of passes each cut: 2

Division: 24 every two to three cuts or 12 every three to four cuts

Pawl: 20 clicks (0.40 mm) to the stop

I start with one plain circle without the rubber touching the rosette. This is deeper than the decoration to prevent nicking the side, so I cut it at 0.08 mm using a 140° cutter 0.60 mm wide. For the first cut, line the point of the cutter up with the inside edge of the circle cut, then displace 0.40 mm.

Make three cuts or make three to four cuts
Move 2 spaces (or 2 pulls of the pawl for 0.80 mm) or move 1 space as usual
Move the division (24) or move the division (12)
Make three cuts or make three to four cuts
Move 2 spaces (or 2 pulls of the pawl for 0.80 mm) or move 1 space as usual
Move the division (24) or move the division (12)
Continue until finished.

This produces a basket weave effect as the name implies. With this pattern there will be material left between the baskets or not, it is up to the operator. This also depends on the type of rosette. For the 24 lobed rosette I let the original material appear between the rows where the division is used. For a 12 × 3 rosette there will not be original material showing and you will not be leaving two spaces between the division rows.

With the attached chart I include numbers using a comparator because it is easier to remember which number I am on rather than having to specify 0.40 mm the first/second/third pass and so on.

Basket weave recipe. *Calina Shevlin*

BASKET WEAVE RECIPE SHEET

	24-lobe rosette	12 × 3-lobe rosette
0.00 mm	1-cut, 1-space	1-cut, 1-space
0.40 mm	1-cut, 1-space	1-cut, 1-space
0.80 mm	1-cut, 2-space	1-cut, 1-space, division
1.20 mm	division, 1-cut	1-cut, 1-space
1.60 mm	1-cut, 1-space	1-cut, 1-space
2.00 mm	1-cut, 2-space	1-cut, 1-space, division
2.40 mm	division, 1-cut	1-cut, 1-space
2.80 mm	1-cut, 1-space	1-cut, 1-space
3.20 mm	1-cut, 2-space	1-cut, 1-space, division
3.60 mm	division, 1-cut	1-cut, 1-space
4.00 mm	1-cut, 1-space	1-cut, 1-space
4.40 mm	1-cut, 2-space	1-cut, 1-space, division
4.80 mm	division, 1-cut	1-cut, 1-space
5.20 mm	1-cut, 1-space	1-cut, 1-space
5.60 mm	1-cut, 2-space	1-cut, 1-space, division
6.00 mm	division, 1-cut	1-cut, 1-space
6.40 mm	1-cut, 1-space	1-cut, 1-space
6.80 mm	1-cut, 2-space	1-cut, 1-space, division
7.20 mm	division, 1-cut	1-cut, 1-space
7.60 mm	1-cut, 1-space	1-cut, 1-space
8.00 mm	1-cut, 2-space	1-cut, 1-space, division
8.40 mm	division, 1-cut	1-cut, 1-space
8.80 mm	1-cut, 1-space	1-cut, 1-space
9.20 mm	1-cut, 2-space	1-cut, 1-space, division
9.60 mm	division, 1-cut	1-cut, 1-space
10.00 mm	1-cut, 1-space	1-cut, 1-space
10.40 mm	1-cut, 2-space	1-cut, 1-space, division
10.80 mm	division, 1-cut	1-cut, 1-space
11.20 mm	1-cut, 1-space	1-cut, 1-space
11.60 mm	1-cut, 2-space	1-cut, 1-space, division
12.00 mm	division, 1-cut	1-cut, 1-space
12.40 mm	1-cut, 1-space	1-cut, 1-space

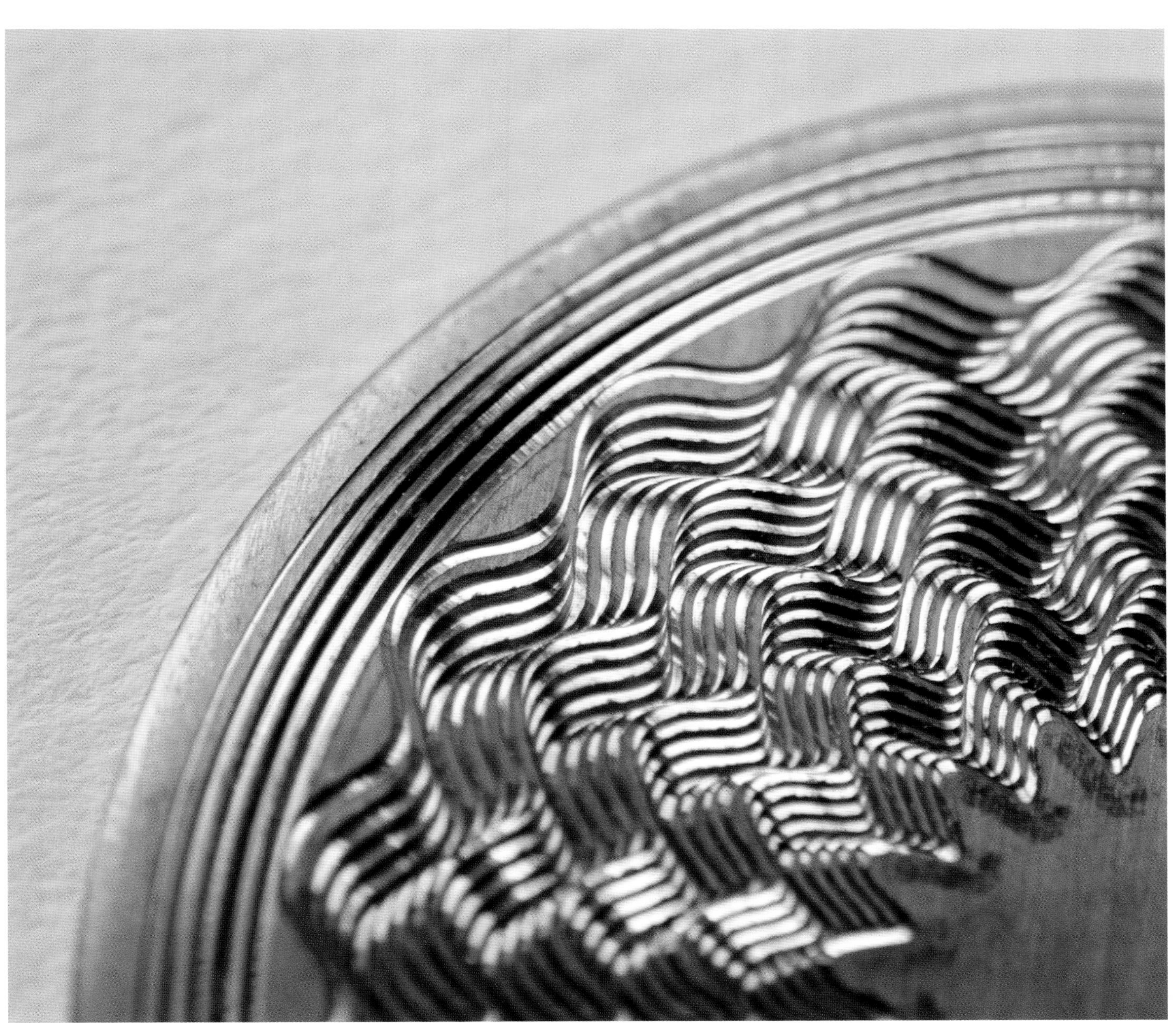

Basket weave. *Calina Shevlin*

Concentric Pattern (Flinqué)

Rose Engine

This pattern can give many different optical illusions and is fun and easy to experiment with many variations.

Rosette/Pattern Bar: 12 × 3 lobe rosette
Amplitude: Low, medium, or high
Cutter: 30°/30° angles and 0.80 mm wide.
Maximum depth: 0.06 mm to 0.07 mm
Number of passes each cut: 2
Division: None
Pawl: 15 clicks (0.30 mm) to the stop

I start with one plain circle without the rubber touching the rosette. This is deeper than the decoration to prevent nicking the side, so I cut it at 0.80 mm using a 140° cutter 0.60 mm wide. For the first cut, line the point of the cutter up with the inside edge of the circle cut, then displace 20 clicks (0.40 mm) for the first cut only. Then continue at 40 clicks (0.80 mm).

This is the most basic and straightforward pattern. You can use any rosette of any amplitude and get a huge variety of results, including mirror images. I have provided a sheet for the 12 × 3 rosette, but do not let that limit you.

For this pattern, you start at the exterior, make 2 passes, and continue at a steady pace. It is quick since you do not have to remember anything other than advancing the pawl.

Concentric pattern. *Calina Shevlin*

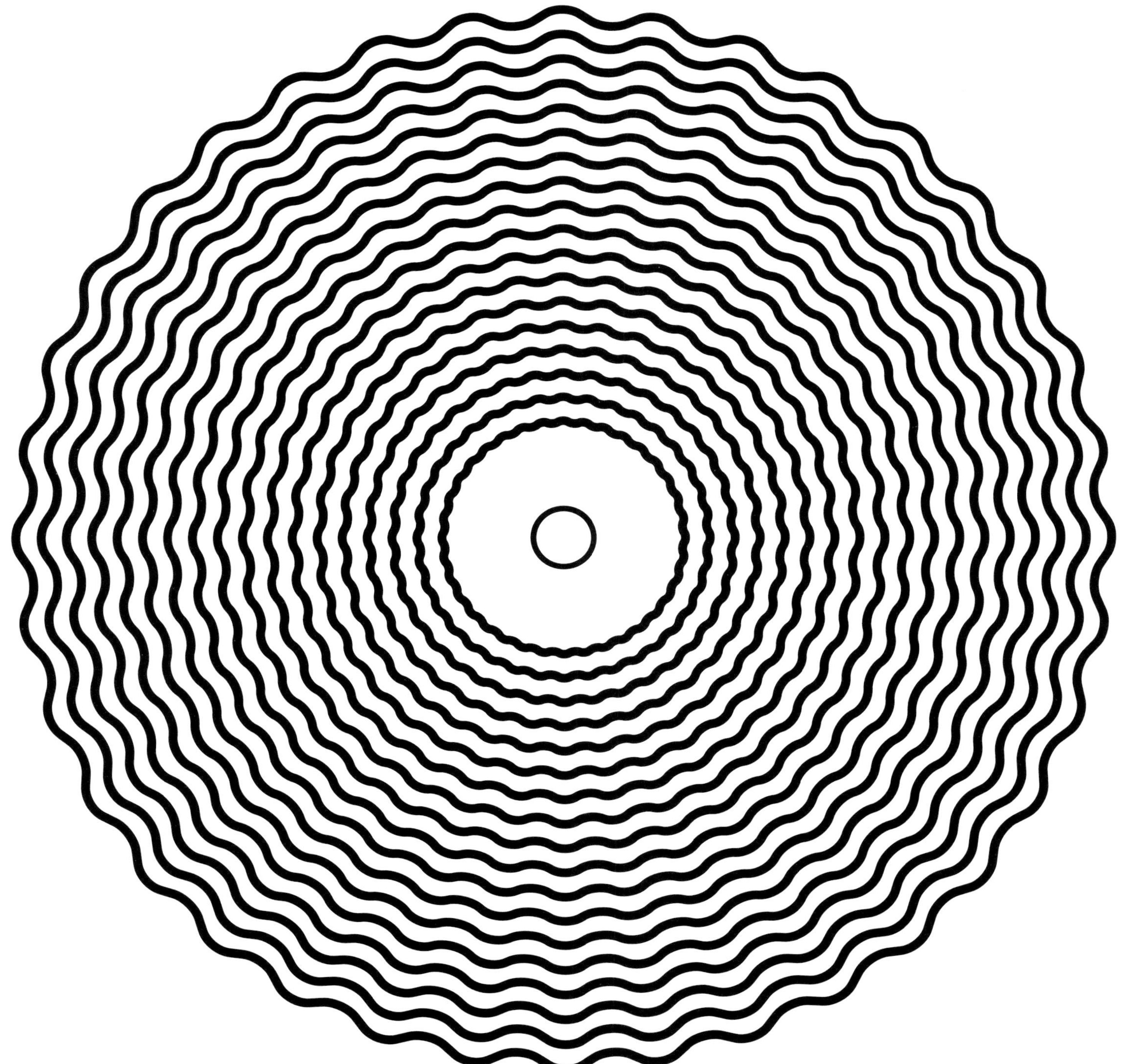

Concentric pattern recipe. *Calina Shevlin*

Lightning/Zig-zag

Rose Engine

For this pattern the goal is to create the illusion of diminishing zig-zags.

Rosette/ Pattern Bar: 24-lobe rosette

Amplitude: Low

Cutter: 155° angle and 0.80 mm wide.

Maximum depth: 0.05 mm

Number of passes each cut: 2

Division: None/Fibonacci

Pawl: 20 clicks (0.40 mm) to the stop

I add one plain circle without the rubber touching the rosette. This is deeper than the decoration to prevent nicking the side, so I cut it at 0.07 mm using a 140° cutter 0.60 mm wide.

There should not be any original material left so you need to make peaks by sight. If there is a bit of material make the cut a bit deeper, but no more than 0.01 mm at a time.

You may use a Fibonacci division on the indexing plate or you can use the worm. I have found the worm to be better, but the same result can be achieved with the division.

With the division you may go from the first to the last and back, or you may go from the first to the middle and back, or you may go from the first to the last and start again at the first. Any which way you choose you need to keep track.

With the worm, turn counterclockwise (CCW) for a sequence of 10 and then clockwise (CW) for a sequence of 10, each time turning the worm 8 times.

ZIG-ZAG RECIPE SHEET

1	CCW	0	2	4	6	8	10	12	14
2	CW	14	12	10	8	6	4	2	0
3	CCW	2	4	6	8	10	12	14	16
4	CW	14	12	10	8	6	4	2	0
5	CCW	2	4	6	8	10	12	14	16
6	CW	14	12	10	8	6	4	2	0
7	CCW	2	4	6	8	10	12	14	16
8	CW	14	12	10	8	6	4	2	0

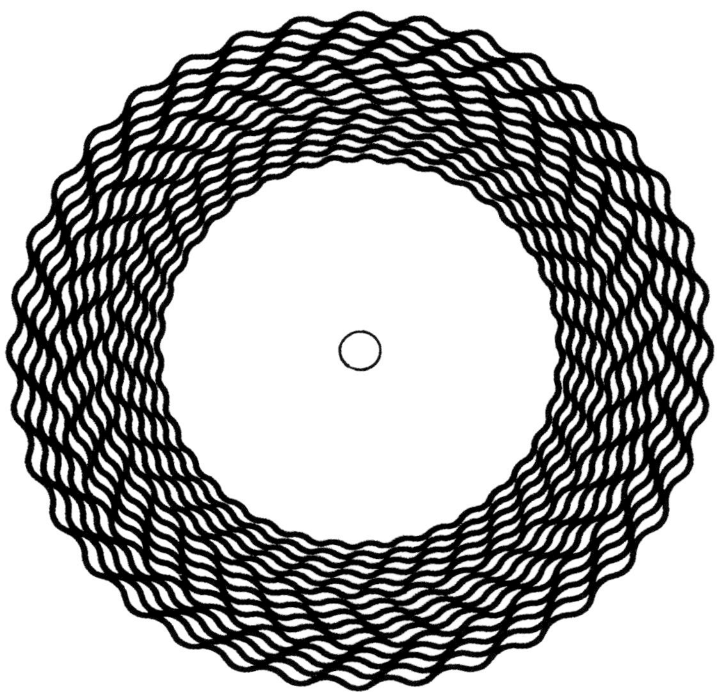

Lightning recipe. *Calina Shevlin*

Lightning. *Calina Shevlin*

Moiré

Rose Engine

The goal is to create an optical illusion of rolling waves that diminish in size.

Rosette/Pattern Bar: 24-lobe rosette

Amplitude: Low

Cutter: 155° angle and 0.80 mm wide.

Maximum depth: 0.04 mm to 0.05 mm

Number of passes each cut: 2

Division: None

Worm: Every cut

Pawl: 20 clicks (0.40 mm) to the stop; I use a digital comparator for this pattern to be precise.

I start with one plain circle without the rubber touching the rosette. This is deeper than the decoration to prevent nicking the side, so I cut it at 0.07 mm using a 140° cutter 0.60 mm wide.

I use a simple chart with CCW and CW for counterclockwise and clockwise, respectively. I find that 68 lines are perfect for a watch dial size.

I start CCW, but either way, you need to keep a chart and tick off as you go. It makes it slower, but helps maintain one's focus throughout the process. Make the outer straight cut, then align the tip of the cutter with the inner edge of the circle and start to displace 0.40 mm. This is the first cut. As always, make 2 passes to ensure it is smooth.

After the first cut, turn the worm 2 clicks CCW, then 4 clicks CCW, 6 clicks CCW, 8 clicks CCW, 10 clicks CCW, 12 clicks CCW, 14 clicks CCW, 16 clicks CCW, 14 clicks CCW, 12 clicks CCW, 10 clicks CCW, 8 clicks CCW, 6 clicks CCW, 4 clicks CCW, and 2 clicks CCW; and then 1 click CW, 2 clicks CW, 4 clicks CW, 6 clicks CW, 8 clicks CW, 10 clicks CW, 12 clicks CW, 14 clicks CW, 16 clicks CW, 14 clicks CW, 12 clicks CW, 10 clicks CW, 8 clicks CW, 6 clicks CW, 4 clicks CW, and 2 clicks CW.

Repeat the above until the piece is finished. This is best accomplished with no distractions.

MOIRÉ RECIPE SHEET

CCW	MAKE FIRST CUT	2	4	6	8	10	12	14	16	14	12	10	8	6	4	2
CW	1	2	4	6	8	10	12	14	16	14	12	10	8	6	4	2
CCW	1	2	4	6	8	10	12	14	16	14	12	10	8	6	4	2
CW	1	2	4	6	8	10	12	14	16	14	12	10	8	6	4	2
CCW	1	2	4	6	8	10	12	14	16	14	12	10	8	6	4	2
CW	1	2	4	6	8	10	12	14	16	14	12	10	8	6	4	2

Moiré recipe. *Calina Shevlin*

Moiré. *Calina Shevlin*

Pyramids (Clous de Paris)

Rose Engine

The goal is to create equal sided pyramids that finish in a point.

Rosette/Pattern Bar: None

Amplitude: None

Cutter: 12°/12° angles and 0.80 mm wide.

Maximum depth: 0.05 mm to 0.06 mm

Number of passes each cut: 2

Division: None

Pawl: 40 clicks (0.80 mm) to the stop

I start with one plain circle without the rubber touching the rosette. This is deeper than the decoration to prevent nicking the side so I cut it at 0.80 mm using a 140° cutter 0.60 mm wide. For the first cut, line the point of the cutter up with the inside edge of the circle cut, then displace 20 clicks (0.40 mm) for the first cut only. Then continue at 40 clicks (0.80 mm). I recommend extra attention to detail; with the pyramids it is extremely easy to detect any change in depth with the naked eye.

Cut the first line in two passes; when you start the second line, the first pass will leave a bit of the original material that will be eliminated with the second pass. The goal is to leave a peak and valley every cut. After you have finished from the left side to the right side turn the work 90°; first cut at 20 clicks (0.40 mm), and then continue with 40 clicks (0.80 mm) displacement. Cut one line slowly for the first pass to avoid tearing the material, then faster for the second pass.

Advance 0.80 mm

Cut the second line slowly for the first pass and faster for the second.

Continue A to Z for both directions.

CLOUS DE PARIS RECIPE SHEET

1st set of lines	2nd set of lines (90°)
Make outer circle (0.80 mm)	Turn work 90°
Start at inner edge of circle depth of 0.05	Start at inner edge of circle depth of 0.05
Pawl 1 time, 40 clicks (0.80 mm)	Pawl 1 time, 40 clicks (0.80 mm)
Make 1st line cut	Make 1st line cut
Pawl 1 time, 40 clicks (0.80 mm)	Pawl 1 time, 40 clicks (0.80 mm)
Make 2nd line cut	Make 2nd line cut
Pawl 1 time, 40 clicks (0.80 mm)	Pawl 1 time, 40 clicks (0.80 mm)
Make 3rd line cut	Make 3rd line cut
Pawl 1 time, 40 clicks (0.80 mm)	Pawl 1 time, 40 clicks (0.80 mm)
Make 4th line cut	Make 4th line cut
Pawl 1 time, 40 clicks (0.80 mm)	Pawl 1 time, 40 clicks (0.80 mm)
Make 5th line cut	Make 5th line cut
Continue alternating cutting and advancing until you have approximately 70 or so cuts	Continue alternating cutting and advancing until you have approximately 70 or so cuts

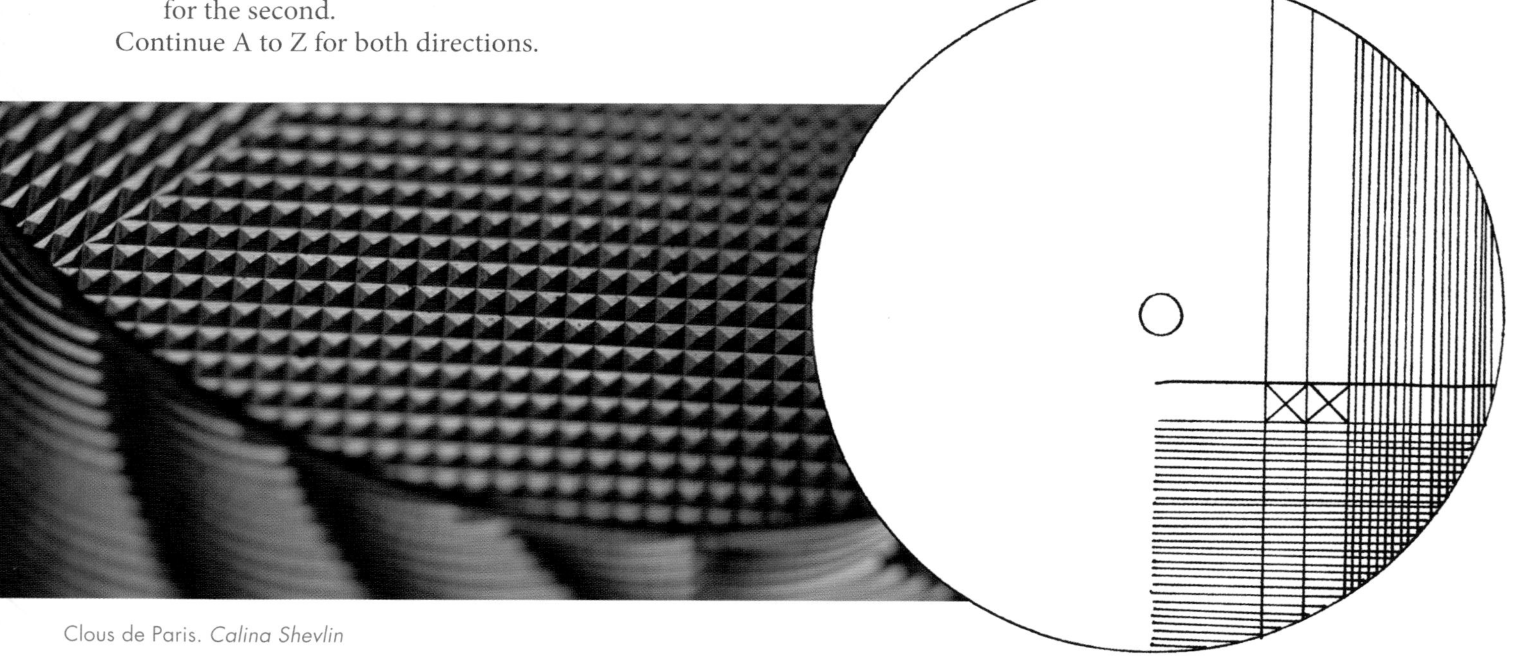

Clous de Paris. *Calina Shevlin*

Clous de Paris recipe. *Calina Shevlin*

Parquet (Damier)

Rose Engine

The goal is to create evenly spaced cuts that are uniform across the whole piece.
Rosette/Pattern Bar: None
Amplitude: None
Cutter: 30°/30° angles and 0.80 mm wide.
Maximum depth: 0.03 mm to 0.04 mm
Number of passes each cut: 2
Division: None
Pawl: 20 clicks (0.40 mm) to the stop; I use a digital comparator for this pattern.

I start with one plain circle without the rubber touching the rosette. This is deeper than the decoration to prevent nicking the side, so I cut it at 0.08 mm using a 140° cutter 0.60 mm wide.

Start by outlining all of the squares. This is like making the pyramids, but not so close. Start at the left hand side and cut at 0.04 mm, displace 2.00 mm (5 pulls of the pawl that is set at 0.40 mm), and continue until the piece is completely crossed. Turn the work 90° and repeat.

For the inner lines, start at the left side bottom and cut the first pass every other square until the top, displace 0.40 mm, and continue. Each square will have 4 cuts. Cut every other square, then turn 90° and repeat with the remaining squares. There will be original material left between the three inner cuts of each square.

I have a hard time concentrating when I am zipping through this pattern, so after I have outlined all of the squares I use a sharpie to color every other square so I do not forget to skip a square when cutting. Feel free to experiment with other depths and displacements: you can add more lines, take lines away, and so on.

PARQUET RECIPE SHEET

1st	2nd	3rd	4th
Outline large squares	Turn work 90°	color every other square with sharpie	Turn work 90°
Start at inner edge of circle depth of 0.06	Start at inner edge of circle depth of 0.06	Start at inner edge of circle depth of 0.03	Start at inner edge of circle depth of 0.03
Pawl 5 times (2 mm)	Pawl 5 times (2 mm)	Pawl 1 time (0.40 mm)	Pawl 1 time (0.40 mm)
Make 1st line cut	Make 1st line cut	Make 1st line cut every other square	Make 1st line cut on colored squares
Pawl 5 times (2 mm)	Pawl 5 times (2 mm)	Pawl 1 time (0.40 mm)	Pawl 1 time (0.40 mm)
Make 2nd line cut	Make 2nd line cut	Make 2nd line cut every other square	Make 2nd line cut on colored squares
Pawl 5 times (2 mm)	Pawl 5 times (2 mm)	Pawl 1 time (0.40 mm)	Pawl 1 time (0.40 mm)
Make 3rd line cut	Make 3rd line cut	Make 3rd line cut every other square	Make 3rd line cut on colored squares
Pawl 5 times (2 mm)	Pawl 5 times (2 mm)	Pawl 1 time (0.40 mm)	Pawl 1 time (0.40 mm)
Make 4th line cut	Make 4th line cut	Make 4th line cut every other square	Make 4th line cut on colored squares
Pawl 5 times (2 mm)	Pawl 5 times (2 mm)	Pawl 1 time (0.40 mm)	Pawl 1 time (0.40 mm)
Make 5th line cut	Make 5th line cut	Make 5th line cut every other square	Make 5th line cut on colored squares
Continue alternating cutting and advancing until you have approximately 15 or so cuts	Continue alternating cutting and advancing until you have approximately 15 or so cuts	Continue alternating cutting and advancing until you have every other square vertically	Continue alternating cutting and advancing until you have every other square filled horizontally

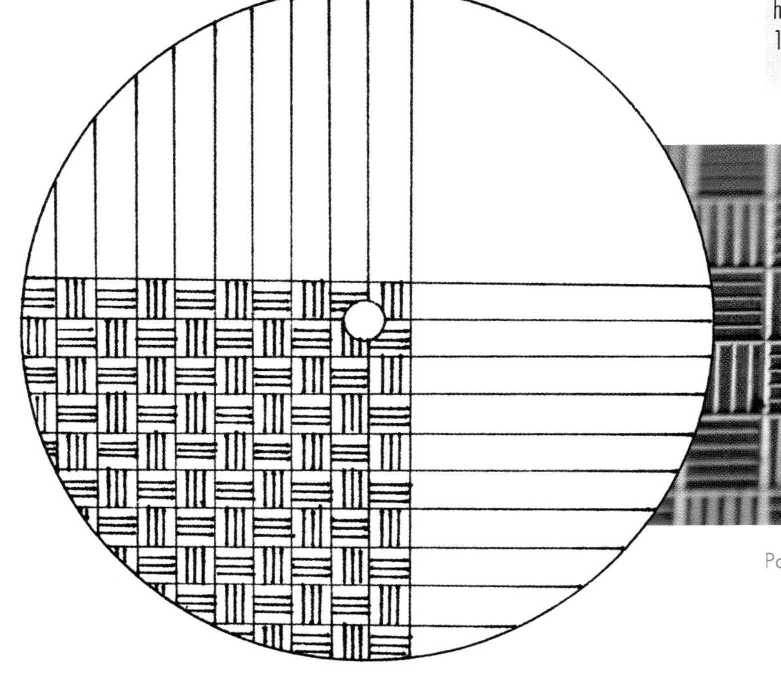

Parquet recipe. *Calina Shevlin*

Parquet. *Calina Shevlin*

Spiral (Escargot)

Rose Engine

The goal is to create a diminishing spiral.

Rosette/Pattern Bar: 12 × 3 lobe rosette or 96 lobe rosette or any rosette you want

Amplitude: Low to medium

Cutter: 12°/12° angles and 0.80 mm wide.

Maximum depth: 0.09 mm

Number of passes each cut: 2

Division: None

Pawl: 15 clicks (0.30 mm) to the stop or try 25 clicks (0.50 mm)

I start with one plain circle without the rubber touching the rosette. This is deeper than the decoration to prevent nicking the side, so I cut it at 0.08 mm using a 140° cutter 0.60 mm wide. For the first cut, line the point of the cutter up with the inside edge of the circle cut, then displace 0.40 mm for the first cut only. Then continue at 0.30 mm.

This pattern requires writing out a chart or using mine; if you do not have a set order of operations you will lose your place and have to start an entirely new piece. By order of operations I mean you do the operations in the same order every time. For example, I cut one line, move the pawl, move the worm, and mark my chart. I never deviate from this order.

Cut the first line, move the pawl 15 clicks (0.30 mm), move the worm 8 clicks away from you CCW, and then mark off the chart. For the marking I start with a dot on each number, then the next round I make a diagonal line, then the next pass I make the other diagonal to make an X and so on with little marks. This allows me to use a smaller chart, but you may want one for each cut and each turn, so go ahead and personalize your chart.

You will never turn back the worm; it is CCW the entire process, which makes it a bit easier to remember. I mark my worm in quarters, then in eighths, and when I say 8 clicks it is in sixteenths. So if you have a machine with a regular worm go ahead and do a measured 1⁄2 turn each cut. I also have a machine with notches cut into it so I can count the clicks.

SPIRAL RECIPE SHEET

cut line, pawl 0.30, worm 8	cut line, pawl 0.30, worm 8	cut line, pawl 0.30, worm 8
cut line, pawl 0.30, worm 8	cut line, pawl 0.30, worm 8	cut line, pawl 0.30, worm 8
cut line, pawl 0.30, worm 8	cut line, pawl 0.30, worm 8	cut line, pawl 0.30, worm 8
cut line, pawl 0.30, worm 8	cut line, pawl 0.30, worm 8	cut line, pawl 0.30, worm 8
cut line, pawl 0.30, worm 8	cut line, pawl 0.30, worm 8	cut line, pawl 0.30, worm 8
cut line, pawl 0.30, worm 8	cut line, pawl 0.30, worm 8	cut line, pawl 0.30, worm 8
cut line, pawl 0.30, worm 8	cut line, pawl 0.30, worm 8	cut line, pawl 0.30, worm 8
cut line, pawl 0.30, worm 8	cut line, pawl 0.30, worm 8	cut line, pawl 0.30, worm 8
cut line, pawl 0.30, worm 8	cut line, pawl 0.30, worm 8	cut line, pawl 0.30, worm 8
cut line, pawl 0.30, worm 8	cut line, pawl 0.30, worm 8	cut line, pawl 0.30, worm 8
cut line, pawl 0.30, worm 8	cut line, pawl 0.30, worm 8	cut line, pawl 0.30, worm 8
cut line, pawl 0.30, worm 8	cut line, pawl 0.30, worm 8	cut line, pawl 0.30, worm 8
cut line, pawl 0.30, worm 8	cut line, pawl 0.30, worm 8	cut line, pawl 0.30, worm 8
cut line, pawl 0.30, worm 8	cut line, pawl 0.30, worm 8	cut line, pawl 0.30, worm 8
cut line, pawl 0.30, worm 8	cut line, pawl 0.30, worm 8	cut line, pawl 0.30, worm 8
cut line, pawl 0.30, worm 8	cut line, pawl 0.30, worm 8	cut line, pawl 0.30, worm 8
cut line, pawl 0.30, worm 8	cut line, pawl 0.30, worm 8	cut line, pawl 0.30, worm 8
cut line, pawl 0.30, worm 8	cut line, pawl 0.30, worm 8	cut line, pawl 0.30, worm 8
cut line, pawl 0.30, worm 8	cut line, pawl 0.30, worm 8	cut line, pawl 0.30, worm 8
cut line, pawl 0.30, worm 8	cut line, pawl 0.30, worm 8	cut line, pawl 0.30, worm 8
cut line, pawl 0.30, worm 8	cut line, pawl 0.30, worm 8	cut line, pawl 0.30, worm 8

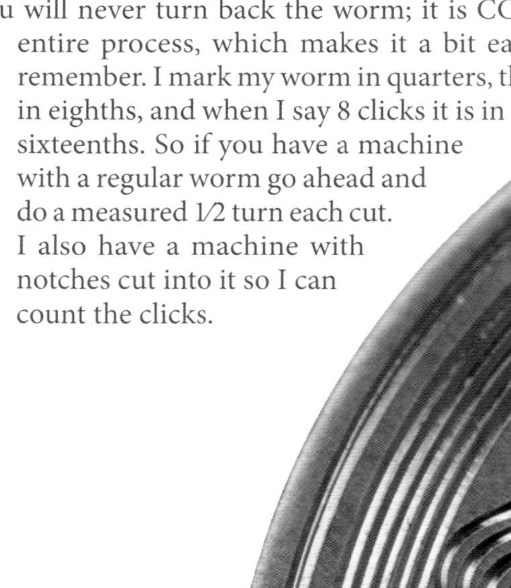

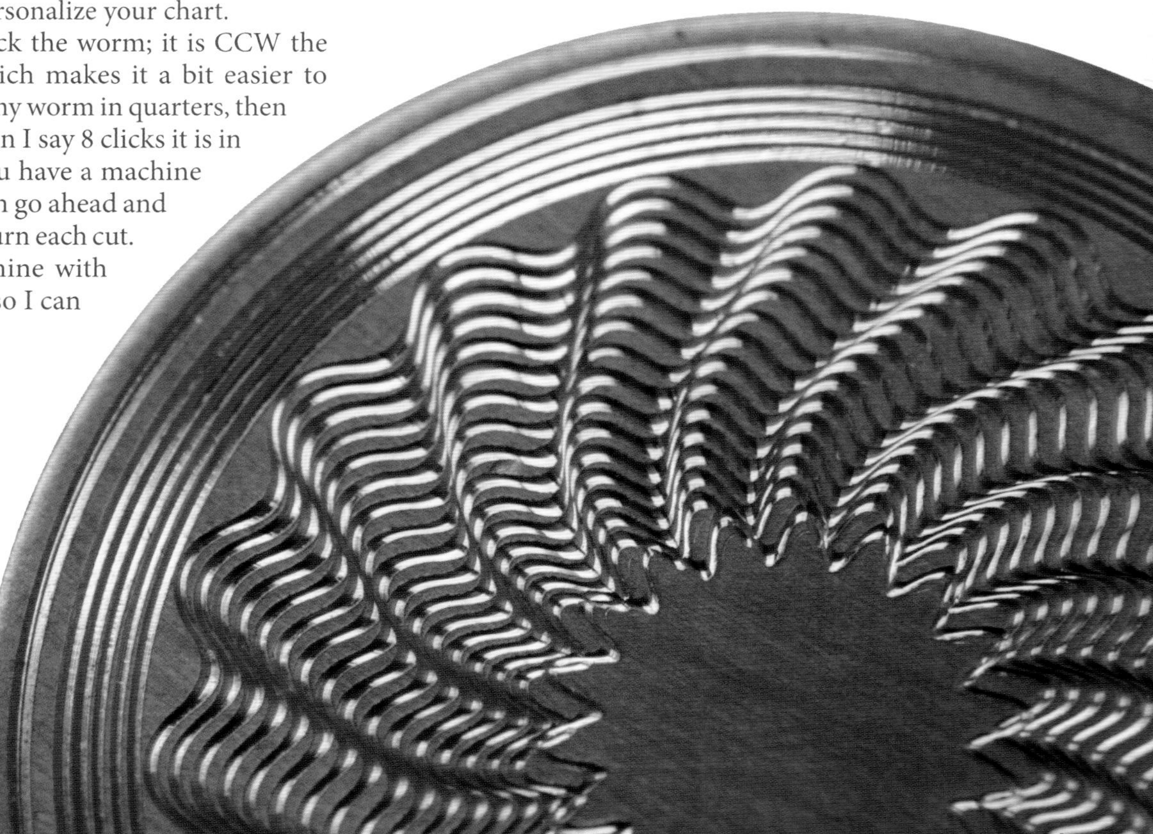

Spiral. *Calina Shevlin*

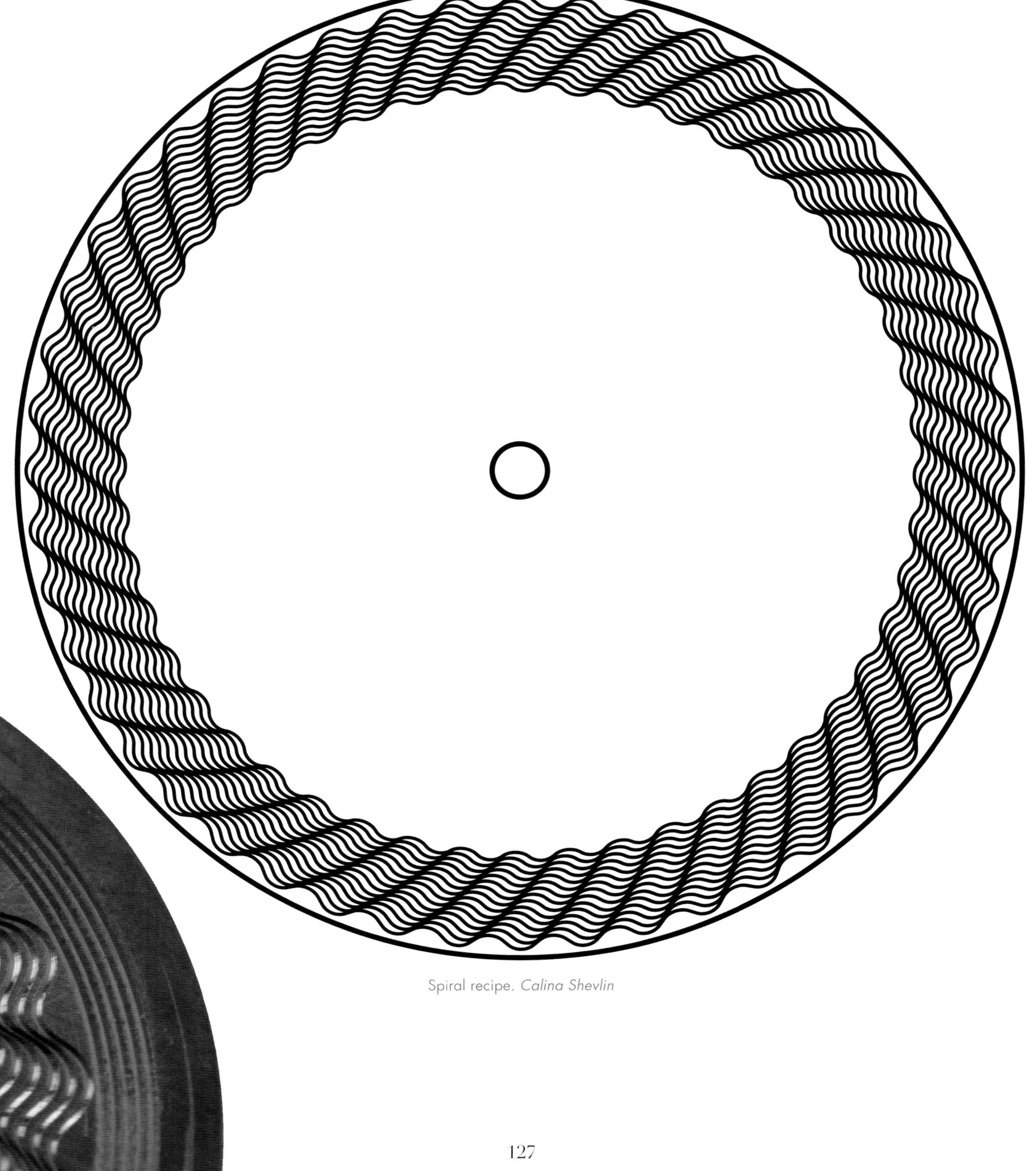

Spiral recipe. *Calina Shevlin*

Alternating Straight Lines

Straight-Line

This pattern is simple but elegant; it is a striped effect and very easy to create.
Rosette/ Pattern Bar: None
Rubber: None
Maximum depth: By sight
Number of passes each cut: 2
Division: None
Pawl: 20 teeth; you can set the stop

This pattern is quick and lends itself nicely to large surfaces. It was quite popular to use in conjunction with the diamonds pattern in the late 1800s. Due to the fact that this requires multiple changes in the advancement and the number of cuts I have included a chart.

ALTERNATING STRAIGHT LINES RECIPE SHEET

6 cuts	6 cuts	6 cuts	6 cuts
Advance 2 times (40)	Advance 2 times (40)	Advance 2 times (40)	Advance 2 times (40)
6 cuts	6 cuts	6 cuts	6 cuts
Advance 3 times (60)	Advance 3 times (60)	Advance 3 times (60)	Advance 3 times (60)
1 cut	1 cut	1 cut	1 cut
Advance 3 times (60)	Advance 3 times (60)	Advance 3 times (60)	Advance 3 times (60)
1 cut	1 cut	1 cut	1 cut
Advance 3 times (60)	Advance 3 times (60)	Advance 3 times (60)	Advance 3 times (60)
1 cut	1 cut	1 cut	1 cut
Advance 3 times (60)	Advance 3 times (60)	Advance 3 times (60)	Advance 3 times (60)

Diagonal Zig-zags

Straight-Line

The goal is to create an illusion of zig-zags that are diagonal while they are cut vertically on the straight-line.
Rosette/ Pattern Bar: 1.2 mm or barley corn pattern bar
Amplitude: n/a
Rubber: 30° with a tapered head; same width as the pattern bar or a tiny bit smaller.
Maximum depth: By sight
Number of passes each cut: 2
Division: 10 teeth
Pawl: 20 teeth and you can set the stop

This pattern assumes you are using one of the original solid blocks of pattern bars; if not, I suggest you experiment and use a pattern bar with low amplitude or just indentations if you have one. Make sure you mark your division for CW and CCW and keep a chart, as you will be making different quantities of cuts and divisions.

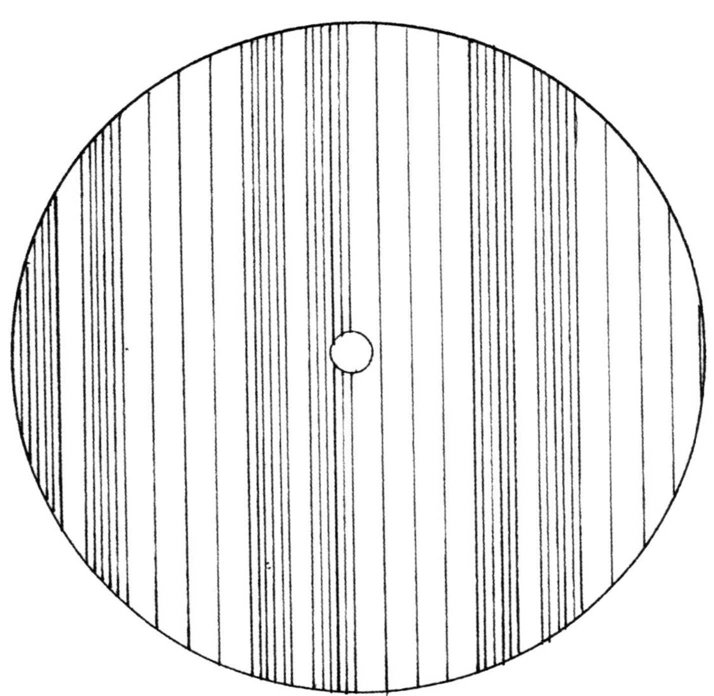

Alternating straight-line recipe. *Calina Shevlin*

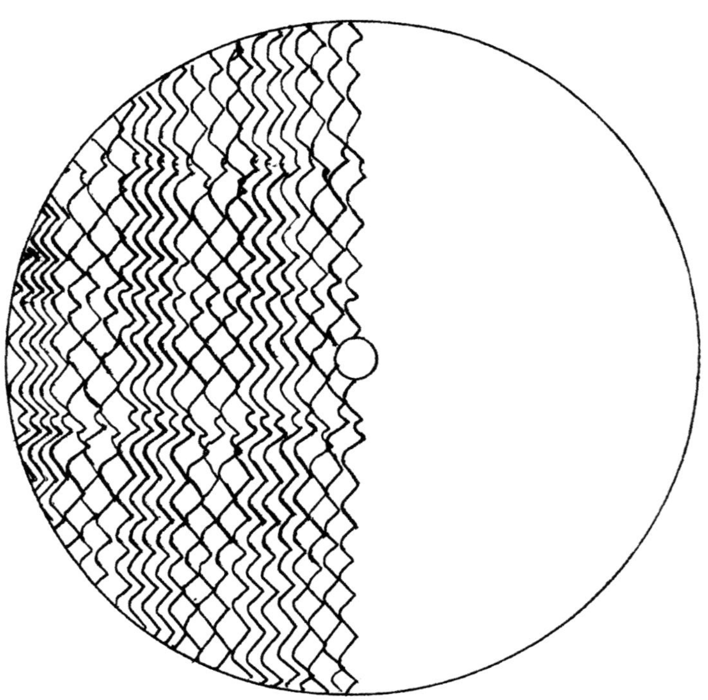

Diagonal zig-zag recipe. *Calina Shevlin*

Make 5 cuts using the pattern bar.
Move 10 teeth (clicks) on the division CW.
Displace/advance 20 clicks.
Make 1 cut.
Move 10 clicks on the division CCW.
Advance 20 clicks.
Make 1 cut.
Move 10 clicks on the division CW.
Advance 20 clicks.
Make 1 cut.
Move 10 clicks on the division CCW.
Advance 20 clicks.

Continue until you have traversed the entire area you wish to decorate. I use the chart to mark off what I have done.

ZIG-ZAG RECIPE SHEET

5 cuts	5 cuts	5 cuts	5 cuts
division 10 CW	division 10 CW	division 10 CW	division 10 CW
1 cut	1 cut	1 cut	1 cut
division 10 CCW	division 10 CCW	division 10 CCW	division 10 CCW
1 cut	1 cut	1 cut	1 cut
division 10 CW	division 10 CW	division 10 CW	division 10 CW
1 cut	1 cut	1 cut	1 cut
division 10 CCW	division 10 CCW	division 10 CCW	division 10 CCW
5 cuts	5 cuts	5 cuts	5 cuts
division 10 CW	division 10 CW	division 10 CW	division 10 CW
1 cut	1 cut	1 cut	1 cut
division 10 CCW	division 10 CCW	division 10 CCW	division 10 CCW
1 cut	1 cut	1 cut	1 cut
division 10 CW	division 10 CW	division 10 CW	division 10 CW
1 cut	1 cut	1 cut	1 cut
division 10 CCW	division 10 CCW	division 10 CCW	division 10 CCW
5 cuts	5 cuts	5 cuts	5 cuts
division 10 CW	division 10 CW	division 10 CW	division 10 CW
1 cut	1 cut	1 cut	1 cut
division 10 CCW	division 10 CCW	division 10 CCW	division 10 CCW
1 cut	1 cut	1 cut	1 cut
division 10 CW	division 10 CW	division 10 CW	division 10 CW
1 cut	1 cut	1 cut	1 cut
division 10 CCW	division 10 CCW	division 10 CCW	division 10 CCW

Diamonds

Straight-Line

This pattern creates small diamond shapes by using three different pattern bars.
Rosette/ Pattern Bar: Pattern bar #1, #2, and #3
Amplitude: n/a
Rubber: 30° with a tapered head; same width as the pattern bar or a tiny bit smaller.
Maximum depth: By sight
Number of passes each cut: 2
Division: 40 teeth
Pawl: 20 teeth; you can set the stop

This pattern assumes you are using one of the original solid blocks of pattern bars; if not, I suggest you experiment and use a pattern bar with low amplitude or just indentations if you have one. You will be needing the three that are generally found together: #1 has two indentations and then space and repeats, #2 has three indentations then space and repeats, and #3 has four indentations then space and repeats. Make sure you mark your division for CW and CCW and keep a chart, as you will be making different quantities of cuts and divisions.

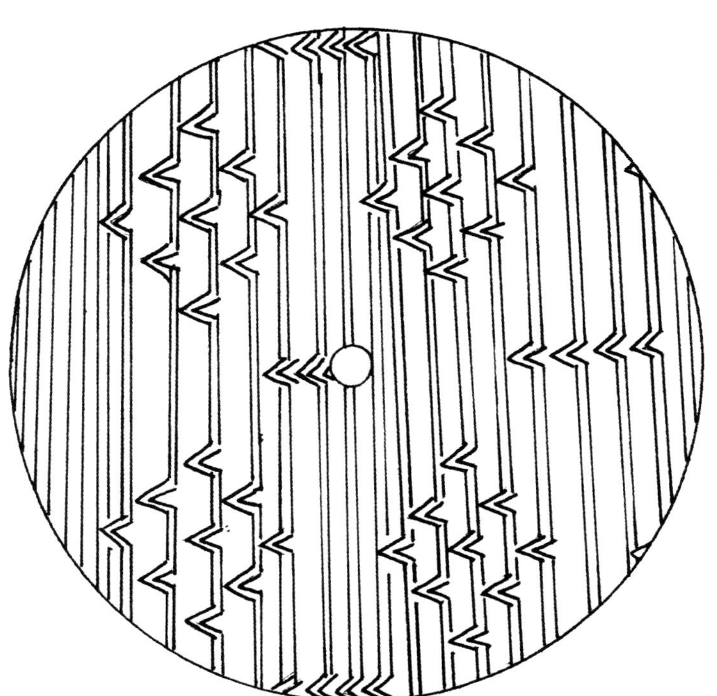

Diamonds recipe. *Calina Shevlin*

Make 8 cuts using the pattern bar #1
Move 40 teeth (clicks) on the division CW
Displace/Advance 20 clicks
Make 2 cuts with pattern bar #1
Advance 20 clicks
Make 2 cuts with pattern bar #2
Advance 20 clicks
Make 2 cuts with pattern bar #3
Advance 20 clicks
Make 2 cuts with pattern bar #2
Advance 20 clicks
Make 2 cuts with pattern bar #1
Move 40 clicks on the division CCW
Advance 20 clicks

Continue until you have traversed the entire area you wish to decorate. I use the chart to mark off what I have done.

DIAMONDS RECIPE SHEET

8 cuts pattern bar (p.b.) #1	8 cuts p.b. #1	8 cuts p.b. #1
div 40	div 40	div 40
advance 20	advance 20	advance 20
2 cuts p.b #1	2 cuts p.b #1	2 cuts p.b #1
advance 20	advance 20	advance 20
2 cuts p.b #2	2 cuts p.b #2	2 cuts p.b #2
advance 20	advance 20	advance 20
2 cuts p.b #3	2 cuts p.b #3	2 cuts p.b #3
advance 20	advance 20	advance 20
2 cuts p.b #2	2 cuts p.b #2	2 cuts p.b #2
advance 20	advance 20	advance 20
2 cuts p.b #1	2 cuts p.b #1	2 cuts p.b #1
div 40	div 40	div 40
8 cuts p.b. #1	8 cuts p.b. #1	8 cuts p.b. #1
8 cuts p.b. #1	8 cuts p.b. #1	8 cuts p.b. #1
div 40	div 40	div 40
advance 20	advance 20	advance 20
2 cuts p.b #1	2 cuts p.b #1	2 cuts p.b #1
advance 20	advance 20	advance 20
2 cuts p.b #2	2 cuts p.b #2	2 cuts p.b #2
advance 20	advance 20	advance 20
2 cuts p.b #3	2 cuts p.b #3	2 cuts p.b #3
advance 20	advance 20	advance 20
2 cuts p.b #2	2 cuts p.b #2	2 cuts p.b #2
advance 20	advance 20	advance 20
2 cuts p.b #1	2 cuts p.b #1	2 cuts p.b #1
div 40	div 40	div 40
8 cuts p.b. #1	8 cuts p.b. #1	8 cuts p.b. #1

Drapes

Straight-Line

This creates a high amplitude horizontal looking wave from small vertical waves.
Rosette/ Pattern Bar: Pattern bar #2 with 3 indentations, space, and so on.
Amplitude: n/a
Rubber: 30° with a tapered head; same width as the pattern bar or a tiny bit smaller
Maximum depth: by sight
Number of passes each cut: 2
Division: None
Pawl: 20 teeth; you can set the stop

This pattern assumes you are using one of the original solid blocks of pattern bars; if not, I suggest you experiment and use a pattern bar with low amplitude or just indentations if you have one. You will use the pattern bar with three indentations, space, and three indentations, etc. Make sure to keep a good chart since you will be turning the worm (see page 52).

This works a lot like the moiré pattern on the rose engine, except in vertical form. You will need to be free of all distractions and do this pattern A–Z without stopping. The abbreviations are as follows:

1 cut: Cutting using the pattern bar #2
adv 20: Advance the work using the pawl, 20 clicks
worm 1–10: Turn the worm 1 click (or however many is stated)

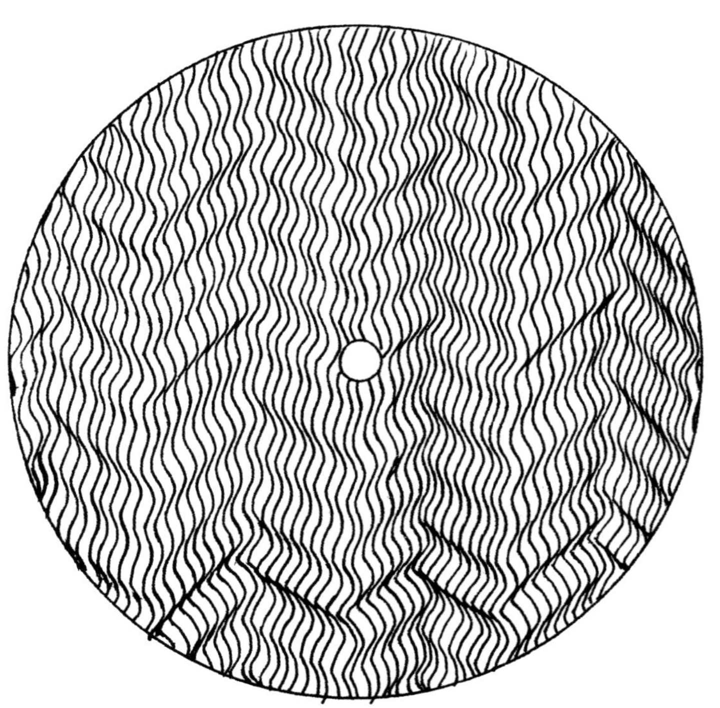

Drapes recipe. *Calina Shevlin*

I find it extremely useful to use a Post-it with an arrow and put that by the worm with the direction you are turning (CW or CCW) so you can remember. Do not forget to switch the direction of the Post-it when you start turning the worm in the opposite direction.

DRAPES RECIPE SHEET

1 cut	1 cut	1 cut	1 cut
adv 20	adv 20	adv 20	adv 20
worm 1 CW	worm 10 CW	worm 1 CCW	worm 10 CCW
1 cut	1 cut	1 cut	1 cut
adv 20	adv 20	adv 20	adv 20
worm 2 CW	worm 9 CW	worm 2 CCW	worm 9 CCW
1 cut	1 cut	1 cut	1 cut
adv 20	adv 20	adv 20	adv 20
worm 3 CW	worm 8 CW	worm 3 CCW	worm 8 CCW
1 cut	1 cut	1 cut	1 cut
adv 20	adv 20	adv 20	adv 20
worm 4 CW	worm 7 CW	worm 4 CCW	worm 7 CCW
1 cut	1 cut	1 cut	1 cut
adv 20	adv 20	adv 20	adv 20
worm 5 CW	worm 6 CW	worm 5 CCW	worm 6 CCW
1 cut	1 cut	1 cut	1 cut
adv 20	adv 20	adv 20	adv 20
worm 6 CW	worm 5 CW	worm 6 CCW	worm 5 CCW
1 cut	1 cut	1 cut	1 cut
adv 20	adv 20	adv 20	adv 20
worm 7 CW	worm 4 CW	worm 7 CCW	worm 4 CCW
1 cut	1 cut	1 cut	1 cut
adv 20	adv 20	adv 20	adv 20
worm 8 CW	worm 3 CW	worm 8 CCW	worm 3 CCW
1 cut	1 cut	1 cut	1 cut
adv 20	adv 20	adv 20	adv 20
worm 9 CW	worm 2 CW	worm 9 CCW	worm 2 CCW
1 cut	1 cut	1 cut	1 cut
adv 20	adv 20	adv 20	adv 20
worm 10 CW	worm 1 CW	worm 10 CCW	worm 1 CCW

Heartbeat

Straight-Line

This pattern creates a heartbeat pattern using only one pattern bar.
Rosette/ Pattern Bar: Pattern bar #2 with three indentations.
Rubber: 30° with a tapered head; same width as the pattern bar or a tiny bit smaller.
Maximum depth: By sight
Number of passes each cut: 2
Pawl: 20 teeth; you can set the stop

This pattern assumes you are using one of the original solid blocks of pattern bars; if not, I suggest you experiment and use a pattern bar with low amplitude or just indentations if you have one. You will use the pattern bar with three indentations. Make sure to keep a good chart since you will be turning the worm CW and CCW.

This works a lot like the zigzag pattern on the rose engine, except in vertical form. You will need to be free of all distractions and do this pattern A–Z without stopping. The abbreviations are as follows:

1 cut: Cutting using the pattern bar #2
adv 20: Advance the work using the pawl, 20 clicks
worm 1–10: Turn the worm 1 click (or however many is stated)

I find it extremely useful to use a Post-it with an arrow and put that by the worm with the direction you are turning (CW or CCW) so you can remember. Do not forget to switch the direction of the Post-it when you start turning the worm in the opposite direction.

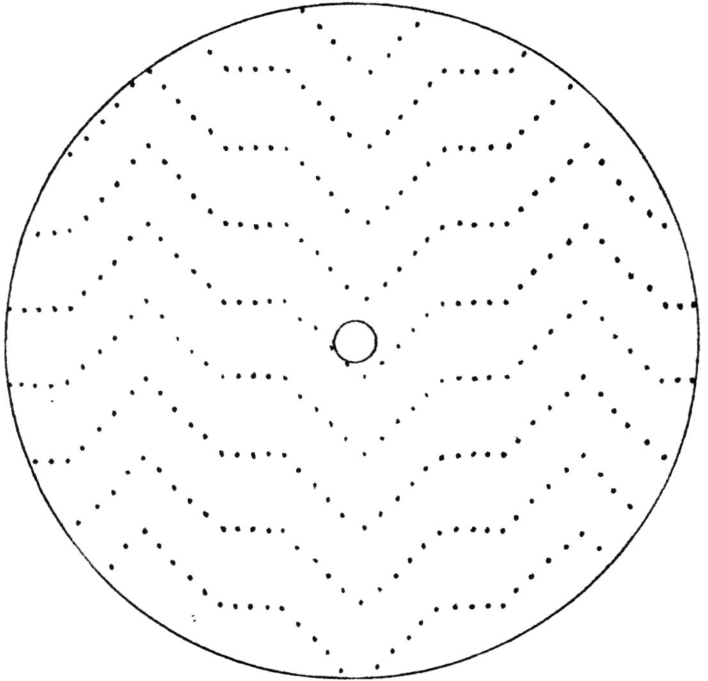

Heartbeat recipe. *Calina Shevlin*

HEARTBEAT RECIPE SHEET

cut 1	cut 1	cut 1	cut 1
adv 20	adv 20	adv 20	adv 20
worm 10 CW	worm 10 CCW	worm 10 CW	worm 10 CCW
cut 1	cut 1	cut 1	cut 1
adv 20	adv 20	adv 20	adv 20
worm 10 CW	worm 10 CCW	worm 10 CW	worm 10 CCW
cut 1	cut 1	cut 1	cut 1
adv 20	adv 20	adv 20	adv 20
worm 10 CW	worm 10 CCW	worm 10 CW	worm 10 CCW
cut 1	cut 1	cut 1	cut 1
adv 20	adv 20	adv 20	adv 20
worm 10 CW	worm 10 CCW	worm 10 CW	worm 10 CCW
cut 1	cut 1	cut 1	cut 1
adv 20	adv 20	adv 20	adv 20
worm 10 CW	worm 10 CCW	worm 10 CW	worm 10 CCW
cut 5, adv 20, no worm	cut 5, adv 20, no worm	cut 5, adv 20, no worm	cut 5, adv 20, no worm
cut 1	cut 1	cut 1	cut 1
adv 20	adv 20	adv 20	adv 20
worm 10 CW	worm 10 CCW	worm 10 CW	worm 10 CCW
cut 1	cut 1	cut 1	cut 1
adv 20	adv 20	adv 20	adv 20
worm 10 CW	worm 10 CCW	worm 10 CW	worm 10 CCW
cut 1	cut 1	cut 1	cut 1
adv 20	adv 20	adv 20	adv 20
worm 10 CW	worm 10 CCW	worm 10 CW	worm 10 CCW
cut 1	cut 1	cut 1	cut 1
adv 20	adv 20	adv 20	adv 20
worm 10 CW	worm 10 CCW	worm 10 CW	worm 10 CCW
cut 1	cut 1	cut 1	cut 1
adv 20	adv 20	adv 20	adv 20
worm 10 CW	worm 10 CCW	worm 10 CW	worm 10 CCW

Barley Corn (Grains d'Orge)

Straight-Line

This creates the barley corn effect in vertical fashion. It looks like the round version between the corns.

Rosette/ Pattern Bar: Pattern bar #4 with 1.2 mm between indentations, also called the barley corn pattern

Rubber: 30° with a rounded, polished head (see p 63)

Maximum depth: by sight

Number of passes each cut: 2

Division: 13 teeth—mark your wheels

Pawl: 26 teeth; you can set the stop

If you do not have a 1.2 mm pattern bar you may use a low amplitude wave without peaks. This pattern is straightforward; there is only cutting and dividing, as in the round pattern.

Cut 1
Advance 26 teeth
Division 13 teeth
Cut 1
Advance 26 teeth
Division 13 teeth

Continue like this until the end. For this pattern I still like to make the exterior circle as in the rose engine patterns, then fill it with the vertical barley corn. It has a nice effect.

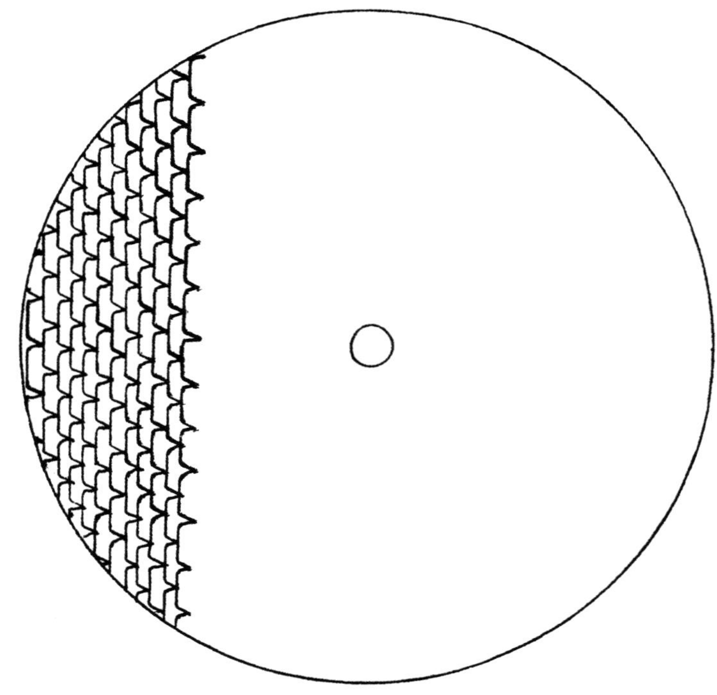

Vertical barley corn recipe. *Calina Shevlin*

BARLEY CORN RECIPE SHEET

cut 1	cut 1	cut 1	cut 1	cut 1	cut 1
advance 26	advance 26	advance 26	advance 26	advance 26	advance 26
division 13	division 13	division 13	division 13	division 13	division 13
cut 1	cut 1	cut 1	cut 1	cut 1	cut 1
advance 26	advance 26	advance 26	advance 26	advance 26	advance 26
division 13	division 13	division 13	division 13	division 13	division 13
cut 1	cut 1	cut 1	cut 1	cut 1	cut 1
advance 26	advance 26	advance 26	advance 26	advance 26	advance 26
division 13	division 13	division 13	division 13	division 13	division 13
cut 1	cut 1	cut 1	cut 1	cut 1	cut 1
advance 26	advance 26	advance 26	advance 26	advance 26	advance 26
division 13	division 13	division 13	division 13	division 13	division 13
cut 1	cut 1	cut 1	cut 1	cut 1	cut 1
advance 26	advance 26	advance 26	advance 26	advance 26	advance 26
division 13	division 13	division 13	division 13	division 13	division 13
cut 1	cut 1	cut 1	cut 1	cut 1	cut 1
advance 26	advance 26	advance 26	advance 26	advance 26	advance 26
division 13	division 13	division 13	division 13	division 13	division 13
cut 1	cut 1	cut 1	cut 1	cut 1	cut 1
advance 26	advance 26	advance 26	advance 26	advance 26	advance 26
division 13	division 13	division 13	division 13	division 13	division 13

cut 1	cut 1	cut 1	cut 1	cut 1	cut 1
advance 26	advance 26	advance 26	advance 26	advance 26	advance 26
division 13	division 13	division 13	division 13	division 13	division 13
cut 1	cut 1	cut 1	cut 1	cut 1	cut 1
advance 26	advance 26	advance 26	advance 26	advance 26	advance 26
division 13	division 13	division 13	division 13	division 13	division 13
cut 1	cut 1	cut 1	cut 1	cut 1	cut 1
advance 26	advance 26	advance 26	advance 26	advance 26	advance 26
division 13	division 13	division 13	division 13	division 13	division 13
cut 1	cut 1	cut 1	cut 1	cut 1	cut 1
advance 26	advance 26	advance 26	advance 26	advance 26	advance 26
division 13	division 13	division 13	division 13	division 13	division 13
cut 1	cut 1	cut 1	cut 1	cut 1	cut 1
advance 26	advance 26	advance 26	advance 26	advance 26	advance 26
division 13	division 13	division 13	division 13	division 13	division 13
cut 1	cut 1	cut 1	cut 1	cut 1	cut 1
advance 26	advance 26	advance 26	advance 26	advance 26	advance 26
division 13	division 13	division 13	division 13	division 13	division 13
cut 1	cut 1	cut 1	cut 1	cut 1	cut 1
advance 26	advance 26	advance 26	advance 26	advance 26	advance 26
division 13	division 13	division 13	division 13	division 13	division 13

Vertical barley corn. *Calina Shevlin*

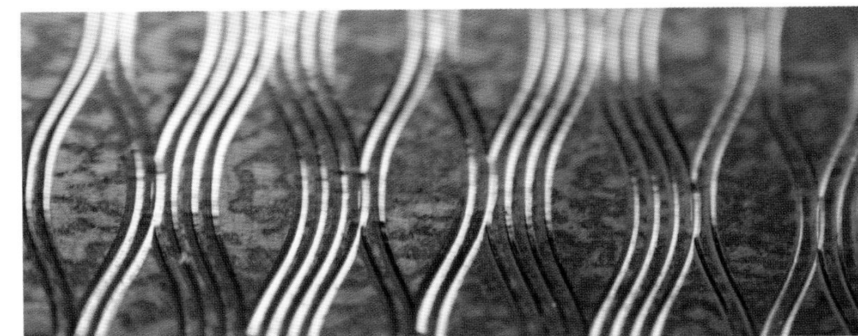

Vertical barley corn. *Calina Shevlin*

Basket Weave (Panier)

Straight-Line

This creates the basket weave effect in vertical fashion. It looks like the round version.

Rosette/Pattern Bar: Pattern bar #2 with 3 indentations (see page XXX).

Rubber: 30° with a gentle point (see page XXX)

Maximum depth: By sight

Number of passes each cut: 2

Division: 40 teeth, mark your wheels

Pawl: 20 teeth; you can set the stop

This pattern is quick and easy. I have included a chart just so you don't get lost in the monotony.

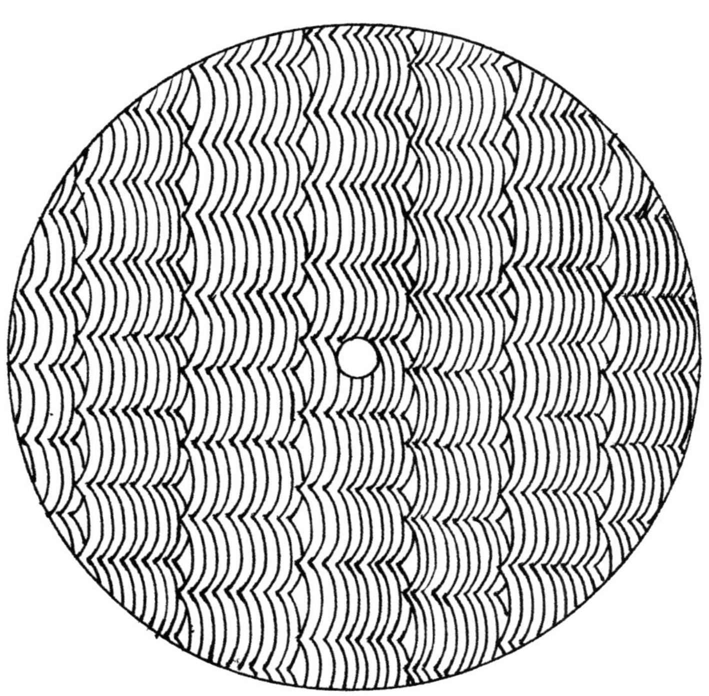

Vertical basket weave recipe. *Calina Shevlin*

BASKET WEAVE RECIPE SHEET

1 cut	1 cut	1 cut	1 cut	1 cut
adv 20	adv 20	adv 20	adv 20	adv 20
Division 40 CW	Division 40 CW	Division 40 CW	Division 40 CW	Division 40 CW
1 cut	1 cut	1 cut	1 cut	1 cut
adv 20	adv 20	adv 20	adv 20	adv 20
Division 40 CCW	Division 40 CCW	Division 40 CCW	Division 40 CCW	Division 40 CCW
1 cut	1 cut	1 cut	1 cut	1 cut
adv 20	adv 20	adv 20	adv 20	adv 20
Division 40 CW	Division 40 CW	Division 40 CW	Division 40 CW	Division 40 CW
1 cut	1 cut	1 cut	1 cut	1 cut
adv 20	adv 20	adv 20	adv 20	adv 20
Division 40 CCW	Division 40 CCW	Division 40 CCW	Division 40 CCW	Division 40 CCW
1 cut	1 cut	1 cut	1 cut	1 cut
adv 20	adv 20	adv 20	adv 20	adv 20
Division 40 CW	Division 40 CW	Division 40 CW	Division 40 CW	Division 40 CW
1 cut	1 cut	1 cut	1 cut	1 cut
adv 20	adv 20	adv 20	adv 20	adv 20
Division 40 CCW	Division 40 CCW	Division 40 CCW	Division 40 CCW	Division 40 CCW
1 cut	1 cut	1 cut	1 cut	1 cut
adv 20	adv 20	adv 20	adv 20	adv 20
Division 40 CW	Division 40 CW	Division 40 CW	Division 40 CW	Division 40 CW
1 cut	1 cut	1 cut	1 cut	1 cut
adv 20	adv 20	adv 20	adv 20	adv 20
Division 40 CCW	Division 40 CCW	Division 40 CCW	Division 40 CCW	Division 40 CCW
1 cut	1 cut	1 cut	1 cut	1 cut
adv 20	adv 20	adv 20	adv 20	adv 20
Division 40 CW	Division 40 CW	Division 40 CW	Division 40 CW	Division 40 CW
1 cut	1 cut	1 cut	1 cut	1 cut
adv 20	adv 20	adv 20	adv 20	adv 20
Division 40 CCW	Division 40 CCW	Division 40 CCW	Division 40 CCW	Division 40 CCW

Honeycomb

Straight-Line

This creates small honeycomb-like cells in a vertical form using the same bars as the Diamonds.

Rosette/Pattern Bar: Pattern bar #1, #2, and #3

Amplitude: n/a

Rubber: 30° with a tapered head; same width as the pattern bar or a tiny bit smaller.

Maximum depth: By sight

Number of passes each cut: 2

Division: 40 teeth

Pawl: 20 teeth; you can set the stop

This pattern assumes you are using one of the original solid blocks of pattern bars; if not, I suggest you experiment and use a pattern bar with low amplitude or just indentations if you have one. You will need the three that are generally found together: #1 has two indentations and then space and repeats, #2 has three indentations and then space and repeats, and #3 has four indentations and then space and repeats. Make sure you mark your division for CW and CCW and keep a chart, as you will be making different quantities of cuts and divisions.

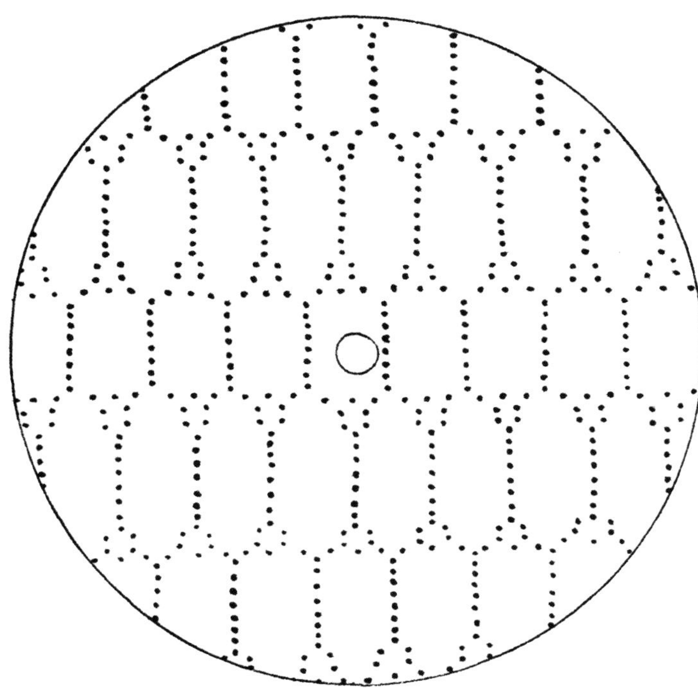

Vertical honeycomb recipe. *Calina Shevlin*

Make 8 cuts using the pattern bar #1
Advance 20 clicks
Make 2 cuts with pattern bar #2
Advance 20 clicks
Make 1 cut with pattern bar #3
Advance 20 clicks
Division 40 clicks CCW
Make 1 cut with pattern bar #3
Advance 20 clicks
Make 2 cuts with pattern bar #2
Advance 20 clicks
Make 8 cuts with pattern bar #1
Advance 20 clicks
Make 2 cuts with pattern bar #2
Advance 20 clicks
Make 1 cut with pattern bar #3
Advance 20 clicks
Division 40 clicks CW
Make 1 cut with pattern bar #3
Advance 20 clicks
Make 2 cuts with pattern bar #2
Advance 20 clicks
Make 8 cuts with pattern bar #1

Continue with the above instructions until you have traversed the entire area you wish to decorate. I find a chart absolutely necessary for this, as there is much changing of pattern bars and the cutting sequence is always changing.

VERTICAL HONEYCOMB CHART

8 cuts p.b.1	8 cuts p.b.1	8 cuts p.b.1
advance 20	advance 20	advance 20
2 cuts p.b.2	2 cuts p.b.2	2 cuts p.b.2
advance 20	advance 20	advance 20
1 cut p.b.3	1 cut p.b.3	1 cut p.b.3
advance 20	advance 20	advance 20
div 40 CCW	div 40 CW	div 40 CCW
1 cut p.b.3	1 cut p.b.3	1 cut p.b.3
advance 20	advance 20	advance 20
2 cuts p.b.2	2 cuts p.b.2	2 cuts p.b.2
advance 20	advance 20	advance 20
8 cuts p.b.1	8 cuts p.b.1	8 cuts p.b.1
advance 20	advance 20	advance 20
2 cuts p.b.2	2 cuts p.b.2	2 cuts p.b.2
advance 20	advance 20	advance 20
1 cut p.b.3	1 cut p.b.3	1 cut p.b.3
advance 20	advance 20	advance 20
div 40 CW	div 40 CCW	div 40 CW
1 cut p.b.3	1 cut p.b.3	1 cut p.b.3
advance 20	advance 20	advance 20
2 cuts p.b.2	2 cuts p.b.2	2 cuts p.b.2
advance 20	advance 20	advance 20
8 cuts p.b.1	8 cuts p.b.1	8 cuts p.b.1
advance 20	advance 20	advance 20
2 cuts p.b.2	2 cuts p.b.2	2 cuts p.b.2
advance 20	advance 20	advance 20
1 cut p.b.3	1 cut p.b.3	1 cut p.b.3
advance 20	advance 20	advance 20
div 40 CCW	div 40 CW	div 40 CCW

Basic Sunray

Straight-Line

This pattern flows out from the center in rays that can be straight or wavy. The center does not necessarily begin in the center; it can begin in a corner, on a side, or just slightly off-center.
Rosette/Pattern Bar: None
Rubber: None
Maximum depth: By sight
Number of passes each cut: 2
Division: None
Pawl: 2 teeth
Counter: (B on p 96) turn

This pattern has many variations; below you will find information for the most basic straight ray pattern. Look at page 98 to see the movement of the headstock from vertical to free turning.

You will be turning the counter 4 clicks every cut marked; since this requires multiple changes in the advancement and the number of cuts I have included a chart.

The pattern is made up of closely spaced rays with only 1 tooth of advancement between the 13 cuts, then 2 teeth of advancement between each single cut. Between all the counter is turned 4 clicks, and this is what rotates the piece.

There will be a total of 240 cuts on the piece with this recipe. The design comprises 20 cuts including the jumping rays repeated 12 times.

Sunray recipe. *Calina Shevlin*

Sunray. *Calina Shevlin*

SUNRAY RECIPE SHEET

13 cuts, Adv. 1 between each ; turn 4	13 cuts, Adv. 1 between each ; turn 4	13 cuts, Adv. 1 between each ; turn 4	13 cuts, Adv. 1 between each ; turn 4	13 cuts, Adv. 1 between each ; turn 4
Adv. 2 clicks	Adv. 2 clicks	Adv. 2 clicks	Adv. 2 clicks	Adv. 2 clicks
Cut 1 ; turn 4	Cut 1 ; turn 4	Cut 1 ; turn 4	Cut 1 ; turn 4	Cut 1 ; turn 4
Adv. 2 clicks	Adv. 2 clicks	Adv. 2 clicks	Adv. 2 clicks	Adv. 2 clicks
Cut 1 ; turn 4	Cut 1 ; turn 4	Cut 1 ; turn 4	Cut 1 ; turn 4	Cut 1 ; turn 4
Adv. 2 clicks	Adv. 2 clicks	Adv. 2 clicks	Adv. 2 clicks	Adv. 2 clicks
Cut 1 ; turn 4	Cut 1 ; turn 4	Cut 1 ; turn 4	Cut 1 ; turn 4	Cut 1 ; turn 4
Adv. 2 clicks	Adv. 2 clicks	Adv. 2 clicks	Adv. 2 clicks	Adv. 2 clicks
13 cuts, Adv. 1 between each ; turn 4	13 cuts, Adv. 1 between each ; turn 4	13 cuts, Adv. 1 between each ; turn 4	13 cuts, Adv. 1 between each ; turn 4	13 cuts, Adv. 1 between each ; turn 4
Adv. 2 clicks	Adv. 2 clicks	Adv. 2 clicks	Adv. 2 clicks	Adv. 2 clicks
Cut 1 ; turn 4	Cut 1 ; turn 4	Cut 1 ; turn 4	Cut 1 ; turn 4	Cut 1 ; turn 4
Adv. 2 clicks	Adv. 2 clicks	Adv. 2 clicks	Adv. 2 clicks	Adv. 2 clicks
Cut 1 ; turn 4	Cut 1 ; turn 4	Cut 1 ; turn 4	Cut 1 ; turn 4	Cut 1 ; turn 4
Adv. 2 clicks	Adv. 2 clicks	Adv. 2 clicks	Adv. 2 clicks	Adv. 2 clicks
Cut 1 ; turn 4	Cut 1 ; turn 4	Cut 1 ; turn 4	Cut 1 ; turn 4	Cut 1 ; turn 4
Adv. 2 clicks	Adv. 2 clicks	Adv. 2 clicks	Adv. 2 clicks	Adv. 2 clicks
13 cuts, Adv. 1 between each ; turn 4	13 cuts, Adv. 1 between each ; turn 4	13 cuts, Adv. 1 between each ; turn 4	13 cuts, Adv. 1 between each ; turn 4	13 cuts, Adv. 1 between each ; turn 4
Adv. 2 clicks	Adv. 2 clicks	Adv. 2 clicks	Adv. 2 clicks	Adv. 2 clicks
Cut 1 ; turn 4	Cut 1 ; turn 4	Cut 1 ; turn 4	Cut 1 ; turn 4	Cut 1 ; turn 4
Adv. 2 clicks	Adv. 2 clicks	Adv. 2 clicks	Adv. 2 clicks	Adv. 2 clicks
Cut 1 ; turn 4	Cut 1 ; turn 4	Cut 1 ; turn 4	Cut 1 ; turn 4	Cut 1 ; turn 4
Adv. 2 clicks	Adv. 2 clicks	Adv. 2 clicks	Adv. 2 clicks	Adv. 2 clicks
Cut 1 ; turn 4	Cut 1 ; turn 4	Cut 1 ; turn 4	Cut 1 ; turn 4	Cut 1 ; turn 4
Adv. 2 clicks	Adv. 2 clicks	Adv. 2 clicks	Adv. 2 clicks	Adv. 2 clicks

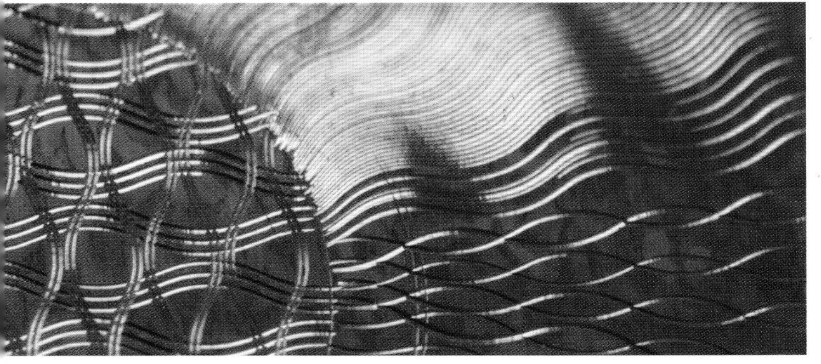

Sunray Honeycomb

Straight-Line

This creates small honeycomb-like cells in the round utilizing the sunray technique and the same bars as the Diamonds.

Rosette/ Pattern Bar: Pattern bar #1, #2, and #3

Rubber: 30° with a tapered head; same width as the pattern bar or a tiny bit smaller

Maximum depth: by sight

Number of passes each cut: 2

Division: 40 teeth

Counter: 4 teeth, always the same direction (CW); this is simply used to rotate the work

Pawl: 1 tooth

This pattern assumes you are using one of the original solid blocks of pattern bars; if not, I suggest you experiment and use a pattern bar with low amplitude or just indentations if you have one. You will need the three that are generally found together: #1 has two indentations and then space and repeats, #2 has three indentations then space and repeats, and #3 has four indentations then space and repeats.

Make sure you mark your division for CW and CCW and keep a chart, as you will be making different quantities of cuts and divisions.

This pattern also has 240 cuts and the pattern will have to be repeated 10 times. The chart has 5 repetitions, so you will need to make a copy or change your markings as you recommence.

SUNRAY HONEYCOMB RECIPE SHEET

6 cuts p.b. #1	6 cuts p.b. #1	6 cuts p.b. #1	6 cuts p.b. #1	6 cuts p.b. #1
Adv. 1 click pawl	Adv. 1 click	Adv. 1 click	Adv. 1 click	Adv. 1 click
Worm; 4 clicks	Worm; 4 clicks	Worm; 4 clicks	Worm; 4 clicks	Worm; 4 clicks
2 cuts p.b. #2	2 cuts p.b. #2	2 cuts p.b. #2	2 cuts p.b. #2	2 cuts p.b. #2
Adv. 1 click	Adv. 1 click	Adv. 1 click	Adv. 1 click	Adv. 1 click
Worm; 4 clicks	Worm; 4 clicks	Worm; 4 clicks	Worm; 4 clicks	Worm; 4 clicks
1 cut p.b. #3	1 cut p.b. #3	1 cut p.b. #3	1 cut p.b. #3	1 cut p.b. #3
Adv. 1 click	Adv. 1 click	Adv. 1 click	Adv. 1 click	Adv. 1 click
Worm; 4 clicks	Worm; 4 clicks	Worm; 4 clicks	Worm; 4 clicks	Worm; 4 clicks
division 40 CCW	division 40 CCW	division 40 CCW	division 40 CCW	division 40 CCW
1 cut p.b. #3	1 cut p.b. #3	1 cut p.b. #3	1 cut p.b. #3	1 cut p.b. #3
Adv. 1 click	Adv. 1 click	Adv. 1 click	Adv. 1 click	Adv. 1 click
Worm; 4 clicks	Worm; 4 clicks	Worm; 4 clicks	Worm; 4 clicks	Worm; 4 clicks

2 cuts p.b. #2	2 cuts p.b. #2	2 cuts p.b. #2	2 cuts p.b. #2	2 cuts p.b. #2
Adv. 1 click	Adv. 1 click	Adv. 1 click	Adv. 1 click	Adv. 1 click
Worm; 4 clicks	Worm; 4 clicks	Worm; 4 clicks	Worm; 4 clicks	Worm; 4 clicks
6 cuts p.b. #1	6 cuts p.b. #1	6 cuts p.b. #1	6 cuts p.b. #1	6 cuts p.b. #1
Adv. 1 click	Adv. 1 click	Adv. 1 click	Adv. 1 click	Adv. 1 click
Worm; 4 clicks	Worm; 4 clicks	Worm; 4 clicks	Worm; 4 clicks	Worm; 4 clicks
2 cuts p.b. #2	2 cuts p.b. #2	2 cuts p.b. #2	2 cuts p.b. #2	2 cuts p.b. #2
Adv. 1 click	Adv. 1 click	Adv. 1 click	Adv. 1 click	Adv. 1 click
Worm; 4 clicks	Worm; 4 clicks	Worm; 4 clicks	Worm; 4 clicks	Worm; 4 clicks
1 cut p.b. #3	1 cut p.b. #3	1 cut p.b. #3	1 cut p.b. #3	1 cut p.b. #3
Adv. 1 click	Adv. 1 click	Adv. 1 click	Adv. 1 click	Adv. 1 click
Worm; 4 clicks	Worm; 4 clicks	Worm; 4 clicks	Worm; 4 clicks	Worm; 4 clicks
Division 40 CW	Division 40 CW	Division 40 CW	Division 40 CW	Division 40 CW

Sunray honeycomb recipe. *Calina Shevlin*

Blocks example. *Calina Shevlin*

Herringbone example. *Calina Shevlin*

Endnotes

1. "Richemont Acquires Stern Group." https://www.richemont.com
2. "PEEK" (accessed January 3, 2017), http://www.curbellplastics.com/engineering-plastics/peek.html
3. "Delrin Acetal Resin," http://www.dupont.com

Bibliography

Bazley, Thomas S. *Index to the Geometric Chuck: A Treatise upon the Description in the Lathe, of Simple and Compound Epitrochoidal or "Geometric" Curves.* (London: Waterlow and Sons, 1875)

Daniels, George. *Watchmaking.* (London: Philip Wilson Publishers,1981)

Diderot, Denis, and Jean le Rond D'Alembert. "Art du Tourner" in *L'Encyclopédie.* (Lyon, France: Tours Bibliotheque de l'Image: 2001 [1701]; selected reprint)

Holtzapffel, John J. *Hand or Simple Turning Principles and Practice.* Vol. IV of V (London: Holtzapffel & Company, 1881)

Matthews, Martin. *Engine Turning 1680–1980: The Tools and Technique.* (Sevenoaks: M. Matthews, 1982)

Glossary

Base Slide/Chariot: This is used to move the entire tool slide system toward or away from the operator to adjust for the size and shape of a piece.

Brocading Machine/Tapisserie: Motorized machine that follows a patterned template and reduces it to create the same pattern on a small disc of metal, often with a small cylinder of rosettes used to create a background pattern.

Chuck/Support: This is the bare headstock point of attachment for any chucks. The basic chuck is just for holding or supporting the work in one place securely while it is being decorated.

Cutter/Burin: Stationary tool that the work piece is turned against to create incised lines.

Division Plate/Indexing Plate/Crossing Plate/Plateau Diviseur: This is the method of moving the rosette a set number of degrees with the aid of a handle. Used when creating patterns that are not simply concentric.

Goniostat/Goniometre: Used to hold the cutter for accurate angles.

Guillochage: The act of creating guilloché, sometimes used as the plural of guilloché.

Guilloché: The incising of thin, shallow, faceted lines into a metal surface using a hand operated lathe called a rose engine or straight-line. This application of decoration does not change the overall form of the original piece.

Guillocheur: Male who creates guilloché.

Guillocheuse: Female who creates guilloché. This term has only been around and in use since 2005.

Hand Wheel/Manivelle: What is turned by the operator to control the speed (on the left-hand side).

Leaf Spring/Ressort: Piece on the rose engine that applies tension to the x axis or y axis. Can be changed for the needs of the operator.

Microscope/Binoculaire: Often attached to the base slide to aid the operator in keeping good posture while seeing the work clearly and without interruption.

Pawl/Clic: Hand ratchet on the right-hand side used to advance the work (the entire tool slide) from left to right. This is used to determine the spacing of the lines.

Rose Engine/Tour a Guilloché: Hand-operated lathe that creates a circular pattern on metal.

Rosette/Came: Rounded, gently undulating, low amplitude patterns that the rubber pushes against to achieve various patterns.

Rubber/Touch Steel: Stock radiused to fit the rosette. The weight of the entire headstock rests here and glides along this to create the pattern.

Straight-Line/Ligne Droit: Hand-operated lathe that creates an up and down pattern or a radial pattern on metal.

Table: The base of the rose engine; often in a thick slab of wood with an indent and the base of the straight-line. Often as one cast piece from the legs to the top of the table.

Tool Slide/Coulisse Porte Outil: What the cutter is mounted on; this is also used for angled pieces not more than 90° as a fine adjustment.

Worm/Vis-sans-fin: In front of the indexing plate, this serves the same function, but is controlled by the operator f or the number of degrees to turn. This aids in patterning offset decoration.

Resources

There are many places that have tools for use in guilloché. Quite a few of these places make tools for other disciplines that have been repurposed to use with guilloché. Here are some examples:

Agathon is pricey, but really accurate, and great for forming the cutters the first time from blanks. There may be other more regional options, but I like this one because it comes with a fixed rail multi-angle tool holder for cutting (http://www.agathon.ch/en/indexable-insert-grinding/tool-grinder/tool-grinder.asp)

Diametal developed quick change tooling with the advice of Georges Brodbeck that allows for many different cutters and a holder that can accommodate them all. After you visit the link scroll down in the PDF until you see the DIADEC information on pp 37–44 (http://www.diametal.ch/pdfs/products/precision/Kat_5_d_e.pdf).

GRS from Diametal is the best system I have found for sharpening cutters. It is precise and includes everything needed to start up in one package. I use the Power Hone Complete Dual Angle System. I love the dual angle tool holder; it is perfect for every step of sharpening (http://www.grstoosl.com/tool-sharpening/power-hone/power-hone-complete-dual-angle-system.html).

Leica has good microscopes that can be mounted to a machine, rest next to the sharpening system, or used to check your pieces. The model I enjoy is the Leica M50 (http://www.leica-microsystems.com/products/stereo-microscopes-macroscopes/routine-manual/details/product/leica-m50).

Orascoptic makes excellent eyewear for seeing guilloché while working. You can find their products at http://www.orascoptic.com/products/loupes.

Ottlite makes little machine mountable lights with a flexible neck perfect for getting close to the work piece so you can clearly see every facet of every cut (http://www.products.ottlite.com/p-436-led-flexneck-desk-lamp-with-usb.asp).

Rio Grande Jewelry Supply has literally everything you could want or need, including red brass (which is the closest in texture to gold if making samples). I really like the Jett Ballistic Fixturing Compound for mounting work to my machine. It lasts forever and you could make one holder and reuse it infinitely or reheat and reform the plastic (http://www.riogrande.com)

Ultrasonic has a nice variety of baths for all your cleaning needs. I like the small bath with plastic insert basket for washing the oil off my work before rinsing and then doing an alcohol and then benzene bath (http://www.riogrande.com/product/mini-ultrasonic-cleaner-06-liter/336337).